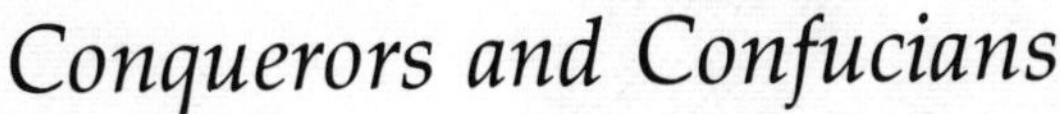

Studies in Oriental Culture Number Nine

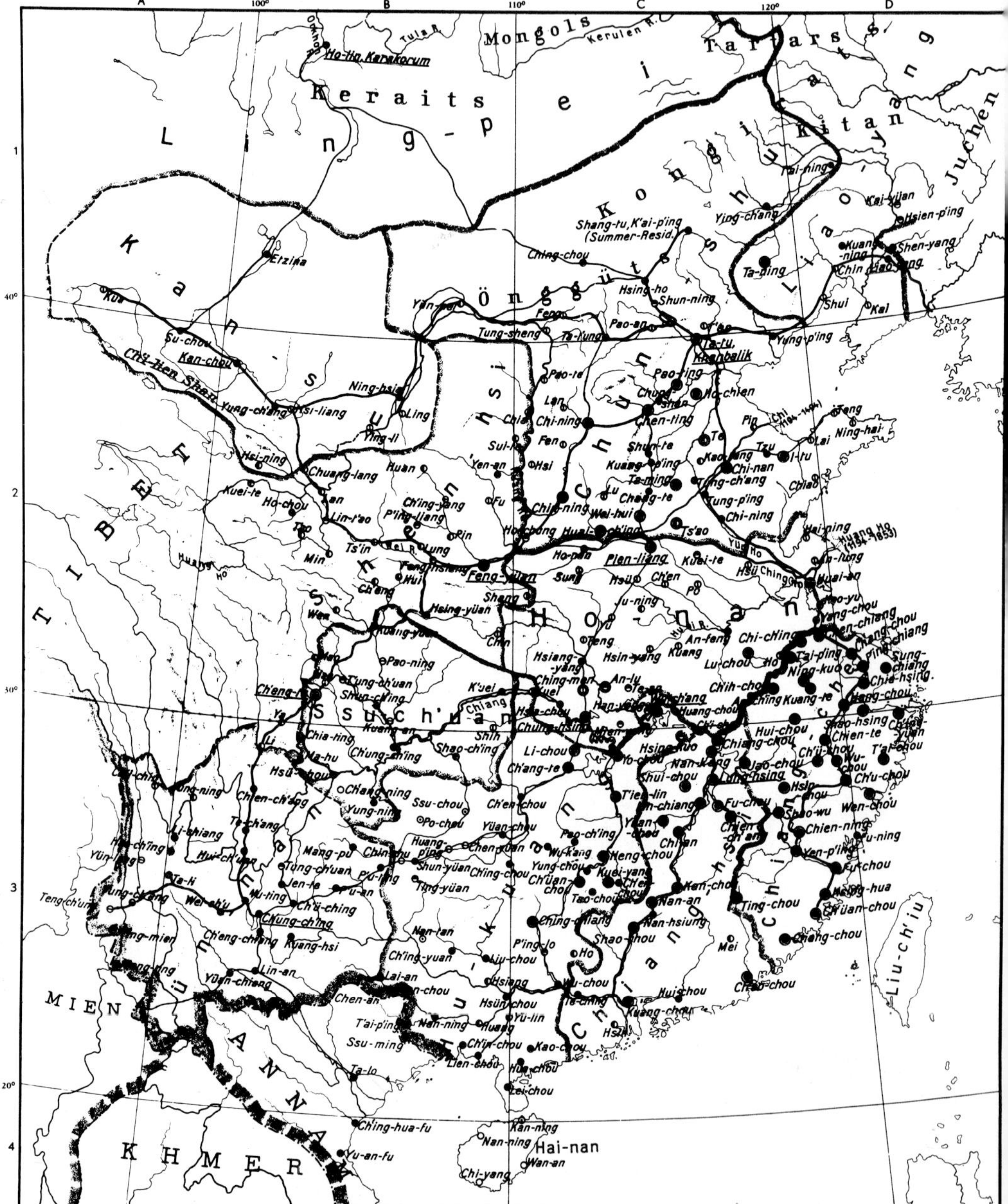

THE YÜAN (MONGOL) DYNASTY, 1280-1368 A.D.

- *Capitals of lu with more than 100,000 inhabitants*
- *Capitals of lu with less than 100,000 inhabitants*
- *Capitals of fu, 1st class*
- *Capitals of fu, 2nd class*
- *Capitals of chou, 1st class*
- *Capitals of chou, 2nd class*
- *Capitals of an-fu-ssu*
- *Capitals of chün*

Capitals of provinces are underlined

Scale 1:15,000,000

0 100 200 300 400 500 600 km

0 100 200 300 400 miles

Conquerors and Confucians

Aspects of Political Change in Late Yüan China

John W. Dardess

Columbia University Press
New York and London 1973

Frontispiece: Reproduced from Albert Hermann's *An Historical Atlas of China,* by permission of Aldine Atherton and Edinburgh University Press.

Library of Congress Cataloging in Publication Data

Dardess, John W 1937-
Conquerors and Confucians.

Includes bibliographical references.
1. China—History—Yuan dynasty, 1260-1368.
I. Title.
DS752.D37 951'.025 72-13308
ISBN 0-231-03689-2

Library of Congress Catalog Card Number: 72-13308
ISBN: 0-231-03689-2
Manufactured in the United States of America

To Margaret

Studies in Oriental Culture
Edited at Columbia University

Acknowledgments

I should like to express thanks to Professor Herbert Franke, to my colleague Lynn Nelson, to Robert Friesner, and to my wife Margaret for their criticisms and suggestions on the present work; and to Professor W. T. de Bary for his most generous help and encouragement. A grant from the General Research Fund, University of Kansas, afforded me free time for writing in the summer of 1970.

Although the present project was conceived independently, I must here acknowledge the original stimulation provided by the Ming Seminar at Columbia University, where under Professors de Bary, L. Carrington Goodrich, and Fang Chaoying I first developed an interest in the problems of early Ming history; and by the Ming Biographical History Project, whose editors, Professors Goodrich and Fang, kindly helped me in the preparation of several late Yüan biographies and opened to me the gate, as it were, to the present undertaking. These teachers also guided my dissertation, which dealt with the late Yüan rebel movements and the Ming foundation.

Some of the material I have used in this book I first gathered in Taiwan and Japan in 1965, thanks to a Fulbright-Hays Award; and I think it proper to mention at this time the very willing advice and assistance given me then by Professors Kuo T'ing-i, Huang Chang-chien, and Yao Ts'ung-wu at Academia Sinica; by Chiang Fu-ts'ung and Ch'ang Pi-te of the National Central Library; and in Japan, by Professor Yamane Yukio of the Tōyō Bunko, by the staff of the Seikadō Bunko, and by Professors Yoshikawa Kōjirō and Saeki Tomi of the University of Kyoto.

J.W.D.

August, 1971

Contents

Introduction 1

CHAPTER I
The Decline of the Steppe in Yüan Politics 7

CHAPTER II
The Restoration of 1328 31

CHAPTER III
Bayan and the Anti-Confucian Reaction 52

CHAPTER IV
The Triumph of Confucian Politics 75

CHAPTER V
The Pursuit of "Merit and Profit" 95

CHAPTER VI
The Growth of Yüan Regionalism 119

EPILOGUE
The Last Days of the Yüan Court in China 147

Summary and Conclusion 157

Biographical Notes 171

TABLE
Emperors of the Yüan Dynasty in China 176

Notes 177

Bibliography 225

Index 237

Introduction

*The Yüan Dynasty in China was one by-*product of the great Mongol conquests of the thirteenth century. Its founding date seems a matter of choice. It began, perhaps, in 1215 when Chinggis Qan (Genghis Khan) seized what is now Peking from the Jürched Chin Dynasty, although North China was not fully conquered by the Mongols until 1234. One can also date the era from 1260, when the China-based prince Qubilai (Kublai) seized the position of Great Qaghan of the Mongol empire, and established its capital in Peking. The Mongol occupation had no Chinese-style dynastic name, however, until 1271, when Qubilai ordered that it henceforth be known as the Yüan. Finally, only by 1279 was south China brought entirely within the Mongol fold. If its formal beginning date is 1271, its equally formal ending date is 1368, when, chased by the armies of the Ming founder Chu Yüan-chang, the emperor and part of the Yüan court evacuated Peking and retreated to the steppes.

For a period of time, the larger political entity of the Mongol world empire overshadowed China, which was simply one of its component parts. As is well known, however, the Mongol empire did not preserve its unity for very long. The rise of Qubilai and his establishment of the imperial center in Peking after 1260 is usually taken as the fateful first step in transforming the larger Mongol entity into a number of mutually independent Mongol conquest states: the Yüan Dynasty in China, the Chaghatai Khanate in Central Asia, the Ilkhans in Persia, and the Golden Horde in Russia.

The present offering is a political study of the Mongol conquest state in China after the Yüan Dynasty seceded, as it were, from the larger Mongol empire. It attempts to show that, although the leading political personalities in this later period were Mongols and *se-mu* (i.e., Turks, Tanguts, etc.), they had become actors in a political drama that was not really of their own making. They came to take leading roles on both sides of a Confucian dispute that was Chinese in origin and went back at least three centuries to the Northern Sung period (960-1126). The conquerors were now largely Confucian adherents themselves. Some of them, however, were Confucians of the "reformist" variety, ideological heirs of the Northern Sung reformer Wang An-shih; and others were Confucians of the "conservative" variety, after the style of Ssu-ma Kuang. In the late Yüan period, the Mongol and *se-mu* conquerors in China fought each other as champions of two profoundly opposed Confucian conceptions of the basic nature and fundamental purpose of the Chinese imperial state. The issues over which they fought were of more relevance to Chinese history than Mongol history. The results of the struggle appear to have strongly influenced the Confucian political orientation of the successor Ming Dynasty (1368-1644), a native Chinese house. The present offering is, therefore, intended primarily as an essay in Chinese history.

For the purposes of this study, I found it necessary to attempt to define politically a "later Yüan period." The first two chapters argue the case for the years 1328-29 as a convenient beginning point. Chapter I tries to explain the final processes of transition from Mongol empire to Chinese-style dynasty from an external point of view, while Chapter II provides parallel analysis from an internal point of view. Succeeding chapters then cover the development of Confucian politics down to the year 1355, when the Yüan state began to break apart. The emphasis of the present work, then, is put upon the twenty-seven years between 1328 and 1355, when Confucianism rose to be the controlling ideology of state. The final chapter attempts to show that after 1355 the central control of the Yüan court over the country had broken down to such an extent that one can no longer speak of a unitary Yüan Dynasty in China.

The segment of an era of "barbarian conquest" here under consideration is one in which the conquerors came more and more to speak and act as Confucians. As a privileged ruling caste, the Mongols and their non-Chinese *(se-mu)* allies became Confucianized to a high degree, but they were scarcely on that account absorbed or swallowed by the Chinese majority, for Confucianism through its insistence upon the principles of ancestral loyalty and filial piety tended to preserve rather than level ethnic and national distinctions. In this connection it must be noted that "Confucianization"—the adoption by outsiders, even Chinese outsiders, of a certain system of ethical and political behavior—was as a process distinct from "Sinicization," which involved not only the loss of national or linguistic identity, but also a most un-Confucian denial of the facts of ancestry, and in the Yüan period carried an additional burden of loss of caste as well.

The purpose of this study, however, is not primarily to explain why Mongol and *se-mu* bureaucrats became Confucians; rather, its purpose is to show that a violent Confucian political debate took place in the late Yüan period, in which the leading protagonists happened to be Mongols and *se-mu*, and that this debate is of some importance for Chinese history in general. The high point of this debate came in the years 1340 to 1355, when reformist and conservative Confucian administrations succeeded each other at roughly five-year intervals, each with a completely different idea of the proper aims and conduct of political life. If the Yüan Dynasty collapsed for any overriding political reason, it was because Yüan institutions were inadequate to control or contain the controversy.

Many historical monographs owe their origin and conception to a process of back-treading: one is originally interested in a different set of problems, but in order to understand them properly, one has to go back in time and study what came before. This monograph derives from an original interest in the founding of the Ming imperial despotism under Chu Yüan-chang, many of whose political choices seemed inexplicable except as personal idiosyncrasies or aberrations. The thrust of the present study is therefore forward; late Yüan political history is considered as if it were a preface to Ming history, which I think it is. I think, and hope in a future work to show, that some idea of the Confucian debate of the late Yüan period is essential to a sound understanding of the early Ming. But that is a project for the future; for the present, I have attempted to make *Conquerors and Confucians* stand as a work complete in itself.

The Yüan period is a difficult one for the non-Mongolist, because the sources bristle with names and terms of Mongol or Turkish derivation cumbersomely garbed in long strings of Chinese characters used purely for their phonetic values. However, at least two generations of philological study by Pelliot, Cleaves, and others have made it possible for outsiders such as myself to use these sources. I have repeatedly acknowledged their philological reconstructions in the notes.

Unfortunately, for Mongolian, as for Chinese, several systems of Latin transcription exist. For Mongolian, I have tried to follow the system used in the *Harvard Journal of Asiatic Studies,* with these simple modifications: C-hacek, J-hacek, S-hacek, and gamma are replaced by "CH," "J," "SH," and "GH" respectively. The consistent use of this system accounts for such correct but perhaps unfamiliar spellings as "Qubilai" (for Kubla, Kublai, Khubilai, etc.), "Chinggis Qan" (for Genghis Khan,), and "Qaraqorum" (for Karakorum). The "q" is not a glottal as in Arabic but a guttural like the "ch" in "Bach." Asterisks prefixed to names (e.g. *Chong'ur) indicate a hypothetical spelling devised by one or another philological authority. I have also tried to retain the generally accepted distinction between the *qan (khan),* originally a clan chief, but also a steppe ruler who holds sway over a "khanate"; and the *qaghan (khaghan),* a supreme overlord or emperor, whose corresponding imperial realm is the "Qaghanate."

Chinese transliteration follows the Wade-Giles, and Korean the McCune-Reischauer system.

Down to 1380, the official organization of the Ming Dynasty was closely modeled on that of the Yüan. In translating the Chinese titles of bureaucratic offices, I have therefore for the most part followed the English nomenclature given by Charles O. Hucker in his "Governmental Organization of the Ming Dynasty," *HJAS*, XXI (1958), 1-66, with index in *HJAS*, XXIII (1960-1), 127-51. My main deviation from Hucker is the use of Central Chancellery instead of Secretariat for *Chung-shu-sheng;* Chancellor of the Right instead of Chief Councilor of the Right for *yu-ch'eng-hsiang;* and Chancellor of the Left instead of Chief Councilor of the Left for *tso-ch'eng-hsiang.* For the Yüan emperors, I have used their personal names rather than their posthumous or temple names. A convenient table of Yüan emperors, with their various names and dates, devised by A. C. Moule, may be found in the *Journal of the North China Branch of the Royal Asiatic Society*, XLV (1914), 124. An abbreviated table of the Yüan imperial house together with biographical notes on the leading personalities of the late Yüan, may be found at the end of this book.

Chapter I
The Decline of the Steppe in Yüan Politics

The civil war and imperial restoration of 1328-29 in many ways marks a watershed in the political history of the Mongol Yüan Dynasty in China. Looking backward in time from that point to Qubilai's ascent to the throne in 1260, a stretch of about seventy years, one can discern at least one tenuous but continuous thread running through the entire period. That thread is the involvement, both friendly and hostile, of the steppe zone (i.e., the original Mongol homeland together with its western neighbor, the Central Asian realm of the heirs of Chaghatai and Ögödei) in the internal and external politics of China. To be sure, Qubilai himself laid the basis for an eventual disengagement of the Chinese realm from the steppe when he moved the capital of the Mongol world empire from Qaraqorum in Mongolia to Ta-tu (Peking) in China shortly after his accession. But the implications of this move did not become fully apparent until 1329. Down to 1329, the emperor of the Yüan Dynasty in China still remained in some degree Great Qaghan of the Mongol Empire precisely because the all-important question of succession was not one necessarily to be determined by domestic Chinese political considerations alone. Until 1329, those who occupied, or operated in, the steppes retained at least a potential voice in succession matters, and as long as they did, there remained the possibility of a continuing involvement on the part of China, Mongolia, and Central Asia in each other's political and economic affairs. This mutual involvement, whether friendly or hostile, bespoke a continuing reality of an eastern Mongol commonwealth, larger than any of its three parts, over which a *qaghan*, in some way chosen by common consultation in a princely diet (*quriltai*), should rightfully rule.

Looking ahead from the same vantage point of 1329 down to the end of the Yüan Dynasty in 1368, a span of about forty years, one finds the succession problem completely geared to the situation of the Mongols and their allies in China. After 1329 the steppe zone was not even hostile, it was simply irrelevant. The Mongolian homeland, fully absorbed into a dynastic system whose power center lay in China, proved incapable of supporting nomadic dissidence or of exerting independent influence in Yüan political life; the Chaghatai Khanate of Central Asia, having failed in an attempt to place a favored candidate upon the Yüan throne, thereafter saw better opportunities on its western, Islamic flank and took no further interest in the affairs of the Mongols of Yüan China. The Yüan Dynasty, having isolated itself from external Mongol concerns, lived out the remainder of its existence as a full and willing participant in the Confucian moral and political culture of China.

This "withdrawal" of the Yüan Dynasty from the larger Mongol empire was, to be sure, no sudden occurrence, but an intricate and gradual process whose beginnings antedate even the Great Qaghan Qubilai's overt preference for a power base centered upon China. I have elsewhere attempted an analysis of the transition from the Mongol steppe empire to the sedentary Yüan Dynasty from the point of view of economic and territorial structure and administrative practice.[1] Here, the focus is on the effects of this transition upon the monarchy. The present inquiry is primarily concerned not with the origin of the Yüan Dynasty, but with its later development as a ruling establishment irreversibly committed to the Confucian persuasion. Consequently this first chapter seeks only to show how it was that by 1329 the monarchical institution lost all vestige of its former importance within the larger pan-Mongol community, and fell complete prey to the desires and preferences of the Mongols and other conquest elements based in the Chinese realm alone.

It is important to establish this point. As long as even a remote possibility remained that extraneous Mongol elements could select a Great Qaghan and Yüan emperor and impose their candidate upon the Mongols in China, or otherwise gain acceptance for him there, the monarchical institution could hold in reserve against complete immersion in the Chinese milieu some vital remnant of its traditional universalism and aloofness from any one particular religious, cultural, or ideological system. On the other hand, once it became definitely established that no monarch was acceptable unless he was selected and backed exclusively by forces within the Yüan order, from that point the monarch as *qaghan* lost all remainder of his true constituency and for all practical purposes moved fully into his alternate persona as emperor *(huang-ti)* of the Yüan Dynasty in China, formally established by Qubilai in 1271. When that happened, the Mongols and their foreign allies domiciled in China could easily proceed along their own path and assimilate themselves into native Confucian culture, safe in the knowledge that their legally protected dominance could not be preempted or threatened by elements from outside the Yüan system. The total integration of the monarchy into the Yüan system by 1329 prepared the way for the full Confucianization of political life that characterized the later Yüan period.

The tensions of political choice between a *qaghan* oriented toward the steppes and the larger Mongol empire, and a *huang-ti* brought up in China and more closely attuned to the desires of the conquest establishment there, were no mere figments of the analytical imagination but realities in a most concrete and dramaturgical sense. Twice in the early decades of the fourteenth century the two opposing monarchical options found living embodiment in conflicting imperial candidacies. The first such instance took place in 1307, the brothers Qaishan and Ayurbarwada, who were great-grandsons of Qubilai, personifying the options. The second and last instance came about in 1328-29, with Qaishan's sons Qoshila and Tugh Temür repeating the situation. The final processes of transition from universal kingship to China-centered monarchy may be discussed in terms of these two dynastic events.

In 1299 the Great Qaghan and emperor of the Yüan Dynasty in China appointed a new princely field commander for the continuing campaign against the conservative and dangerous alliance of the heirs of Chaghatai and Ögödei in Central Asia. The reigning emperor and Great Qaghan was Temür, grandson and successor of the great Qubilai; the new commander was Qaishan, the emperor's nephew.

The Central Asian alliance had come into being in 1268 or 1269 on the banks of the Talas west of Lake Balkhash. Its driving spirit was Qaidu, a grandson of the *qaghan* Ögödei (r. 1229-41), whose descendants had lost the headship of the Mongol Empire to Möngke of the line of Tului in 1251. At the diet, Qaidu and his Chaghatai allies among other things made a mutual pledge to retain the nomadic life and customs of their ancestors. This pledge, while related to the exigencies of the moment, had a certain conservative appeal because long ago Chinggis Qan had appointed his son Chaghatai to be the special guardian of his sacred laws, the "yasa" *(jasagh)*, which the Great Qaghan Qubilai of the Tului line in Ta-tu (Peking) had notably but tacitly forsaken. Together, the allied Mongols of Central Asia under Qaidu maintained a stern defiance of Qubilai's pretensions to the qaghanate. Qubilai's armies in the steppes had defeated Qaidu and his allies on at least four occasions between 1264 and 1293. Nevertheless, when Qubilai died in 1294, Qaidu was still alive and his armies still dangerous.[2]

When the eighteen-year-old prince Qaishan departed for the steppes in 1299 to command the anti-Qaidu operation, there were two young men in his entourage whose association with him in the war effort would prove to be politically crucial to them about thirty years hence, at a very different stage in Yüan history. One of the young men was El Temür, a Qipchaq, whose forebears had been chieftains of sorts in the steppes north of the Caspian at the time of the Mongol attacks of 1223 and 1237; the other was Bayan, a Mongol of the Merkid tribe. Despite their political importance later, their contributions were definitely of a minor order at this time.

Qaishan's job was to position himself at Qaraqorum and take whatever measures were necessary to prevent the steppe homeland from falling into Qaidu's hands. In this he was aided by two senior commanders, the Grand Preceptor *(t'ai-shih)*

*Yochichar and El Temür's father *Chong'ur. Qaishan's first action was a retaliatory attack upon Qaidu's base camp in the western steppes east of Lake Balkhash in September and October 1300. Following this, in August and September 1301, Qaidu and his ally Duwa, chief of the Chaghatai Khanate, together with some forty princes of the Ögödei and Chaghatai lines, marched eastward through the Altai mountains for what turned out to be their last major offensive against the eastern steppes. Qaidu's forces gained an initial victory on a hill probably somewhere west of the upper Orqon River on September 5, and on the following day surrounded a part of Qaishan's army there. Qaishan, who was observing from a distance, grew excited. Only with difficulty did a young member of his personal guard, the Qangli Toghto, of whom more will be heard later, prevent him from rushing personally into the foray. The Merkid Bayan, apparently caught inside the encirclement, fought bravely and hard. Finally *Yochichar and a myriarch led a successful escape from the trap, and the Yüan forces were then able to retreat. But while Qaidu gained a victory, his ally Duwa lost a simultaneous encounter a short distance away to El Temür's father *Chong'ur, and withdrew nursing a wounded knee. Although they had gained a partial victory in their campaign, the Central Asian forces did not press the attack further but marched back west again through the Altai mountains to their winter quarters. That winter (1301-2) Qaidu died, and the Central Asian Mongols thereupon gave up their aggressive strategy.[3]

With Duwa's support, Qaidu's son Chapar succeeded to the Ögödei Khanate in the spring of 1303 and, as is well known, the two sued for peace, sending envoys to Ta-tu where Temür was ruling as well as to Maragha in Persia where the Il-khan Öljeitü was in charge in an effort to reopen the trade and communications among the various parts of the Mongol world empire that the recent wars had disrupted.[4] Although Qaishan, since promoted to the second-class princedom of Huai-ning, willingly acted as an intermediary in the peace negotiations between the Central Asian allies and the Great Qaghan in Ta-tu, he was also eager to heed Temür's secret instructions and intervene in the civil war that broke out between Duwa and Chapar in 1305-6.[5] Temür backed Duwa in this affair, and together they all but destroyed the Ögödei Khanate. In obedience to Temür's orders, Qaishan marched west through the Altai in August and September, 1306, capturing several ranking members of Chapar's family, plus part of Chapar's horde and their tents. After that, he advanced to the Irtysh River and brought two other Mongol princes to surrender. Chapar fled and gave himself up to Duwa, who had defeated him earlier in Transoxania and had seized his lands. Prince Qaishan then withdrew and entered winter quarters in the Altai.[6]

Such, in brief, was the record of Qaishan's accomplishments as princely overseer of the Yüan forces in the steppe. In the course of his eight years' guard duty in Mongolia, Qaishan had assembled a staff of veteran advisers and young adherents who proved themselves by defending the territory of the Great Qaghan against a spent but dangerous rival. They had the good fortune to confront Qaidu not at his prime but in his old age, after he had already suffered severe defeats. After Qaidu's death, they easily helped administer the *coup de grace* to what remained of the Ögödei Khanate. But in the present discussion what matters is not how much of the credit for putting down the Ögödei line should be assigned to Qaishan and his men; what is important is that a set of primary personal loyalties had been formed around Qaishan during the course of the operations. In short, a Qaishan clique had come into being, and this clique would have a major political role to play in future Yüan history.

The Qaishan clique did not have to wait long before making its first entry into Yüan dynastic politics. The emperor Temür had been ailing for some time and died without an heir on February 10, 1307. News of this event reached Qaishan and his men in the Altai in the spring of that year. Qaishan at once marched back to Qaraqorum where he held an assembly of imperial princes and sons-in-law to decide upon rewards and plan strategy. It was at this time that the Merkid Bayan was granted the title of *ba'atur* for his efforts in capturing two of Chapar's adherents the year before.[7] No doubt

Qaishan's issuing of such rewards at this time was linked to his designs upon the throne.

There were, however, two other candidates. One was the prince of An-hsi Ananda, grandson of Qubilai through his third son Manggala, who held a momentary advantage in that he was already on the scene in Ta-tu. From the point of view of seniority, he had a strong claim to the throne. He had even once been heir apparent, from 1285 down to 1293, when Qubilai removed him and replaced him with Temür. The empress dowager Bulughan backed him, as did the Chancellor of the Left Aqutai and some others. But beyond a few court figures and handful of imperial princes, some of them former steppe enemies of the Yüan, Ananda commanded little support. He was rather unpopular. Although he had participated in the Yüan wars against Qaidu, mainly by defending west China and the Tangut territory, his disorderly and expensive administration of his princely fief in Shensi had on several occasions displeased the court and the bureaucracy.[8] He was, moreover, a pious Moslem.[9] The power realities dictated the need for some other choice.

All eyes fell upon two brothers, Qaishan and Ayurbarwada, great-grandsons of Qubilai through his second son Jingim, who had been a popular heir apparent, but had died in 1285 before reaching the throne.[10] It was widely agreed that the imperial succession should lie with Jingim's heirs; Qubilai had decided as much when he named Temür, who was Jingim's third and youngest son. The father of Qaishan and Ayurbarwada was Jingim's second son, Darmabala.

Qaishan's younger brother Ayurbarwada, the second candidate, commanded substantial support, much more than his distant cousin Ananda; and the sources of his support were such as to place his candidacy in conflict with that of his brother in the steppes. Unlike Qaishan, Ayurbarwada had no experience of the steppes. In 1305, when he was twenty years old, he was assigned his late father's fief at Huai-ch'ing (Ch'in-yang, Honan), and Ayurbarwada took up residence there with his and Qaishan's mother, the Qunggirad *Targi.[11] Several well publicized acts served to establish his reputation for Confucian piety and virtue. His filial devotion to his mother, for example, was touching and reassuring. His conspicuous refusal to accept the sumptuous hospitality of the local officials through whose districts he passed on the way to his fief pointed up his tender and solicitous concern for the burdens such extravagances imposed upon the common people. Another sign of the same concern was his appointment of one of his Chinese staff members to see to it that his military escort did not molest the villages.[12] All of this was in large part show, calculated to have a certain political effect within a geographically Chinese context. He had a chance to exhibit more calculated behavior on his way to Ta-tu in March, 1307, having been secretly summoned by the Chancellor of the Right Harghasun and others. Arriving at the supposed tomb of Pi-kan, loyal counselor to the "bad last" king of the Shang Dynasty in the second millennium B.C., he reminded his entourage that the ancient king's lust had lost him his empire, and ordered a temple built in Pi-kan's honor, "as an encouragement to later ages." That was in Wei-hui (Chi-hsien, Honan). Farther along, at the Chang River, Ayurbarwada and his party encountered a heavy snowstorm. An old peasant appeared with an offering of coarse gruel, which the prince's aides spurned. "Anciently when emperor Kuang-wu of Han was hard-pressed by the enemy," lectured Ayurbarwada, "he ate bean gruel. A man who has never fully experienced hardship never learns of the toil involved in agriculture and as a result he becomes idle and arrogant." Ayurbarwada then ate the gruel and rewarded the old peasant. At Han-tan he told the local officials his fear that his guards and the clerical subbureaucracy might force too many exactions from the population, and assured them that he would have his staff watch out for these things.[13] These anecdotal reports of Ayurbarwada's behavior—his filial piety, his understanding of the primacy of agriculture, his openness to loyal advice (or to clique pressure), his concern for the peasantry, and his acquaintance with Chinese historical precedent—made it clear enough to all who cared to observe that as an imperial candidate he was offering a conception of empire which was essentially China-centered. It was focused not upon the problems of the Mongol commonwealth, of which China was one part, but upon the problem of the Mongol dynasty in China as an entity in itself. It was designed in large part to appeal to those conquest elements that had built their careers within the framework of the Yüan bureaucratic state, and not in steppe war.

The elimination of Ananda as a candidate posed no special difficulty. Ayurbarwada and his supporters, who arrived in Ta-tu on March 20, 1307, arranged his removal by storming the palace, killing the Chancellor of the Left Aqutai, and arresting Ananda together with the empress dowager Bulughan, Temür's widow.[14] But the choice between Ayurbarwada and Qaishan was momentarily an agonizing one. The mother of the two candidates consulted fortunetellers and thus betrayed her quandary. If Ayurbarwada was on the spot in Ta-tu and commanded the allegiance of the majority of the bureaucrats, Qaishan surely held a military edge; his steppe warriors might conceivably declare for an independent khanate in Mongolia, or make common cause with the Chaghatai Khanate, even if they did not undertake an invasion of China. After frantic consultations it was decided that Ayurbarwada should voluntarily cede the throne to Qaishan, on condition that Ayurbarwada and not one of Qaishan's sons should be made heir apparent. Qaishan was notified of this decision, and after his initial suspicions were allayed, he marched south to the Yüan summer capital of Shang-tu (To-lun, Chahar), where Ayurbarwada met him. He was already assured the backing of the steppe princes, with whom he had been in session in Qaraqorum. A second diet at Shang-tu gave him the support of the China-based princes, and on May 21 he formally assumed the throne.[15]

In the edict Qaishan issued on this occasion, he listed his three qualifications for the imperial dignity: his military record, his genealogy, and his election by a diet of the imperial princes. He strongly implied by this that he considered his credentials better than Qubilai's, for everyone knew that Qubilai's election to the throne in 1260 was essentially illegal because he was backed by a rump diet which he had hastily convened and not by a full assembly of princes. The collapse of the Ögödei-Chaghatai alliance, moreover, came about while Qaishan was commanding; and in his edict, Qaishan likened his accomplishments to those of Chinggis Qan in a way which was indirect but obvious to anyone who knew the basic facts of the recent past. Chinggis Qan, he said, "by military success pacified the empire *(t'ien-hsia).*" Qubilai, on the other hand, whose conquest of south China and attempted invasions of Japan and Southeast Asia were a matter of public record, "by civilized (i.e., nonmilitary) virtue harmonized all within the four seas."[16] The contrast Qaishan was making was in large part spurious. Chinggis's military efforts fell short of empire *(t'ien-hsia)* in the usual Chinese sense; that was actually Qubilai's work. But Chinggis did pacify the nomad *t'ien-hsia,* and so too, in a sense, did Qaishan.

The new emperor of course brought his personal adherents with him when he came to take the throne, and he saw to it that they received generous rewards and important posts in the new administration. To give some notable examples, among the principal beneficiaries of Qaishan's enthronement were the Tangut Ch'i-t'ai-p'u-chi and his sons Yeh-erh-chi-ni and Li-jih. During the steppe wars, the father had organized a special military unit for Qaishan and had served him as an adviser. The first son was a guards commander, and the second, originally a follower of the Prince of Chin Kammala, Qaishan's cousin and nominal superior, went so far out of his way to keep Qaishan's household supplied with meat and his troops with grain that Qaishan eventually decided to lure him away from Kammala's staff and attach him to his own. All three at various times obtained the very highest bureaucratic positions in the Yüan state after Qaishan became emperor.[17] The Qangli Toghto and his older brother A-sha Buqa, both of whom had performed a crucial diplomatic role in Qaishan's enthronement by maintaining a communications link between the steppe and the capital, received their due rewards; Toghto at various times held the positions of Chancellor of the Left, head of the Chief Military Commission, and Censor-in-Chief.[18] A-sha Buqa, who unlike his brother did not accompany Qaishan into the steppes, received the lesser position of Chief Administrator but was also made commander of a newly created Qangli guard.[19] The Qipchaq *Chong'ur was especially close to Qaishan, and as emperor Qaishan did more than provide him with bureaucratic position; as a reward for his defeat of Duwa's army in 1301, Qaishan married to him a girl of the imperial house, and made him commander of the Qipchaq guards.[20] In 1309, moreover, *Chong'ur was invested with the newly created sixth-class princely fief of Chü-jung.[21] *Chong'ur spent most of the rest of his career not in bureaucratic positions but in command of Yüan troops in the steppes. *Chong'ur's third son El Temür was made a Vice Commissioner in the Office for Imperial Cuisine *(Hsüan-hui yüan)*.[22] The Merkid Bayan during Qaishan's reign became successively President of the Board of Civil Office, Vice Censor-in-Chief, Chief Administrator in Qaishan's new secretariat (the *Shang-shu sheng*), and was for part of this time concurrently imperial commissar *(darughachi)* of the newly organized right Asud (Alan) Guards.[23]

The point to be drawn here is this: the Qaishan enthronement meant that military service in the steppe in this one instance constituted a public stepping stone, a means of joint entry, into the Yüan central bureaucracy at various levels depending upon individual age and experience. Yet such service was by no means an ordinary prerequisite for those aspiring to higher bureaucratic position. For the Mongols and their foreign *(se-mu)* allies in China, service in the imperial guard at Ta-tu followed by a regular scale of upward promotion through the bureaucratic ranks was by far the most common route to high office.[24] It was chiefly bureaucrats of this sort who provided support for Qaishan's brother Ayurbarwada. The position of the Qaishan group in the Yüan state depended entirely upon the unusual and essentially irregular circumstance of Qaishan's promotion from princely field commander to emperor. Had he not come to the throne, it is safe to guess that most of the clique would have ended their days in one or another obscure military post. What welded the members together was a common realization of their having participated in a significant event in the steppe, but even more, of their singular good fortune in riding into high office on Qaishan's coattails. It is therefore not surprising that the clique later on came to revere Qaishan as a virtual dynastic founder, the father of an imperial line of succession.

While much seems to have given the Qaishan clique a sense of common identity as the emperor's "old ministers," circumstances acted to produce a split within this group. After a reign of four years, Qaishan died in January, 1311, at the age of thirty, and was succeeded by his younger brother Ayurbarwada. He left two sons, both by secondary wives; the older was Qoshila, born in 1300, and the younger Tugh Temür, born in 1304.[25] In the sources as we have them, there is no conclusive evidence of any agreement having been made on the question of the succession to Ayurbarwada. Perhaps the matter was left hanging, to be decided by some future diet of the princes. Only by Qaishan's partisans was it definitely asserted that one of Qaishan's sons was according to the agreement of 1307 to succeed Ayurbarwada.[26] Their witness, however, is not unimpeachable. In any event, Ayurbarwada, his mother, and their supporters decided that the succession should stay in Ayurbarwada's line. In August, 1319, accordingly, Ayurbarwada's second son Shidebala was confirmed as heir-apparent, and in March, 1320, upon Ayurbarwada's death, he succeeded to the throne as emperor.[27]

In 1315 Ayurbarwada began to prepare the way for Shidebala's succession by taking steps to remove Qoshila from the political scene. In that year, he conferred upon Qoshila the first-class princedom of Chou, together with a large princely office *(ch'ang-shih fu)* consisting of forty-three ranked officials, and contributed a handsome sum of 400,000 ingots *(ting)* in paper cash for the maintenance of his escort guards. The Merkid Bayan was originally made one of the seven chief officials *(ch'ang-shih)* in Qoshila's establishment, but for reasons which are obscure he was shortly afterwards transferred to be Vice Censor-in-Chief of the Kiangnan Censorate.[28] Thus in 1316, when Qoshila was ordered to proceed with his officials to the distant southwestern province of Yunnan and take up residence there, Bayan did not accompany him and all further contact between the two came to an end.

Qoshila never reached Yunnan, his proper destination, for events brought a radical change in his itinerary. Late in the year 1316, Qoshila and his party arrived in the city of Yen-an in north Shensi. There they met three of Qaishan's old followers, among them the Tangut Li-jih, once Censor-in-Chief, but apparently unemployed since Ayurbarwada's succession.[29] Qoshila and his officials renewed ties and made a compact with Li-jih and the others; they then made contact with the Shensi provincial capital of Feng-yüan (Sian) to the south, and got the leading officials of both the provincial administration and the Shensi Branch Censorate to join them in a plan to stage a rebellion in the name of Qaishan. The leading Shensi officials were inclined to go along in this, for they were enemies of Ayurbarwada's court officials, who had driven them from the capital into what they considered to be political exile. The rebels' apparent aims were to force the removal of some of the high court officials and probably also to persuade the emperor, Ayurbarwada, to change his plans for the succession.[30] An army was gathered; the rebels began to march east from Shensi, but the expedition ended when two of the lower ranking Shensi officials abruptly decided that the venture was bound to end in disaster and so murdered their leaders.[31]

The abortive uprising in which Qoshila's staff involved him bears all the hallmarks of poor planning and an unrealistic assessment of the current political situation. This fact may have contributed to a desire on the part of Qaishan's old ministers who stayed behind in China to dissociate themselves from their colleagues who followed Qoshila. Probably more important in engendering the split in the ranks of the Qaishan clique, however, was Qoshila's flight to the steppes after the failure of the uprising, and his subsequent isolation from China. Instead of proceeding to Yunnan, Qoshila and his group marched northwest into the grasslands, where on the western side of the Altai the reigning prince Esen Buqa of the Chaghatai Khanate warmly welcomed them. As an important political refugee from China, and as a claimant to the throne of the Great Qaghan, Qoshila might be of some possible future use to the Chaghataids. They assigned him summer and winter campgrounds and space for the planting of spring crops somewhere in the Tarbagatai.[32] From here, in 1328, Qoshila would emerge again as a candidate for the Yüan throne.

Qaishan's second son Tugh Temür would also emerge in 1328 as an imperial candidate and an alternative rallying point for those of Qaishan's old followers who did not accompany Qoshila into the Tarbagatai. Ayurbarwada's son and successor Shidebala removed this younger heir of Qaishan's to the subtropical island of Hainan in 1321 in order to forestall the incipient gathering of disaffected elements behind him.[33] He was entirely isolated there; apparently none of the Qaishan clique was permitted to accompany him. In 1324, however, the emperor Yesün Temür recalled Tugh Temür from Hainan, gave him the designation prince of Huai, and sent him out to reside in the Yangtze city of Nanking, surely a more favorable and central spot than Hainan.[34] There he was able to patronize several well-known Chinese artists and litterateurs and demonstrate in his own way a sensitivity for Chinese cultural values.[35] In this he resembled strongly his uncle Ayurbarwada. As twin candidates, one from the steppe and the other based in China, Qoshila and Tugh Temür in 1328 appeared to be replaying the roles Qaishan and Ayurbarwada had played in 1307. The difference was that in 1328-29 the "Chinese candidate" and his backers did not have to compromise with their rival, but were able to force him off the political stage entirely.

This peculiar repetition of events on the dramatic but superficial level of dynastic politics leads one to suspect the existence of some more basic conflict of interest between the Mongols of the steppe and those settled in China, of which the recurring dual candidacies were in some way a reflection. But the very different resolution of the dual candidacy problem in 1328-29 would seem to indicate that an important realignment of forces in favor of China and to the disadvantage of the steppe had taken place over the preceding twenty years. In fact, as the discussion below should make clear, Qaishan in 1307 and his eldest son Qoshila in 1328-29 found themselves in profoundly different political circumstances largely because of the political and administrative transformation of the Mongolian steppe homeland.

For the gradual imposition of administrative control over the steppe regions, as with almost everything else in Yüan history, the origins inevitably go back to Qubilai. One major result of Qubilai's accession in 1260 was the transfer of the political center of the Mongol empire from Mongolia to North China. This transfer entailed a basic reorganization of the state along traditional Chinese bureaucratic lines, whereby a tightly centralized regime built on the Chinese model came to exercise a predominant authority over the collection and disbursement of revenues. Regular official taxation collected by a centrally controlled bureaucracy came finally to replace the earlier irregular exactions of Mongol commanders, princes, and their Moslem tax farmers. While the state did not confiscate the North China appanages earlier parceled out to the princely descendants of Chinggis Qan and his brothers, it did gain the ability to interfere more and more in the administration and taxation of these appanages.[36] Consequently, from Qubilai's accession in 1260, the Mongol princes who remained in the steppes or who were domiciled in other parts of the Mongol empire found a China-based bureaucratic state, with a Mongol emperor as its chief executive, controlling direct access to their individual sources of revenue in China. To finance their struggles against Qubilai, they had to look to other, less lucrative sources of revenue.

But Qubilai's strategy of locating the seat of the Great Qaghanate of the Mongol empire somewhere in the vicinity of its economic center of gravity in China meant that he had eventually to sacrifice the political and military leverage over the other parts of the world empire that the more central location in Mongolia had afforded. By moving into China, he lost forever the ability of his predecessors to manipulate succession in the Khanate of Chaghatai in Central Asia, and he transformed for a time the Mongolian homeland from the imperial center to an unstable and anarchic frontier zone. A number of important "rebel" movements were organized across the whole breadth of Inner Asia after Qubilai's ascent to the throne; these ranged from Manchuria in the east across Mongolia to the Chaghatai Khanate in Central Asia, precisely in those areas where political and administrative control was forfeited after the Great Qaghan's removal to China. The leading rebels were Arigh Böke in Mongolia and Central Asia (1260-64); Nayan in upper Manchuria (1287); and Qaidu in Central Asia (1269-1301).[37]

The fundamental issue in Qubilai's confrontation with these dissident movements was the proper ordering of the Mongol empire, or at least its eastern parts. Was it more advantageous to control the agrarian realms from a power center in the steppes, or to control the steppes from a power center in the agrarian realms? Qubilai's younger brother Arigh Böke made the first attempt to preserve the older political and administrative order, with its headquarters in Qaraqorum. His surrender to Qubilai in 1264 symbolized the collapse of an independent steppe regime in Mongolia before the superior military forces of a *qaghan* who had the supplies and resources of China at his disposal, and who could directly subsidize those princes who took his side as well as offer relief and remissions of levies and tributes to the steppe tribes who came over to him.[38] Arigh Böke's greatest weakness lay in his inability to gain access to any major source of agrarian revenue; the Chaghatai khan Alughu (r. 1261-66), jealous of his newly gained independence, resisted Arigh Böke's attempt to secure the resources of Central Asia, and Arigh Böke in his extremity was forced to resort to savage measures in an unsuccessful effort to prevent defection in his camp.[39] It was under these circumstances that he decided to give in to Qubilai. Qubilai hoped to make an object lesson of Arigh Böke by treating him leniently. He received an agreement from Berke of the Golden Horde, Alughu in Central Asia, and Hülegü in Iran that Arigh Böke should be spared.[40] No doubt he hoped to impress upon the other steppe princes the futility of revolt and to encourage them to depend upon the benevolence of the Great Qaghan and his administration in Ta-tu for sustenance and leadership.

Qubilai's gesture, however, was clearly insufficient to alter the nature of an entire frontier. While he turned to busy himself with the conquest of South China and other projects, Qaidu was able to put together another steppe movement which was a little more firmly based than Arigh Böke's had been. Qaidu's own patrimonial state, the *ulus* of Ögödei, centered between the Altai and Lake Balkhash, was not in itself sufficiently productive an area to permit the organization and supply of an armed force large enough to threaten Qubilai to any degree. But from the famous diet of 1269, held on the Talas, Qaidu imposed himself upon the Chaghatai Khanate to the extent that, unlike Arigh Böke, he was able to influence the basic orientation of that state and gain access to the agricultural resources of Transoxania and the oasis cities of the western Tarim basin. In 1274, as we have see, Qaidu helped place Duwa upon the Chaghatai throne, and thus cemented even more closely the Chaghatai and Ögödei patrimonies.[41] Qaidu's initial strategy appears twofold: to gain control of all of the oasis region west of the Yellow River in order to expand his resource base, and to seize Mongolia for its geographical advantages and its supply of military manpower. Having gained this, he would possibly be in a position to begin dictating terms to Qubilai in China. Qaidu's effort peaked in the 1270s and 1280s. Qubilai lost the Uighur oasis cities of Beshbaliq and Qaraqojo; his Pacification Office *(Hsüan-wei ssu)* in Qaraqorum defected to the enemy; the walled grain depot of Ying-ch'ang (in present-day western Jehol province) did the same, and most threatening of all, in response to Qubilai's attempt to impose a centralized provincial administration over his territories and subject tribes, Nayan rebelled in upper Manchuria in 1287 and allied himself with Qaidu.[42]

Qubilai's ability to put down Nayan and turn Qaidu out of Mongolia derives in large part from his richer supply base and greater administrative capabilities. Qaidu and Nayan were obliged to rely heavily on the thin margin of surplus that the steppe tribes, such as the Ba'arin on the Irtysh, or hunters and fishers, such as the Water Tatars (Shui Ta-ta) and Jürcheds of upper Manchuria and the Sungari region were able to provide.[43] When this did not suffice, they had to make raids into settled areas—Nayan into Korea and the

Liao valley of lower Manchuria, and Qaidu into the eastern Tarim and Tangut territory.[44] When Qubilai campaigned in the steppe regions, however, he first assembled his horses, weapons, and supplies in China; and far from having to rely on exactions from the tribes, he was able to cancel their official obligations, provide them with relief, and in some cases resettle them.[45] Moreover, as soon as Qubilai recovered an area, he secured communications by organizing horse relay stations which served to deny the possibility of rapid communications and mobility to the opposition.[46] By the time he died in 1294, Qubilai had secured Manchuria from Nayan and his allies and reestablished the province of Liaoyang there, and had succeeded in gaining the upper hand over Qaidu in Mongolia. For the Yüan Dynasty, the crisis period of steppe reaction was definitely over with. It remained only to complete the process of shifting the imperial center from Mongolia to China by bringing the Mongolian steppe region under the direct administrative control of Ta-tu. Qubilai initiated this process in Manchuria; it was left to Qaishan, after the death of Qaidu and the collapse of the Central Asian opposition, to impose a similar provincial regime over Mongolia itself when he became emperor.

Qaishan's integration of the Mongolian homeland into the Chinese administrative system made it all but certain that another opposition movement of potential danger to the Yüan state could not be raised in the steppe regions. His reduction of Mongolia to provincial status in 1307 combined with the construction in 1308 of a new imperial walled capital called Chung-tu (north of present-day Kalgan) were the two most obvious steps taken in this direction.[47] Qaishan's imposition of a centralized bureaucratic network over Mongolia was important in a number of respects: it confirmed the policy trend begun earlier under Qubilai and Temür of securing and extending the postal relay system; of ensuring military control through the use of Chinese garrison troops, particularly at Qaraqorum; and of extending this control through the development of military agricultural colonies *(t'un-t'ien)* in certain favored spots in the northern steppes.[48] Equally important, the establishment of a provincial capital at

Qaraqorum and a provincial bureaucracy staffed partly by Chinese afforded the central government an effective means of intruding into the relations between the steppe princes and the native tribesfolk. Owing to its near monopoly of grain and other commodities, the provincial administration could provide direct relief to the common people and thus deny to the steppe princes the possibility of rallying a significant portion of the population to themselves as new recruits.[49]

At the same time that he sought to alleviate popular distress directly, Qaishan also continued to provide relief grants and subsidies to the steppe people through the mediation of their ruling princes so that the princes and the provincial administration might to some degree keep each other in check. Qaishan furthermore undertook to draw the steppe princes themselves closer to China by awarding them fiefs for the most part named after, and nominally identified with, territorial divisions inside China. To be sure, Qubilai and Temür had begun to award such fiefs, although on a limited scale. It was Qaishan who first gave them out in large number.[50] His intent seems to have been to substitute for the older generalized ranks of prince *(wang)* and grand prince *(ta wang)* a new and more precisely graduated scale of princely ranks of Chinese origin through which the emperor could control promotions and demotions.[51] The net result of this dual strategy—of bureaucratizing Mongolia, and integrating the princes into a Chinese-style prestige system of rank and nomenclature, while granting jurisdiction over the settlement of princely disputes to one or another government agency—was to reduce the northern steppes to a postion of political, economic, and administrative dependency upon the central government in China.[52]

With the steppe lands of Mongolia swallowed into the Chinese imperial system, the zone of anarchy and instability which permitted the existence of opposition movements such as those of Arigh Böke and Qaidu, not to speak of Nayan in Manchuria, was severly reduced. For fifteen years after the administrative assimilation of Mongolia, however, frontier anarchy continued to exist along the Altai and Tarim border between the Yüan Dynasty and the Chaghatai Khanate, where intermittent raids and counterraids took place through the first half of the reign of the Chaghatai *qan* Kebek (r. 1318-28).[53] The Prince of Chou Qoshila was posted in Chaghatai territory west of the Altai, as we have seen; and although what we know of him at this time is scant, it is clear that he was involved in these frontier raiding operations at least in 1317, when he took a position hostile to the Yüan Dynasty.[54] The raids stopped after 1323, when Kebek offered peace to the Yüan court. The reigning emperor Shidebala was happy to accept. "I do not at all want his land or his people," he remarked. "It is enough of a blessing if my people do not suffer frontier disturbances and my troops are not overstrained. Now that he has come to submit, we should make his reward generous to put him at ease."[55] In 1325 Shidebala's successor Yesün Temür sent a friendly embassy to Qoshila, treating him not as a prince subordinate to Yüan control—in spite of his title Prince of Chou—but as an autonomous prince on a level with the Chaghatai house, the Ilkhans of Persia, or the Golden Horde on the Volga. This fact can be seen in Qoshila's two return embassies to Ta-tu, where, according to the terminology employed, he presented "tribute" of furs and other items.[56] Clearly, by the 1320s, sixty years after Qubilai's emergence, the Yüan empire had achieved its territorial maximum and was reaching administrative maturity behind a closed and stabilized frontier.

It was in these circumstances that Qoshila came forth as the "steppe candidate" for the Yüan throne in 1328-29. The death of the emperor Yesün Temür in Shang-tu in September, 1328, precipitated a civil war between his partisans and another faction based in Ta-tu, spearheaded by several of Qaishan's "old ministers," most prominently the Qipchaq El Temür. By November, Yesün Temür's partisans were crushed. Qoshila's younger brother Tugh Temür was brought up to the capital where he provisionally assumed the throne on October 16, voicing an intention to abdicate as soon as his elder brother could be reached. The Ta-tu court duly made contact with Qoshila, who set out eastward from the Tarbagatai. On February 27, 1329, north of Qaraqorum, he assumed the throne as emperor. On May 5, El Temür came in person to deliver to him the imperial seal. Tugh Temür stepped down and became heir apparent.[57] It was then arranged that Qoshila should move south from Qaraqorum while his younger brother traveled north from Ta-tu, and that they should meet each other in joyous reunion at a place roughly equidistant between Shang-tu and Ta-tu.[58] It is evident, however, that Tugh Temür and his supporters did not intend Qoshila's reign to be a long one. Qoshila may have suspected something; once inside China he ordered stricter night watches.[59] The meeting of the two brothers took place on August 26; four days later, at the age of twenty-nine, Qoshila was dead. The annals *(pen-chi)* explicitly state that the death was by violence; outsiders suspected the use of poison.[60] Tugh Temür became emperor once again.

Behind the candidacy of Qoshila, however, lay Chaghatai support, and an episode in Chaghatai history which the standard accounts neglect. Qoshila's candidacy was one last case of major political interaction between two major realms of the Mongol empire. As is well known, the Chaghatai Khanate was hard put to achieve internal stability owing to the striking political, geographical, and religious polarities that existed within the confines of its realm. It first of all freed itself from the political manipulation of Qaraqorum only after 1260 when Qubilai transferred the Great Qaghanate to China. Shortly after that, however, the Chaghatai realm fell under Qaidu's domination. Qaidu's general policy of drawing in orderly fashion upon the revenues of both Transoxania (Moslem) and the Tarim oases (Moslem, Buddhist, Nestorian) in order to help finance the conquest of Mongolia as a central point from which to control the conquered agricultural areas round about, succeeded for a time in providing some inner logic and consistency to Chaghatai affairs. But after the passing of Qaidu, the Chaghatai Khanate regained its independence only to fall victim to the latent contradictions within it. The rulers were confronted with the choice either of partial denomadization, leaning westward towards Transoxania and Islam, with the possibility of lucrative raiding operations into Persia, Afghanistan, and India; or of retaining the full nomadic regime and looking eastwards from the Ili and the Tarbagatai towards China and the possibility of political intervention in Yüan affairs. Qoshila, of course, personified this second alternative. His enthronement, supported by the Chaghatai Khanate, would demonstrate the viability of the eastern alternative and would serve to show that the Mongol empire was still in some sense a living reality, greater than any of its component parts, precisely because the key issue of succession to the throne of the Great Qaghanate could be settled on the basis of common consultation among all the leading Mongol princes, and not purely on the basis of political maneuvering within the Chinese Yüan realm alone.

A few facts may help illustrate the Chaghatai options. The Chaghatai *qan* Kebek, after making peace with the Yüan Dynasty in 1323, turned his attention to the western or Transoxanian portion of his realm where, without accepting Islam himself, he posed as a protector of the faith and entered into the settled administrative life of the country to a sufficient degree to build a palace near Nakhshab and strike in his own name the first Chaghatai coinage.[61] After his death in 1326 or 1327, his successor Eljigitei apparently turned the whole orientation of the state away from Transoxania back to the Ili region, where he joined Qoshila with a view to supporting the latter's claim to the Yüan throne. The "Chaghatai prince" who escorted Qoshila eastward to Qaraqorum was apparently Eljigitei himself.[62] In April, 1329, Qoshila, who had assumed the throne and was still at Qaraqorum, informed an emissary from the Ta-tu government that he planned to convoke a grand Mongol diet for the purpose of confirming his accession. "When I arrive at Shang-tu," he ordered, "the princes of the various khanates *(tsung-fan chu-wang)* will definitely all come to gather together. This is not to be compared to an ordinary court assembly. The Chaghatai prince, for one, has followed me for a long distance. The authorities must make all preparations to receive him. You and your colleagues in the Central Chancellery *(chung-shu)* will discuss the matter."[63]

The diet was never held, and Qoshila's nominal reign as Yüan emperor ended four months later with his assassination at the hands of his younger brother's partisans. Apparently Qoshila had not expected any major hindrance to his enthronement in China, since it seems clear that he and his Chaghatai ally were not prepared to invade that country in case of opposition.[64] It would probably have been difficult in any case for Qoshila to gather a large army on the spot in Mongolia because there was a severe drought there in the summer of 1329, and when Qoshila ordered the issuance of grain relief, he did so through the administrative agencies back in China, which indicates that he probably had no massive stocks of grain himself.[65] One is tempted to conclude that Qoshila and his backers had no knowledge or grasp of the power realities inside China and were led to believe that Mongol political unity could be restored from within, as it were—through the automatic operation of the laws of succession, without a determined and organized movement behind them to substantiate their claim. They seem to have been unaware that the workings of Yüan domestic politics were responsible for the civil war that cleared the way for the restoration of Qaishan's line, and that the Mongol and *se-mu* bureaucrats in China who guided that effort might oppose Qoshila's exploitation of their victory in the interest of an extraneous group that had no part in the affair. Tugh Temür's partisans were too clever flatly to oppose Qoshila's assumption of the throne; to do so might have given Qoshila an excuse to organize a determined steppe opposition. As it was, Qoshila's backing dissolved immediately after his assassination. Eljigitei apparently went home without a struggle, for he entered into amicable relations with Tugh Temür's court which lasted until his own death or removal in 1330 or so.

It is significant that Qoshila made plain in his imperial pronouncements his intention to preserve in its entirety the administrative organization of the Yüan empire.[66] In Qaraqorum he dismissed Yesün Temür's provincial officials and replaced them with his own appointees, but he made no effort to wreck the administration his father had created.[67] In 1307 his father had emerged from an autonomous and anarchic Mongolia to assume the Yüan throne in China. Had he been assassinated at that time the consequences might have been serious for Ayurbarwada and his supporters. Qaishan was in command of a battle-tested army, which at the time was the key to determining whether Mongolia fell within the Yüan or the Chaghatai-Ögödei orbit. He had the support of the steppe princes, who were expecting certain benefits from his enthronement. To a very great degree, therefore, Qaishan's accession was the product of an as yet unstabilized frontier. But Qaishan himself created the conditions that would make it impossible for his eldest son to follow in his footsteps. By 1328 Mongolia was integrated into an imperial system whose controlling levers lay in China and not in Mongolia. Unless Qoshila had somehow been willing to demolish this structure, his steppe candidacy lacked all substance. Since he did not attempt to demolish it, and thus reduce the steppe zone to anarchy once again, his idea of reaffirming the unity of the Mongol empire was completely unreal. His assassination proved that the Yüan Dynasty had triumphed over the Mongol empire. Thus did Yüan domestic politics win at the expense of Mongol unity; thus was it finally determined that the Mongol ruler in China was Yüan emperor first and foremost and Great Qaghan only in name.

Chapter II
The Restoration of 1328

The transition of Mongolia from imperial center (until 1260) to a state of anarchy (1260-1307) and finally to a position of administrative subordination to the Yüan Dynasty (after 1307) was mirrored in China by an almost inverse process: from subordination to rule from Mongolia (until 1260) to the consolidation of a centralized bureaucratic state under Qubilai in China (1260-94), and finally to the extension of this political and administrative centralism over the Mongolian steppe region (after 1307). The abortive attempt of Qoshila to become emperor in 1329 shows that the decline of steppe anarchy and independence had destroyed any further possibility of using Mongolia as a base from which an extraneous force might seize power in China. After the enthronement of Qaishan in 1307, Yüan political and dynastic history was almost entirely a reflection of struggles internally generated. This was certainly true of the restoration of 1328, which put Qaishan's younger son Tugh Temür upon the Yüan throne.

The restoration of 1328 not only marked the definite passing of the steppe frontier as a factor in politics; it constituted an important turning point in the internal political history of the Yüan Dynasty as well. The event involved a major turnover in bureaucratic personnel at the higher levels of the central government. It erased an earlier set of cliques and alliances, and brought into prominence a new group of individuals and clans, many of which retained their influence down to the end of the dynasty forty years later. Perhaps more significant, the restoration signaled the beginning of a new shift in the ideological orientation of the Yüan state. The year 1328 laid the groundwork for the thorough Confucianization of government, which, except for a short reactionary period under the Merkid Bayan from 1335 to 1340, characterized Yüan rule down to its end.

On the face of it, there was little that could be termed Confucian in the tumultuous events of 1328 and 1329. The Qipchaq El Temür and the Merkid Bayan, the coup leaders, were themselves hardly Confucian in orientation, and they did not consciously strive to achieve Confucian ends. Nor was the imperial line they restored, that of Qaishan, at all historically associated with the promotion and encouragement of Confucian bureaucrats or their doctrine. The restoration, nevertheless, opened the way to the emergence of Confucianism as the dominant working ideology of government. The time was ripe for it. The Mongol war machine had completed its tasks, and the point had long since been reached where, in the traditional scheme of things, the conqueror on horseback must step down and the peaceful administrator take over. For the Yüan, this also meant that side by side with the gradual shift from war to peace there must come a changeover in bureaucratic groups. The finance experts who had made up the earlier ruling cliques had been essential in gathering the revenues necessary to support the monarch as commander in chief during wartime. Yet once the need for warfare on the frontiers declined, the role of the finance experts became less obviously important. Always the incarnations of evil in the Confucian typology of official morality, the finance experts increasingly became vulnerable to attack from within the bureaucracy.

That Yüan leadership had to change as historical conditions changed was perhaps clear enough. However, the circumstances prior to the restoration of 1328 which allowed the specific emergence of Confucianism, or rather Neo-Confucianism, require some preliminary explanation, inasmuch as Neo-Confucianism, the former heresy of Southern Sung times, was not the only possible ideological alternative to the Legalism or crypto-Legalism of the ruling financial ministers. There was, for example, the Tung-p'ing school, or as it is sometimes termed, the "literary faction." As its name indicates, it was a regional group of Northern Chinese officials from Tung-p'ing in present-day Shantung province.

It achieved its high point of influence early in Qubilai's reign. In 1262 its patron, the prime minister Wang Wen-t'ung, accused of conspiracy with the Shantung satrap Li T'an, was executed, and the Tung-p'ing faction was in time replaced in power by another group, the finance experts, largely but not entirely of Central Asian origin. Tung-p'ing men, however, remained prominent in government, especially in the Han-lin Academy, down to the beginning of the fourteenth century. The Tung-p'ing school and its ideology served for a time as an important counterfoil to the Neo-Confucians. Tung-p'ing thought, vaguely Confucian rather than insistently and stridently Neo-Confucian, was less narrowly moralistic, concentrating as it did upon the cultivation of the purely literary Chinese art forms, both new and traditional, as well as upon the reintroduction of traditional Chinese methods of administration *(Han-fa)* into the Mongol conquest regime. For reasons which remain to be explored, however, the Tung-p'ing school failed to perpetuate itself. By the early fourteenth century, the burden of opposition to the ruling administration became almost entirely a monopoly of the Confucian group.[1]

Confucianism as a bureaucratic ideology enjoyed certain long-term political advantages under the conditions of Mongol rule that the incipiently nationalistic Tung-p'ing movement lacked. It was an importation from South China and, as such, was less tied to purely regional associations than Tung-p'ing thought. This was true even though the Neo-Confucian movement in its early stages in North China was itself organized partly as a regional response to Tung-p'ing domination, and eventually took over the Imperial University just as the Tung-p'ing men had taken over the Han-lin Academy.[2] Membership in the Confucian movement was, moreover, inherently more open than was the case with the Tung-p'ing. Not only was the Confucian movement in the bureaucracy eager to overarch regional differences within China; it was also eager to cross ethnic boundaries and bid for members from among the conquest groups—the Mongols and *se-mu* (mainly Central Asiatics). This it could do partly because it did not demand Sinification as the price of admittance. The Confucian approach to the problem of ethnic cleavage in the Yüan period was to transcend it. Above Mongol and Chinese, conqueror and conquered alike, sat the eternal, immutable, and essentially simple political and moral principles of the doctrine, true in all times and places. While the obligations of filial piety linked Mongols to Mongol forebears and Chinese to Chinese, not permitting either to "forget their origins" *(wang-pen)*, the cumulative demands of the other key tenets of Confucianism as a system of moral suasion *(chiao-hua)* required the debasement of national culture, Mongol or Chinese, to the level of folk custom *(feng-su)*, of which the moral value might range from neutral through successive levels down to the positively evil. It was, indeed, the duty of *chiao-hua* to act upon and improve *feng-su*.[3] Far from requiring the mastery of the Chinese literary tradition for its own sake, as did the Tung-p'ing school, Confucianism as a political and moral ideology placed primary emphasis upon the the acceptance and cultivation of its behavioral principles, considering literary training as no more than one means to this end, an ancillary discipline at best. As an ideological system to which the national literary tradition stood in an ambiguous and not a fundamental relationship, Confucianism undoubtedly was the more accessible to the alien in China, either directly or through translation. Perhaps the movement even welcomed alien blood. "The basic character of the Mongol is solid and simple and as yet undifferentiated," the Neo-Confucian Hsü Heng is quoted as having said. "He is capable of giving undivided attention and effort. If placed in a suitable company of his peers and allowed to develop himself for a few years, he will inevitably become an excellent servant of the state."[4]

It would appear that the Yüan monarchy consistently favored Neo-Confucianism over the Tung-p'ing tendency, if the record of officially sponsored translation from Chinese into Mongolian is any guide. Most popular were the *Four Books*, the *Hsiao ching*, the *Tzu-chih t'ung-chien*, the *Ta-hsüeh yen-i* and the *Chen-kuan cheng-yao*, either in whole or in part. Conspicuously absent are any translations from the masters of Chinese literature: no Tu Fu, for example; no Po Chü-i.[5] This notable lack of imperial favor, if such it is, is difficult to explain in view of the willingness of the Tung-p'ing group to help Qubilai achieve a centralized monarchy at the expense of the "feudal" establishment, the appanaged Mongol nobility *(t'ou-hsia)*, a class whose continued existence Confucian theory tended to favor and to whom Confucian bureaucrats often looked for patronage and support.[6] It may be surmised, however, that Qubilai as monarch found it advantageous to encourage the Confucian movement rather than the Tung-p'ing, even though at the time the Confucian attitude toward uncontrolled autocracy appeared somewhat less favorable. As is well known, Qubilai's tightly centralized government in China came to be staffed in accordance with a system of ethnic classes which, in order of precedence, were (1) Mongols; (2) *se-mu;* (3) Han-jen, or Northern Chinese, plus Sinicized Jürcheds, Khitans, and Koreans; and (4) Nanjen, or Southern Chinese. According to Meng Ssu-ming's analysis, the system was designed for two over-all purposes; to ensure the dominance of the Mongols and *se-mu* in the Yüan bureaucracy at Chinese expense, and to safeguard monarchical leverage over the bureaucracy by using one ethnic group to check another within any major organ of the government.[7] But if in these circumstances factional divisions should coincide with the ethnic classes—and the Tung-p'ing movement looked very much like a strictly ethnic Han-jen faction—the system would be in great danger of degenerating into bureaucratic civil war. Consequently, the monarchy was careful to put members of every faction into each level of the ethnic hierarchy. Qubilai, for example, saw to it that each faction had its proper ethnic mixture and was patronized at the top by Mongols and *se-mu*.[8] The ethnic class system itself came to be looked upon as sacrosanct in theory. In spite of the large amount of latent dissatisfaction with it on the part of the Chinese, it was violated only surreptitiously by various modes of irregular and illegal circumvention, and was never raised to the dignity of a major political issue.

A milestone in the Yüan bureaucracy was reached in 1315, when Ayurbarwada for the first time in the Yüan period instituted the civil service examination system. Its institution had long been delayed owing in large part to the dispute between the Confucian and Tung-p'ing factions over what the proper subject matter should be.[9] Ayurbarwada settled the issue in favor of the Confucians. He scrapped the traditional Sung examination, with its emphasis upon metrical composition, demanded by the Tung-p'ing school, and specifically directed that the contents be restricted almost entirely to questions on Confucian ideology, principally the *Four Books* with Chu Hsi's commentary. Metrical composition was explicitly excluded on the grounds of its irrelevance and frivolity *(fou-hua).* While acting to prevent a complete bureaucratic revolution by restricting the triennial quotas to a mere 300 *chü-jen* and 100 *chin-shih,* the emperor strengthened the multinational character of the Confucian movement without prejudicing the ethnic class system itself. He did so by dividing the quotas equally among the four ethnic groups, thus giving the numerically fewer Mongols and *se-mu* a distinct advantage over the Chinese.[10]

In addition, the system of guaranteed recommendations *(pao-chü),* put into practice as a bureaucratic recruiting device for the first time in 1298, was revived, Confucianized, and extended to the prospective examinees. The Tung-p'ing faction had originally urged *pao-chü* upon the government as a corrective to the prevailing *yin* system which provided access to office through hereditary privilege.[11] According to the *pao-chü* system, officials at various levels were made to recommend two or three "honest and capable" men for employment, and were held liable for punishment if their recommendations turned out to be false or inaccurate.[12] The system was, however, sparingly used. The revived *pao-chü* system was based upon more typically Confucian qualifications for office. As a preliminary screening device for examination candidates, the new *pao-chü* demanded evidence of filial piety, fraternal submission, righteousness, knowledge of the classics, and correct behavior rather than "honesty and capability."[13] The intent behind this change was to replace functional criteria with ideological and moral desideratives as the more prestigious basis for official recruitment.

By the reign of Ayurbarwada, only two major factional alignments remained in the central bureaucracy: the rising

Confucians and their bitter opponents, the successors of the financial managers of Qubilai's time. Ayurbarwada utilized both. He counterbalanced his Confucianizing tendencies by simultaneously employing the financier, Temüder, as his head of government and chief financial adviser. Temüder's job was not an easy one, however. Since the squeezing of revenues was no longer related to the exigencies of warfare but rather to increasing court and administrative costs, Temüder's financial operations provoked an insurmountable resistance in the bureaucracy and in society. In 1276 the financier Aḥmad had been able to stifle the Confucian opposition to his policies temporarily but effectively. Temüder, however, had a much more difficult task in 1315. He was not only obliged to bargain with his opposition, allowing it to institute the examination system, but was forced to cancel a fund-raising scheme of his own when the landlords of South China threatened to rebel rather than submit their tax registers to inspection and verification by his agents.[14] Temüder and his faction managed with the help and support of the monarchy to survive this serious defeat, but they found themselves constantly on the defensive against an emboldened Confucian enemy, especially within the Censorate.

Matters came to a severe crisis in 1320. The emperor, Ayurbarwada, died on March 1 of that year, and was succeeded by his son Shidebala, the candidate favored by Temüder and Ayurbarwada's mother, the Qunggirad empress dowager *Targi.[15] The opposition considered the succession to be a violation of an agreement supposedly made between Qaishan and Ayurbarwada, whereby the throne was to have passed from the latter to one of Qaishan's sons. Resistance to Temüder mounted; already in 1319 he had been forced into temporary retirement as a result of a savage censorial attack upon him.[16] He returned to power as Chancellor of the Right upon Shidebala's accession, and used the opportunity to execute three of his chief detractors.[17] In so doing, he unwittingly produced a Confucian martyrology for the future.

In 1323 the crisis reached an extreme and ended in the assassination of the reigning emperor, Shidebala. When both Temüder and the empress *Targi died in 1322, apparently of natural causes, Shidebala shifted his political ground, gave his blessing to the Confucian opposition, and permitted it to undertake a purge against Temüder's relatives and supporters in the bureaucracy, executing them and confiscating their properties.[18] But the purge was arrested in mid course. Temüder's party rallied its forces, assassinated the emperor and his Confucianizing Chancellor of the Right, and arranged to have an imperial cousin, the Prince of Chin Yesün Temür, come down from his quarters in Qaraqorum to ascend the throne as their patron and protector.[19]

Yesün Temür ruled as emperor from 1323 to 1328. Although he repudiated the cabal immediately responsible for the murders, he refused to go further and allow an all-out purge of the anti-Confucians in the bureaucracy. In fact, after disposing of the assassins, he came to base his rule upon a policy of reconciliation for all sides. This satisfied Temüder's former adherents, but was a severe disappointment to those Confucian elements whose memory of Temüder's unavenged victims was keen.[20] They were eager to resume the purge that Shidebala's assassination had ended.

Thus did matters stand on the eve of the restoration. The bureaucratic conflict, which Yesün Temür had succeeded in suppressing for five years, came to the surface again in August, 1328, when he died in the summer capital of Shang-tu. The desire for revenge on the part of the Confucians, unleashed by the emperor's death, was ultimately responsible for the success of the *coup d'état* which brought Tugh Temür to the throne because it assured the leaders of the coup, men not consciously acting for Confucian ends, the indispensable element of substantial bureaucratic support.

It had been known since early spring of 1328 that Yesün Temür was critically ill. Just before his departure for Shang-tu on May 5 a conspiracy was planned and organized. Its aim was to put Tugh Temür on the throne as soon as Yesün Temür died. Some conspirators positioned themselves at the main capital of Ta-tu in preparation for seizing control of government. Others were placed among Yesün Temür's entourage at Shang-tu for the purpose of murdering his chief partisans among the high officials and imperial princes there. When Yesün Temür did die on August 15, however, his supporters at Shang-tu managed to outmaneuver the conspirators there, arresting and later executing eighteen of them.[22] The other group of conspirators at Ta-tu had therefore to go ahead with their part of the plot alone. On September 8, at dawn, the leader of these men, the Qipchaq El Temür, at the time Assistant Commissioner in the Chief Military Commission, led a squadron of troops into one of the palaces and arrested a group of Yesün Temür's officials who were in conference there.[23] This move gave the conspirators immediate control of the central bureaucracy, as well as access to the financial resources of the Buddhist monasteries of the capital, which ordinarily served as mercantile and banking institutions to the imperial household. El Temür at once appointed a new staff of ministerial officials, used the monastic funds to purchase military supplies, and made arrangements for the defense of the capital. He then dispatched envoys to bring the imperial candidate Tugh Temür up from Chiang-ling on the Yangtze.[24] Tugh Temür departed Chiang-ling on September 18 and on October 1, escorted by the Chief Administrator of Honan province, the Merkid Bayan, he arrived in Ta-tu.[25] On October 16 he provisionally assumed the throne, pending the arrival of his elder brother Qoshila from the steppes.[26]

Yesün Temür's supporters at Shang-tu were evidently caught off guard by this sequence of events in Ta-tu. El Temür had seized control of the government, installed an emperor, and by throwing a blockade north of the capital, was challenging the Shang-tu party to come south and fight its way back into power. One small point in Shang-tu's favor was the blatant illegality of Tugh Temür's accession, together with the fact that the conspirators were obliged to issue edicts without the validating mark of the imperial seal, which Shang-tu retained. Responding to the difficulty into which El Temür's swift moves had forced them, Yesün Temür's ministers proceeded to organize themselves for retaliation. Sometime during the ninth lunar month (October 4 to November 1) the Shang-tu party put up its own emperor, Yesün Temür's eight-year-old son and heir apparent, Aragibag.[27] It made use of what resources it had at hand to issue its own paper currency and gather armies to attack Ta-tu.[28] Of the provinces of the Yüan empire, five at one point or another declared themselves for the Shang-tu side: Liaoyang and Lingpei (i.e., Manchuria and Mongolia), Shensi, Kansu, Szechwan, and Yunnan.[29] The loyalist armies, led by various princes, nobles, and provincial officials, penetrated El Temür's defenses on the north and east and advanced as far as the outer walls of Ta-tu by late October and early November, forcing the insurgents to conscript the civilian inhabitants to help defend the city.[30]

El Temür's over-all strategy rested upon the exploitation of two broad advantages. One was that his initiative in seizing the bureaucratic and administrative center of the realm assured him an incalculable material advantage over Shang-tu. The provinces that declared for Shang-tu were geographically peripheral and economically poor compared to the core regions of China. The province of Shensi, potentially one of the richer provinces, was in the throes of a ruinous famine in 1328 and 1329 and consequently was of less aid to the Shang-tu side than it might otherwise have been.[31] El Temür held the metropolitan province of Chung-shu, together with Honan, and above all the three rich Kiangnan provinces of Hukuang, Kiangsi, and Kiangche. To be sure, certain imponderable factors, such as a bandit insurrection in Kiangnan, or treachery on the part of the Merkid Bayan, or active Korean support to the Shang-tu side, might have tipped the scales against the restoration.[32] As it turned out, however, the core provinces held firm, thanks partly to El Temür's swift removal and execution of opposition elements in the provincial governments. Despite the absence of the imperial seal, the insurgents were able to command the provincial and local bureaucracies and through them impose extra duties of forced labor, weapons manufacture, and rations deliveries upon the population.[33] The Shang-tu armies were at a comparative disadvantage. Once they entered North China, they had to forfeit popular sympathy and supply themselves by looting the villages. El Temür was quick to provide relief to the areas the Shang-tu forces disrupted, and so capitalized upon one major weakness of the loyalists.[34] Since he controlled the economic heart of the Yüan realm and could use the regular bureaucracy to exploit it, El Temür forced his opponent to act the part of an invader dependent upon casual local plunder for supplies. Though an insurrectionist, he made his own side appear the true defender of security and order.

A second advantage of great importance to the restoration was the fact that no one single important political or military power group in insurgent territory proved entirely loyal to the Shang-tu side once El Temür seized control in Ta-tu in the name of Qaishan's line. Two groups potentially capable of determining the outcome of the struggle were the imperial princes and the elite military units. The great majority of the princes, however, remained aloof. Only twelve fought actively on the Shang-tu side, some of them for obvious personal reasons.[35] Not one of the elite military guards units at Ta-tu, which in the circumstances were remarkably free to bolt sides, threw all of its support to Shang-tu. Several of them were cleanly split, with one half fighting for Shang-tu and the other for the restoration.[36] The palace guards and the elite units at Shang-tu were not entirely loyalist in sympathy either; some of the commanders there defected to Ta-tu with their troops.[37] The two great noble Mongol clans, the Qunggirad and the Jalair, with semi-autonomous appanages in eastern Mongolia and Manchuria plus large holdings in China, saw no special advantage in giving full support to either party, and in fact committed a few members to both sides.[38] For the geographically and materially disadvantaged Shang-tu loyalists to succeed in their aim of regaining control at the center, it was of course imperative that they hold the allegiance of at least a few key power groups there. Even though El Temür's active supporters may have been no greater in number than those backing Shang-tu, the very widespread apathy, or calculated neutrality, on the part of many groups toward the loyalists was a condition distinctly in El

Temür's favor. The young emperor Aragibag and his partisans at Shang-tu were fatally disadvantaged by the lack of die-hard enthusiasm for their cause inside China.

The Shang-tu loyalist effort collapsed on November 14, 1328, after two months of warfare. El Temür's forces having surrounded the city, the Chancellor of the Right Daula-shah came out and surrendered, bringing with him the imperial seal. This he presented to Tugh Temür at a ceremony in Ta-tu on November 23. On December 26 Daula-shah was executed and his corpse exposed in the market place. The Prince of Liang, Ongchan, one of the few loyalist commanders not killed in battle, was ordered to commit suicide.[39] The fate of the unfortunate young emperor Aragibag is unclear; there is a slight possibility, however, that he survived the debacle.[40] Not through luck, but through their initiative and superior strategy, exploiting popular apathy and bureaucratic discontent, the restoration forces triumphed.

Not a single issue, but a complex tangle of personal and group interests brought together the forces that produced the *coup d'état* of 1328. The restoration of the imperial line of Qaishan was the slogan which lent all the participants a cloak of righteousness and a degree of unity but, because only a handful of men with real personal ties to Qaishan actually took part in the event, its true political meaning was neither so simple nor so profound as it might appear. Only for the leaders of the coup did Qaishan serve to symbolize personal interests and bureaucratic identities.

It is related that when plotters first approached El Temür with a plan for a *coup d'état,* he was shocked and alarmed at the idea.[41] But as he weighed the pros and cons in his mind, his thoughts must have flickered briefly over the fortunes of his recent ancestral history. There was his great-grandfather, who surrendered to the Mongols, fought under Möngke in the Caucasus and under Qubilai in China and Mongolia, and in reward for his exertions was put into the Imperial Guards *(su-wei),* with a girl of the imperial house for a wife. His Qipchaq followers were accorded the privilege of being made koumiss-brewers *(qarachi)* to the imperial household. There was his grandfather Tughtugha (d. 1297), who succeeded to the Imperial Guards position, and over a period of a quarter century compiled a brilliant military record against Arigh Böke, Nayan, and Qaidu. For his efforts, he too was given a girl of the imperial house, and in addition was made a member of the appanaged nobility, being awarded extensive grants in lands and households in North and South China. Nor was that all. In 1286 Qubilai set up a new elite military unit, the Qipchaq Guards *(wei)*, consisting of Qipchaqs, Qanglis, and other Turkish soldiers, over which Tughtugha was given partial control.[42] Finally there was his father *Chong'ur (d. 1322), who ably carried on the tradition of this remarkable family, commanding his troops under Qaishan in the steppes, as was recounted in the previous chapter. After *Chong'ur's death, however, the family inheritance suffered serious losses, possibly through the influence of Temüder, who like his financier predecessors was intent upon reducing the appanages. The elite troops, the households, and the lands passed out of the family's control, and the princely fief of Chü-jung, awarded to *Chong'ur by Qaishan in 1309, was not reassigned to his heirs.[43] Surely El Temür calculated that he stood to regain all of this, and more, if he led a successful revolution in the name of Qaishan, under whom both he and his father had served, and who was the last to confirm and augment the family privileges.

El Temür first gained official position on the occasion of Qaishan's enthronement in 1307, and for the Merkid Bayan, too, Qaishan was the bridge into the bureaucracy. With the death of Qaishan and the accession of Ayurbarwada in 1311, however, both El Temür and Bayan were obliged to relinquish their positions. El Temür gave up his office in the Court of Imperial Cuisine and from 1312 to 1325 commanded an elite unit called the Left Guards.[44] Bayan left court altogether and took up new duties in the southern provinces.[45] The man the court at the time considered to be the leader of the Qaishan bureaucratic clique, the Qangli Toghto, was sent out to be Chancellor of the Left of Kiangche province. Once during Ayurbarwada's reign he was called to the capital, imprisoned, and interrogated about his attitude toward the naming of Shidebala as heir apparent. He was arrested again in 1322 after Shidebala became emperor; this time he was flogged at court, imprisoned, and sentenced to banishment.[46] When Yesün Temür came to the throne in 1323, however, he acted upon his policy of reconciliation and relaxed the controls that his two imperial predecessors had imposed upon the Qaishan clique. He released the Qangli Toghto, reopened contact with Qoshila, recalled Tugh Temür from exile in Hainan, gave El Temür civil office again, and transferred Bayan from South China to Honan province, which was in the north and nearer the court.[47]

Despite the emperor Yesün Temür's conciliatory moves, which served to put El Temür, Bayan, and their imperial candidate Tugh Temür into the strategic positions they occupied on the eve of their *coup d'état,* there was no longer any real Qaishan clique in existence, no horde of old Qaishan bureaucrats eager and ready to reoccupy their lost positions in the central bureaucracy. With the exception of *Chong'ur's son El Temür, none of the descendants of Qaishan's senior staff are known to have been involved in any aspect of the restoration, and few seem to have profited politically by it.[48] As for the leading figures in Qaishan's bureaucracy, those associated with his central chancellery (the *Shang-shu sheng)* were actively persecuted by Ayurbarwada upon his accession in 1311, and six of them were put to death.[49] Others joined Qoshila in his abortive revolt in Shensi in 1316 and then followed him into the steppes, thereby removing themselves from Yüan politics.[50] Still others either suffered persecution, died, or changed their political affiliations. Only for a few former members of Qaishan's junior staff—El Temür, Bayan, and the Qangli Toghto (who died in 1327)—was the idea of a restoration a living and concrete symbol of their identities and interests. Since among the chief figures in the restoration were a number of men whose lives are reasonably well documented but who had no known official or personal connection with Qaishan, other ties of common interest must have helped provide a basis for the mutual trust and cooperation that existed inside the restoration clique.

An examination of the family and tribal backgrounds of El

Temür and the Qangli Toghto provides a clue to the existence of a wider bond, whose origins lie in the Mongol conquests of the previous century. The two men belonged to closely related Turkish tribes, the Qipchaq and the Qangli. On the eve of the Mongol invasions, the Qipchaqs dominated the Russian steppes from the Black Sea to the Caspian and Aral, while their neighbors, the Qanglis, held the steppes from the Aral eastward to Lake Balkhash.[51] Toghto's was a chiefly clan among the Qangli, which, according to the ancestral record, surrendered and came to Qaraqorum during the reign of Ögödei.[52] Similarly, El Temür's ancestors, a chiefly clan among the Qipchaqs, with its center of power in the area between the Yaik and Volga Rivers north of the Caspian, surrendered to the Mongol armies in approximately 1237.[53] The descendants of both these clans, uprooted from their own native grasslands, eventually came to settle in China in the service of the *qaghan*. By Qubilai's time, when the ethnic class system was established, they were designated as *se-mu* and ranked right after the Mongols themselves. As members of a deracinated steppe aristocracy serving in China, El Temür and Toghto could reach out to a much wider circle of men of similar background than they could as former personal adherents of Qaishan. It was this consideration which must have helped to tie a number of important individuals to the restoration cause.[54] To a degree, the restoration of 1328 may be characterized as a seizure of power by the foreign, largely Turkish, elements in China officially known as *se-mu*.[55]

A third bond, which the Qangli Toghto was particularly active in cultivating, linked the restoration clique to the Confucian movement within the bureaucracy and provided the necessary assurance of base support to the coup makers both during and after the short civil war of 1328. After his second release from prison, the Qangli Toghto spent the last years of his life at his private villa in Hsüan-te (now Hsüan-hua, Chahar), where with the cooperation of the court he established a Confucian academy for the instruction of his nine sons and the other people in his district.[56] Although he died in 1327 and thus took no part in the coup, his Confucian interests were shared by other *se-mu* backers of the restoration, and his Confucian studies were avidly pursued by at least two of his sons.[57]

Only the Qangli Toghto was at the same time a former personal adherent of Qaishan, a *se-mu*, and a patron of Confucianism. El Temür was a Qaishan adherent and a *se-mu*, but had no Confucian sympathies. Bayan was neither a *se-mu* nor a Confucian, but simply a Qaishan adherent. The restoration idea was the only common denominator among them. Little wonder, then, that they and their followers should raise the restoration slogan as a mask to cover other and potentially conflicting interests.

Tugh Temür's reign as emperor lasted from 1328 only until 1332; although shortlived, the period was on the whole peaceful and stable. Some understanding of the institutional nature of the period may be obtained through an analysis of the offices held by El Temür, whose efforts on behalf of the restoration found consummation in a far-reaching domination of Tugh Temür's court.

A position in the Chief Military Commission had enabled El Temür to initiate the insurgency in September, 1328. In October, 1328, Tugh Temür appointed him Chancellor of the Right, a post which afforded him control over the central bureaucracy; from this eminence, El Temür's power soon flowed outward into the military, censorial, and other branches of government and downward through the lines of command into the lower levels of the bureaucratic machinery. By a decree of December, 1328, only El Temür and Bayan were permitted to hold three offices concurrently, and by the same decree they were designated the exclusive channels through which matters of state expressed in memorials might reach the emperor.[58] El Temür was reappointed Chancellor of the Right in March, 1329, and he reached an apogee of power and influence in March, 1330, when Bayan agreed to step down as Chancellor of the Left and leave him as sole Chancellor and sole channel between emperor and bureaucracy.[59] An imperial edict of June 1, 1330, justified El Temür's paramount position on the basis of his meritorious accomplishments, listed his honors and offices, emphasized his power of final decision over all matters concerning orders and directives, punishments, official appointments, fiscal policy, and construction, and warned not only the regular bureaucracy but also the princes, princesses, imperial sons-in-law, and their attendants against circumventing his authority.[60]

El Temür's military powers rested upon his designation as *Lu chün-kuo chung-shih*, which allowed him a final word over the policies of the Chief Military Commission but did not necessarily involve him in its daily administration; and also upon his more direct control of the *Ta-tu-tu-fu*, a new institution which constituted a kind of special directorship over six of the elite guards units, one of which he also commanded personally.[61] The *Ta-tu-tu-fu*, it may be noted, had under it the various Qipchaq guards units; El Temür's power over them, thus legalized and institutionalized, was a resumption and a further growth of an inheritance dating from the time of his grandfather; and, equally important, he had at his disposal a loyal force which he could deploy on short notice against seditious movements in the capital.[62]

In contrast to his influence within two of the great organs of state, the Central Chancellery and the Chief Military Commission, El Temür's power over the third, the Censorate, appears to have been tenuous. In February, 1329, he was indeed appointed Censor-in-Chief, but merely for the purpose, it would seem, of gaining some familiarity with its personnel and operations, since he apparently occupied the post for only about a month. Yet, owing undoubtedly to firm partisan control, the Censorate during Tugh Temür's reign confined its scope of attack and impeachment chiefly to certain former members of the political opposition. El Temür and his close political associates were never attacked.[63]

Other offices which El Temür held may be summarized briefly. Already in October, 1328, he was given general editorship of the National History (which implied ultimate control over its contents); in February, 1330, he was given general editorship of the great institutional compendium of the Yüan period, the *Ching-shih ta-tien;* these were followed in March, 1332, by a charge over the K'uei-chang-ko Academy, a collegium of scholars of literary and artistic bent which Tugh Temür set up in 1329.[64] It may be assumed with some confidence that El Temür's literary positions did not involve him in any actual literary work, and that his directorship over the Academy was in part intended as an impediment to the members' independent access to the emperor.[65] El Temür was also given control over the *Kung-hsiang tu-tsung-kuan-fu*, a palace office which managed an extensive empire of textile manufacturing bureaus and other enterprises such as rice farming, leatherworking, and hunting in North and South China.[66]

If the restoration and civil war of 1328 propelled El Temür into a public position suggestive of a dictatorship, it also provided him an opportunity to amass private privilege and fortune to a degree that far outdistanced the best efforts of his father and grandfather. The princely fief of Chü-jung, once held by his father *Chong'ur, passed to a younger brother, and an entirely new fief, that of T'ai-p'ing, was created for El Temür himself in October, 1328. Income for the fief was provided by revenues from the *lu* of T'ai-p'ing (now Tang-t'u, Anhwei) on the Yangtze; by a special decree of February, 1330, El Temür was given the privilege of bypassing the regular bureaucracy and collecting these revenues himself.[67] And he gained yet more: 500 *ch'ing* (*ca.* 8,000 acres) of government land in the Soochow area; other confiscated tracts of land of unspecified dimensions on the Yangtze delta region; a park, pond, water mill, and fields in Lung-ch'ing *chou* (now Yen-ch'ing, Chahar); and a restored outright control of around 1,500 households in south central China which once belonged to his grandfather.[68] He was moreover in November, 1328, granted the ancient and coveted title of *darqan*, which carried with it the hereditary privileges of unrestricted access to the emperor, juridical immunity, and exemption from taxation.[69] In pursuance of this latter right was Tugh Temür's order of September 12, 1331, to the effect that the Commercial Tax Bureau *(Hsüan-k'o t'i-chü-ssu)* was not to let its agents enter El Temür's residence for the purpose of taxing the commercial articles he stored there.[70] Other gifts in gold, silver, cash, precious objects, slaves, women, residences, and lesser goods came one after the other from 1328 to 1332; of these gifts, not least perhaps was the construction at imperial command of a temple *(sheng-tz'u)* on the outskirts of Ta-tu, dedicated to the worship of El Temür's spirit and genius, with an accompanying stone stela bearing an inscribed account of El Temür's merits, for the edification of contemporaries and the enlightenment of posterity.[71] The emperor himself honored the site with occasional visits.

But there was yet more than this to El Temür's ascendancy: offices and privileges were further extended and cemented through the bonds of kinship. His stepmother, the princess *Chagir, apparently gave El Temür significant aid and counsel in the early stages of the coup.[72] Of El Temür's four sisters, three married princes of the imperial house.[73] El Temür himself is said, no doubt with exaggeration, to have taken no less than forty girls of the clan of Chinggis Qan to wife.[74] The true significance of these marriages and the manner of their arrangement are nowhere described, but may be surmised. If El Temür had it in mind to displace the Qunggirads, the imperial consort clan par excellence, with his own Qipchaqs, then this was a policy which did come briefly to fruition. His daughter, married to Toghon Temür, became empress in 1333.[75]

Other ties of relationship operated in different spheres to aid and reinforce El Temür's dynasty. An uncle, Buqa Temür, who commanded an elite guard against Shang-tu in 1328, received as reward a confiscated residence, promotion to a senior post in the Chief Military Commission, and the princely fief of Wu-p'ing.[76] El Temür's younger brother Sadun and Sadun's son *Tangkish, both active in the coup, received their measure of booty as well as the title of *darqan;* both served at different times as directors of the Office for Imperial Cuisine, a sort of palace commissary. Through that office patronage could be dispensed, because it appointed its own functionaries, and political loyalties could be cultivated, owing to the many recipients of its favors.[77] El Temür's younger brother *Darindari, who inherited the fief of Chü-jung, also held military office and served as a director of the *Ta-hsi tsung-yin-yüan,* which nominally managed the imperial cult, but which also dispensed cash and grain and undertook imperial construction. Access to the *Ta-hsi tsung-yin-yüan* meant access to a whole world of semiprivate imperial finance.[78]

As sole Chancellor of the Right and the chief minister of the realm, El Temür's power substantially surpassed that of any of his predecessors. To be sure, previous chancellors had packed the bureaucracy with their relatives and personal supporters and had concurrently controlled individual guards units; but none gathered so many powers and functions into his own hands, or combined bureaucratic leadership with princely status, as did El Temür. By the same token, no previous emperor of the Yüan Dynasty was ever so circumscribed in his powers as Tugh Temür. From this it would appear that the restoration idea served not only to unify a coalition of disparate insurgent elements, but also to justify what might be termed a temporary but radical alteration of the Yüan constitution. In fact, the leading partisans of the restoration looked not upon Qubilai as their justifying founding father, but upon Qaishan; and not upon Qaishan as emperor, but as their commander in the steppe wars. As emperor, Qaishan's strongly legalistic policies were neither revived nor invoked as precedents by the restorers of his line.[79] As the personal symbol of the unity of a group, however, Qaishan lived on in the figure of his son Tugh Temür. In these circumstances, Tugh Temür's function in the restoration was not to rule as emperor in the fashion of either Qubilai or Qaishan, but simply to reign as a living representative of his father and a rallying-point for the restoration forces. There was little Tugh Temür could do to alter this situation, for the whole composition of government rested upon the intensely personal relationship between himself and El Temür. Neither could have achieved his position without the other, and both were knowing accomplices in the murder of Qaishan's eldest son Qoshila, the emperor from the steppes who invoked Qubilai and promised to institute a very different style of rule.

The restoration regime led by El Temür moved quickly and eagerly to satisfy a Confucian demand of long standing—the removal and punishment of Temüder's former clique. The Moslem officials were the first to suffer. One of the first acts of the new regime was the abolition on October 3 of the office of the Moslem *qāḍī* in Ta-tu.[80] The Chief Administrator Ubaid-ullah, arrested in Ta-tu on September 8, was executed on October 15; the Chancellor of the Right Daula-shah, who surrendered Shang-tu to the insurgents, was put to death on December 26, as was related above.[81] These men were highly placed protectors of Moslem commercial wealth in Yüan China, and powerful enough to exempt their co-religionists from labor service obligations.[82] Their names were given specific and pointed mention as traitors in Tugh Temür's edict of enthronement of October 16, a document intended for the widest publicity.[83] No less pointed was the official name which El Temür later gave to the *coup d'état:* "The Pacification of Daula-shah."[84] Since the officially protected commercial operations and other privileges of the Moslems had long provoked Confucian enmity, their special privileges were canceled, and imperial favor was henceforth bestowed upon their commercial competitors, the Buddhist monasteries.[85] It would appear that the entire recent past was being surreptitiously marked with the stigma of Islam. These official moves soon stimulated a popular wave of anti-Moslem sentiment in both North and South China, and the government was obliged to take steps to curb it.[86]

During November and December, 1328, the restoration regime stepped up the purge, giving special attention this time to the Chinese and Mongols who were officials in the former administration. In addition to dismissals and punishments, the purge involved the confiscation of families and family property. By a special edict of November 24, El Temür was appointed the sole authority for redistributing confiscated property, and under his direction about 125 individual properties changed hands.[87] While it certainly did not oppose El Temür, a clue to the already strong Confucian orientation of the new Central Chancellery may be seen in its repeated but unsuccessful attempts to halt the confiscations of wives and children.[88]

By the time of Qoshila's murder in August, 1329, and Tugh

Temür's reassumption of the throne, the basic work of the restoration was accomplished, and a major bureaucratic revolution had been achieved. With its opponents at last thoroughly vilified and totally crushed, the Confucian movement stood as the only coherently organized faction remaining in the bureaucracy. Even so, it was not yet strong enough to force its ideology upon the leadership. Until Tugh Temür's death in 1332 the non-Confucian El Temür and his personal Qipchaq dynasty were all-powerful. His position rested upon the tentative but close harmony of the men he carried with him to office when he acted to restore Qaishan's line, and upon his peculiar relationship with Tugh Temür—to whose care, in ostentatious token of mutual harmony between ruler and minister, he entrusted his son.[89] The over-all stability of the period is easier to assume than to demonstrate, although the quiescence of the Censorate, obstreperous in Yesün Temür's day, seems indicative of it. The regime was in any event stable enough to put down rebellions in Szechwan and Yunnan and, in accordance with its official policy of fiscal sobriety, to carry out a partial demobilization of the Imperial Guards.[90]

Yet the whole structure of government was fragile and transitional. The leadership at the top was united only through Tugh Temür, who served as a personal representative of his father. As it turned out, the death of Tugh Temür in 1332 led to a split between El Temür and Bayan. In addition, the alliance between the leadership and the Confucian movement in the bureaucracy was only a temporary one, for El Temür and Bayan were not themselves leaders or champions of the Confucian movement. The two sides were allied only because in 1328 they needed each other to effect the purge of Temüder's faction, which was their common enemy. In 1335, after Bayan had annihilated El Temür's relatives and supporters, he repudiated his alliance with the Confucians and tried to crush them. In the face of this anti-Confucian reaction, however, the Confucian movement was to show its true strength.

Chapter III
Bayan and the Anti-Confucian Reaction

The relationship of the Merkid Bayan to the restoration of 1328 was a peculiar and ambiguous one. He was not a Confucian, and he formed no known friendships with people who were. He was not a *se-mu*, either, but a member of a Mongol tribe, the Merkids, whose unfortunate history resembled strongly that of the defeated and uprooted Turkish noble clans of Central Asia. The Merkids were not allies of Chinggis Qan, but one of the chief victims of his wars of unification in Mongolia. The leading clan of the Merkids was utterly annihilated in two main battles, one in about 1209 on the Irtysh, and the other around 1217 somewhere further west, possibly on the Chu River.[1] Having been denied asylum by the Uighur kingdom of Qaraqojo, remnants of the routed Merkids continued to flee westward, some of them seeking refuge among the Qipchaqs. After the Mongol general Sübü'ütei defeated the Qipchaqs and the Russians in the famous Battle of the Kalka in 1223, he formed chiliarchies, including a Merkid Chiliarchy, from among the captives he took.[2] Although Bayan's ancestral connection with these events is not directly attested anywhere, it is possible that his ancestors were among the Merkids taken at that time.[3]

Unlike El Temür, who struggled to restore an endangered family inheritance, Bayan acted for himself alone, His forebears were undistinguished and obscure.[4] His only apparent relationship to El Temür lay in the fact that they both served as junior staff under Qaishan in Mongolia. It was this former relationship that El Temür had in mind when he began the coup in Ta-tu in Qaishan's name. It would have been disastrous for the whole undertaking had Bayan chosen to give strict observance to the usual administrative regulations and refused to acknowledge the illegal orders issuing from the capital.[5] The attitude of Honan province, of which Bayan was Chief Administrator, was crucial for at least two reasons. First of all, El Temür's imperial candidate Tugh Temür was in residence at Chiang-ling on the middle Yangtze and would have to cross Honan in order to reach the capital; and second, Honan lay sandwiched between North and South China and could conceivably have interdicted the flow of grain and other resources which only South China could provide. In these circumstances, Bayan was in a position to throw the province either to Ta-tu or to Shang-tu. He chose, however, to give El Temür's agents free access to Tugh Temür; and when the imperial candidate and his cortege on their journey north reached the Honan provincial capital of Pien-liang (K'ai-feng), Bayan immediately assumed personal responsibility for the safety of the candidate for the remainder of his progress to the capital. Bayan's act of loyalty to the insurgents at Ta-tu was executed at a moment of critical importance to the success of the restoration movement. El Temür must have been well aware of this: upon entering Ta-tu with Tugh Temür on October 1, Bayan was accorded high honors, put in charge of the Imperial Guard, and appointed Censor-in-Chief. Honan was left for others to defend.[6]

During Tugh Temür's reign, Bayan's position in the state was second only to El Temür's. While El Temür remained as Chancellor of the Right, Bayan was shifted from high office to high office but finally settled into the headship of the Chief Military commission on a permanent basis. Like El Temür, however, Bayan also occupied a number of concurrent positions in other areas of the government. During Tugh Temür's reign he commanded an elite guards unit and a myriarchy of Alan troops, and held, like El Temür, the designation of *Lu chün-kuo chung-shih.*[7] Within the palace, Bayan held position in, but had no exclusive control over, the institution established for the guidance and support of the heir apparent; and he was also named one of nine chiefs of a new board called the *Shih-cheng-fu*, which managed those members of the Imperial Guards who served as the emperor's personal valets.[8] Finally in November, 1331, Bayan was appointed one of the heads of the new *Chao-kung wan-hu tu-tsung-shih-ssu*, a palace revenue-producing agency—which seems to have lost much of its sources of wealth when one of its components, headed by El Temür, was removed from its jurisdiction.[9] In addition to these official posts, Bayan, like El Temür, was also the recipient of property confiscated from the political opposition.[10] He too was granted a princely fief, with income from the tax revenues of two counties (*hsien*) in Honan province, and was given the daughter of an imperial prince in marriage.[11] On imperial order, temples (*sheng-tz'u*) and laudatory stelae were set up for him in his bailiwick of Pienliang and elsewhere in North China.[12] Bayan's power was thus distributed in the same fashion as El Temür's; they both held high posts in the central government, in one or more inner palace agencies, and both had personal command of elite guards troops. Bayan's position was lesser only in degree; and with the disappearance of El Temür from high politics, it was a position which he could, and did, easily build upon.

The death of Tugh Temür on September 2, 1332, at the age of twenty-eight removed the keystone from the whole restoration settlement. The heir apparent Aradnadara had died in February, and Tugh Temür had named no replacement. In these circumstances, Tugh Temür's widow, the Qunggirad Budashiri, stepped into the political foreground, brandished a will said to have been left by Tugh Temür on his deathbed, and declared that it was the late emperor's intention that the throne should first go to a son of Qoshila rather than to his and Budashiri's second son, El Tegüs.[13] Although there is no evidence that he originally opposed the move, El Temür was eventually persuaded to give his endorsement to the succession of Qoshila's younger son Irinjibal.[14] Irinjibal ascended the throne in October, 1332, and died two months later, at the age of six. It would appear significant that while there was enough time during Irinjibal's short reign to reconfirm Bayan in most of the same positions he held under Tugh Temür, El Temür was not reconfirmed; in fact no chancellor at all was named.[15] El Temür, quite clearly, was being outmaneuvered by the Qunggirad empress dowager. She appointed a seven-man advisory board to discuss the "renovation of government" and aid her in rule.[16] El Temür was excluded. She had, it might be noted, sufficient finances of her own to use in support of her political purposes.[17] The leading position she held and the influence she suddenly wielded were a first and telling blow to El Temür's Qipchaq ascendancy. Tugh Temür was gone, and the restoration clique was put in confusion.

The empress dowager's determination to replace Irinjibal not with El Tegüs, but with Qoshila's elder son Toghon Temür, was obviously aimed at preventing El Temür from returning to power; and although his position was already severely damaged, El Temür was able to prevent the enthronement for a time. For half a year, until July, 1333, the throne remained vacant. There is some doubt whether, as his biography explicitly states, El Temür died before Toghon Temür's enthronement; some evidence suggests that he died in the following year, 1334.[18] He appears in any event to have withdrawn from active politics owing to illness, and was dead at least by July, 1334, when posthumous honors were accorded him.[19] In the meantime, Bayan made an open political break with El Temür and shifted his support to the empress dowager. According to an unofficial account, Bayan was in Honan province at the time that Toghon Temür was recalled from exile in Kwangsi; and once again, as in 1328, he placed himself prominently in the escort as the imperial candidate proceeded northwards across Honan to the capital. Until the last possible moment, however, Bayan gave no indication of his attitude towards Toghon Temür, thus dramatizing once again his power to permit or obstruct imperial successions.[20]

Bayan's willing collaboration with Tugh Temür's widow, the empress dowager Budashiri, together with his support of the enthronements of Qoshila's sons Irinjibal and Toghon Temür, forced him to move further and further away from his old colleagues of 1328. The total collapse of the restoration order did not come about, however, until the summer of 1335. In June of that year the empress dowager signaled her support for Bayan when she refused his request to cede the

Chancellorship of the Right to El Temür's son *Tangkish.[21] Then in July, suddenly and without warning, Bayan fielded his elite units and attacked and destroyed El Temür's sons on the dubious charge that they were plotting "rebellion" *(ni)*.[22] Following that, he dismissed their personal adherents from their positions, and poisoned Toghon Temür's empress, who was a Qipchaq and the daughter of El Temür.[23] The official justification for this purge was shallow; there was no appeal this time to former days, no rehearsal of ancestral glories, but simply charges of rebellious and criminal behavior against an old and powerful clan.[24] The restoration clique was irreparably damaged, and the restoration myth, centered about Qaishan's achievements and his frustrated legacy, could no longer perform any cohesive function. It was hard for Bayan, the parvenu Merkid who climbed to the very top of the bureaucratic pyramid and into El Temür's shoes on the ruins of these associations, to escape the imputation of undisguised political opportunism and selfish ambition.

A sense of personal insecurity may have contributed to Bayan's incessant quest for private wealth and honor. After the purge, Bayan took over much of the Qipchaq inheritance himself.[25] Also profitable, but more picturesque, were the 40,000 pearl-diving households allotted to him in March, 1337.[26] There was more: several grants of land in various parts of the realm, and a new fief at Kao-yu on the Grand Canal.[27] New laudatory stelae were emplaced in a triumphal arch north of the capital.[28]

In rank, Bayan climbed notably higher than his predecessor El Temür had done. In November, 1339, he was elevated beyond (sole) Chancellor of the Right to "Great" Chancellor *(ta ch'eng-hsiang)*.[29] Even more, he had already held since 1333 the first-class princely fief of Ch'in.[30] Ch'in was the second on the list of first-class fiefs, all of them traditionally reserved for members of the imperial clan, except for three further down the list which were held at various times by members of the Qunggirad clan.[31] The princely fief of Chü-jung awarded to *Chong'ur in 1309 was of the sixth, or lowest grade; that of T'ai-p'ing, held by El Temür, was only of the second grade. Surely Bayan was going to excess. In a spirit of malevolent and persistent pedantry, a Chinese opponent wrote down in his personal notebook Bayan's thirty-five concurrent positions and official honors, which, he troubled to note, added up to 246 characters. Four other entries cite instances of the Great Chancellor's personal cupidity, and another lists three cases in which minor officials demanded gross and absurd tokens of privilege and esteem for their patron.[32] No one but Bayan was authorized to hold three or more concurrent positions; no one was second to him as he had once been to El Temür.[33]

While institutionally Bayan's position as Chancellor appeared to be nothing more than an improved version of El Temür's, the positions of the two men actually rested upon entirely different political foundations. Bayan's working relationship with the monarchical institution, so different from El Temür's, gives one clue to the changes that had taken place. From 1332 to 1340 the monarchy was under the control of the empress dowager, ruling for her nephews, both children whose own mothers (Qoshila's consorts) were dead or missing.[34] In this capacity, she was entitled to the designation, "empress dowager" (*huang t'ai-hou*), but not to the title, "grand empress dowager" (*t'ai-huang t'ai-hou*), which she assumed in September, 1335, over the strenuous objections of both Chinese and non-Chinese in the Central Chancellery and in the Censorate.[35] The meaning in her elevation was, however, clear: not one, but two imperial lines were open and operative. If Toghon Temür of Qoshila's line sat on the throne, her own son by Tugh Temür, El Tegüs, was alive, in the palace, and was designated as heir apparent and Toghon Temür's successor.[36] Toghon Temür was only twelve years old when he assumed the throne; the precariousness of his tenure must have been impressed upon him by the widespread and officially encouraged rumor that he was not really Qoshila's son.[37] It seems significant that Bayan made no attempt to define a new single line of legitimate succession, but cooperated with the Qunggirad Grand Empress Dowager Budashiri and maintained a friendly attitude toward both Toghon Temür and his cousin, El Tegüs. Bayan's indeterminate position on the monarchical issue was clearly related to his difficulty in defining a political role for himself after the passing of El Temür and the restoration order.

El Temür's restoration order was firmly and fully committed to Tugh Temür. Bayan, however, was not in a position to repeat El Temür's actions and make himself a restoration hero, this time in favor of another legitimate but wronged line, that of Qoshila. On the face of it, it would appear that he ought to have been able to make a forthright attempt to champion Qoshila's line, since he was not directly involved in Qoshila's assassination. But the truth seems to be that Bayan was almost as closely identified with Tugh Temür and his line as El Temür had been; and while he was able to accommodate himself to the reversion of the throne to Qoshila's sons in 1332, he was in no position to lead a glorious restoration on their behalf. Bayan and El Temür seem to have made efforts to avoid an overt political clash during Tugh Temür's reign, and Bayan made no noticeable attempt to nurture a clique of his own during that time, even though there was ample opportunity for him to do so.[38] In 1330, for example, there were at least two conspiratorial movements afoot in the capital, which according to later allegation had attempted to rally behind Toghon Temür as their factional symbol. In both cases, Bayan stood aside while El Temür executed the leaders, confiscated their families, and finally exiled Toghon Temür himself to Korea.[39] In January, 1331, a few months after the failure of these plots, Bayan was personally involved in the nomination of Tugh Temür's eldest son Aradnadara as heir apparent, for it was he who was sent to announce the event to the gods in the suburban temple.[40]

Thus by 1332, when Tugh Temür died, the time and opportunity for the factional exploitation of monarchical cleavages had come and gone. Not only that; the bureaucracy was relatively calm and showed no perceptible movement or desire to champion any particular imperial candidate as it had in 1328. As a consequence of this, Bayan lacked any acceptable justification for his emergence at the expense of the restoration order; he had no glorious and deserving imperial cause to promote, and no righteously vocal following within the bureaucracy. Once having achieved the highest position of ministerial power, however, he then attempted to formulate a program and win bureaucratic supporters for it. If his precipitate advance into the supreme ministerial position did little more than cause raised bureaucratic eyebrows, the subsequent revelation and implementation of his controversial political ideas, seemingly contrived in careless haste, antagonized and eventually alienated those elements in the bureaucracy that had earlier supported the restoration order. By 1340 bureaucratic revulsion against Bayan and his policies grew widespread and intense enough to occasion his political downfall.

Bayan's attempt to effect basic changes in the restoration political settlement, though inauspicious and eventually unsuccessful, nevertheless merits close attention. At the outset, his "anti-Confucianism" was a distinctly limited notion, more pragmatic than ideological; he rejected, for example, the policies of fiscal aggrandizement that earlier financiers had pursued, and he was even willing on occasion to accord official patronization to leading Confucian temples.[41] Bayan did not at all intend to destroy Confucianism altogether, but rather aimed to reduce what he saw as its inordinate influence in the bureaucracy, to deprive it of some of the gains it had made in the restoration of 1328, and to reinstitute some facsimile of the more varied mixture of factional alignments that had characterized the Yüan bureaucracy in its earlier years. The Confucian movement, however, put a more extreme interpretation upon Bayan's ultimate intentions than the facts of the case really warranted, but in the end it succeeded in showing conclusively that a non-Confucian factional alternative could not be restored in the bureaucracy. The Confucian gains of 1328 were not, as it turned out, temporary but permanent and preparatory to the even greater gains of 1340.

On November 17, 1335, Bayan had the emperor decree the abolition of the civil service examination system as a route of entry into bureaucratic office.[42] This was the earliest and most notorious of Bayan's anti-Confucian acts. There followed in December, 1335, almost as an afterthought, a change of reign-title *(nien-hao)*—an act which traditionally often symbolized a major change in official policy.[43] What was new and historically unprecedented in the reign-title change of 1335 was the fact that it revived and reimposed the Chih-yüan title that Qubilai had used from 1264 to 1294. Although Bayan never gave an explanation of what he meant by this peculiar act, it is certain that he was attempting to resuscitate the figure of Qubilai, shunted aside in favor of Qaishan since 1328, as the constitutional authority for the legitimacy of his policies. No civil service examinations had been held under Qubilai. In May, 1337, Bayan also issued regulations reserving once again the leading positions in the central, provincial, and local government organs to the Mongols and *se-mu*.[44] The aim of this move was to preserve the delicate system of bureaucratic control through the ethnic class system that Qubilai had devised. Bayan's order forbidding Chinese to learn the Mongol or *se-mu* languages must have been intended to deny them a popular but irregular route of official advancement.[45] Bayan's revival of the legacy of Qubilai did not, however, extend much beyond matters of bureaucratic recruitment and appointment; in the fiscal and economic spheres, he laid Qubilai's acquisitive precedents entirely aside. Thus one finds Bayan humbly beseeching the emperor to cease all activities that interfered with agriculture, to stop all imperial construction within the empire for four years, to close down two government ironworks, to reduce *corvée* among certain occupational groups, to reduce the annual quotas in three important salt-producing areas, and to relieve the large numbers of famine victims in north and south.[46]

Of all of Bayan's measures, the examination controversy aroused the most heated passions, yet few critics were so bold as to challenge the issue squarely. In opposition circles at court, responsibility for the cancellation of the examinations was not laid directly upon Bayan, but upon a subordinate, one Cherig Temür, who as Chief Administrator first made the proposal. Cherig Temür, it is said, was concerned over the expenses involved in arranging and holding the examinations, and thought that the proceeds from the lands set aside for the support of Confucian students might be put to better use if instead they provided maintenance for the Imperial

Guards *(keshig)*.[47] A Confucian opponent imputed Cherig Temür's dislike for the examination system to a "personal grudge."[48] Similar in its ascription of motive is an anecdote, probably apocryphal, that Bayan stopped the examinations when he found out that his missing Chinese groom had gone to try his luck at them: "As for the Chinese who study books," Bayan supposedly confessed, "they always deceive people. Formerly I had a groom. For some time I did not see him. When I asked about him, I was told that he had gone to take the examinations. I never realized that the examinations were taken by *these* kinds of people. . . ."[49]

If Confucian dismay at the cancellation of the examinations is perhaps readily understandable, Bayan's purpose in canceling them is less so, for between the years 1315 and 1333 only 539 *chin-shih* of all ethnic classes were graduated, constituting a mere 2 percent of a total ranked bureaucracy of around 22,500 men.[50] Obviously, the bureaucracy was hardly on the point of being taken over by the holders of the highest degree. This point was made forcibly in what appears to be an accurate report of a conversational exchange at court between Bayan and the Confucian Hsü Yu-jen. Since few transcripts of this sort survive, perhaps a direct translation would not be out of place here:

Hsü: If the examination system is abolished, the talented men of the empire will lose all hope.

Bayan: Many of the graduates have become corrupt, and some of them have assumed Mongol or foreign names.

Hsü: Countless officials were punished for corruption before the examination system was reinstituted, so this involves not only the graduates. The graduates are not blameless, but they are hardly as corrupt as the others.

Bayan: Of all the graduates, you are the only one capable of assuming office.

Hsü: Men like Chang Meng-ch'en, Ma Po-yung, and Ting Wen-yüan are all fit for high responsibility. And who can match Ou-yang Hsüan in composition?

Bayan: Even though the examination system is abolished, any scholar who wants fine food and clothing can study on his own and get any high office he wants.

Hsü: The true scholar does not concern himself with fine food and clothing. His business is to rule the state and bring peace to the empire.

Bayan: But selection for office through the examination system cuts off other avenues.

Hsü: As Mencius says, one should employ worthy men regardless of where they come from. Are not the scholars who come through the examination system much better than those who come from the ranks of the translators or seal-keepers? In the whole empire there are presently 3,325 translators and others, about 456 per year. The gatekeepers, imperial physicians, and imperial guardsmen all get to become regular officials, as do the local *(lu)* clerks and the sons of officials. So there are many avenues. This year from the fourth to the ninth month, 72 non-scholars were given office, yet the examinations only graduate about 30 men per year. I ask you, does the examination system really block other avenues?[51]

Bayan's appeal to the large but inarticulate mass of non-Confucians of all ethnic categories within the bureaucracy—careerists frankly interested, as Bayan put it, in the pursuit of wealth and rank, or men who prided themselves upon technical expertise—was to a degree based upon a compassionate and realistic assessment of the composition and mood of Yüan officialdom. Among many officials known collectively as *li-chin,* or men promoted upward from the clerkly ranks, there existed a good deal of smoldering resentment against the Confucian examination graduates, whose entry into the regular bureaucracy was so much easier and whose rates of official promotion were, or were believed to be, so much faster than their own.[52] The *li-chin* were officially discriminated against. During Ayurbarwada's reign, for example, there was a regulation in effect which prohibited *li-chin* from advancing beyond the fifth grade in the civil service.[53] At the higher levels of government, Confucian officials did struggle to see that their own men were given preference over *li-chin* in the matter of bureaucratic appointments.[54] By canceling the examinations, Bayan was making a definite political overture to this large and frustrated mass of clerks and lower bureaucrats whose status had not been quite so despised and hopeless under Qubilai.

What Bayan did not calculate was the enormous prestige, far greater than the statistics would indicate, that the Confucian movement commanded within the ranks of the 98 percent non-*chin-shih* majority of the bureaucracy There were, for example, about 2,100 holders of the lower *chü-jen* degree, which did qualify a man for office; combined with the 539 *chin-shih,* Confucian degree-holders of all kinds must have constituted about 11 percent of the bureaucracy.[55] Even more, there was a strong tendency on the part of many *li-chin* to identify themselves with the Confucian movement and to pin their career hopes upon eventual success in the examinations.[56] The Confucians, for their part, tended to look kindly upon those *li-chin* who professed shame for their clerkly origins.[57] Thus for all the men who might conceivably have been pleased by Bayan's attack on Confucianism, there must have been a large number of others who were dismayed and disappointed. In any case, it was certainly widely felt that the cancellation of the examinations would have a profoundly adverse effect upon the Confucian movement precisely because of the all-important role played by the state in channeling and regulating sociopolitical ambition. As the Kiangsi Confucian Chieh Hsi-ssu put it, with the prospect of an examination career dangled before them, men will drop their plows, their weapons, or their clerkly tools in order to follow it; but with that prospect gone, even the sons of the great Confucian literati will abandon Confucian study for other pursuits.[58]

Outside immediate court circles, the Confucian reaction to Bayan's moves was not limited to technical points, but cautiously hinted consequences of a much more fundamental sort. Chieh Hsi-ssu indicated this in a missive to a young Turkish protégé, a Qarluq from a family of garrison commanders domiciled in the provinces, who had married a Cantonese girl and pursued the *chin-shih* degree program only to find the door summarily shut by Bayan. The situation is distressing, urged Chieh, but not hopeless, for the Confucian Way in the final analysis exists independently of examinations or other official encouragement. One must continue to devote oneself to study even in the absence of career opportunity in so doing, for the pursuit of the *chin-shih* degree as a means of social self-advancement is not really its legitimate purpose. Its legitimate purpose is to nourish and build a corps of Confucian talents whom the ruler may employ in leading positions so that Confucian ideals may be translated into concrete policy for the benefit of all society. This purpose, Chieh emphasized, has not been achieved in the Yüan period anyway, despite the examinations. Ideologues who cleave sincerely to the Way have been ridiculed as pedants and hypocrites; eager and assertive talents who share in anxiety for the dynasty have been buried in inferior positions. The state has wrongfully contented itself with the reputation for, and not the real aim of, employing Worthies. Chieh ended his missive with a veiled threat and a note of hope. Whether Confucians are employed or not is a matter out of our hands, he confessed; the obstruction of our Way has to do with the movement of the cosmos and the dynastic cycle. Grieve as we will, there is nothing we can do about this, yet perhaps someone will soon come forth who, unable to bear any longer this cruelty and oppression (*k'o-pao ts'an-k'o*), will rectify matters for the dynasty.[59]

Chieh's indirect warning of disastrous consequences for the Yüan Dynasty was seriously intended. The Confucianists' bargaining point with any dynasty was their unqualified assertion that only they knew how to assure that ultimate guarantee of dynastic safety, the harmony of the social order. The vital point of contact at issue lay at the local level, where the *chiao-hua* (Confucian moral suasion) of the government met and acted upon the *feng-su* (prevailing customs and attitudes) of the common people. *Feng-su* was the fund of precedent and habit which is the very stuff of any tradition-bound society on the popular level. In Confucian eyes, however, the value-content of unadjusted *feng-su* was at best neutral in its harmlessly quaint or picturesque forms, and at worst positively evil when it degenerated into criminality, heresy, competitive strife, gross ignorance, or mindless excitability. Hence the purpose of *chiao-hua* was to improve and rectify —"beautify"— *feng-su*. Like the experienced peasant who cherishes the grain sprouts and roots up the weeds, the good local official, appointed to his post by a Confucian government sincerely committed to the Confucian program, must protect his crop of good people, feeding and clothing them, and positively encouraging their growth through the suppression of the heretical and violent, the guidance and enlightenment of the ignorant, and the soothing of the minds of the excited and disturbed. Prohibitions are not enough to extirpate undesirable forms of *feng-su*; positive remedial measures are necessary. All people are ultimately transformable to the good, and the sources of *chiao-hua* which effect this derive not from any code of laws but from Confucian self-cultivation and self-restraint, which alone legitimizes the use of sanctions, and which Bayan had now decided officially to discourage. A government dominated by *li-chin,* men who by their very nature believe that the possession of power carries with it the license to gouge and oppress (thus Chieh's reference to "cruelty and oppression"), will inevitably encourage the worst excesses of *feng-su.* That in turn will eventually bring about a total social cataclysm.[60] Chieh warned in his missive that in the six decades of the Yüan period to date, *chiao-hua* had never flourished and *feng-su* had grown progressively worse. The whole Confucian argument was ancient and powerful, if not logically necessary. In attempting to refute it, Bayan was laughing at the already weak bulwarks of *chiao-hua* which shielded the dynasty from the effects of violent and erratic *feng-su,* thus recklessly calling the Confucian bluff.

The first tangible signs of what the Confucians did interpret as proof of their warnings soon began to appear. In 1337 and 1338 a number of popular uprisings broke out in Central and South China. In February, 1337, rebels in Kwangtung set up a Great Chin "dynasty" and made common cause with another rebel group whose symbolic leader was claimed to be a reincarnation of the Dipamkara Buddha.[61] In March a group of rebels led by one "Stick" Hu, emboldened by a belief in the imminent appearance of the Maitreya Buddha and his millennium, initiated a rising which spread into four cities of the Huai area.[62] In May one Han Fa-shih, evidently a Buddhist devotee of some sort, set himself up as "king" of a Sung restoration state in Szechwan.[63] These commotions were followed in the summer of 1338 by a rising in Kiangsi, inspired and organized by the heretic Buddhist monk, P'eng Ying-yü. There were also troubles in Fukien.[64] Bayan's remedies for these disturbances, though negative and prohibitory, were successful. His provincial authorities put the rebels down without much difficulty. In October, 1337, he set up Branch Military Secretariats in four provinces, and twice issued regulations forbidding the possession of weapons to all Northern and Southern Chinese and Koreans.[65]

A Confucian by the name of Yeh Tzu-ch'i asserted that there was a connection between Bayan's "wrecking of the old norms" and the occurrence of these risings.[66] Precisely what the connection was, if indeed there was any, cannot be said for certain. However, whether from paranoia or from well-founded suspicion, Bayan himself was certain of the existence of some collusion between some of his Chinese officials and the rebels. His certainty in this matter had the unfortunate effect of enlarging his anti-Confucianism into a kind of anti-Chinese racism. On the explicit grounds that the rebels were all Chinese, he and his associates summoned the Chinese court officials and laid the evidence before them, hoping that "the Chinese officials would avoid answering and could then be accused of complicity."[67] In this he was not successful, but another case did develop concerning the illegal possession of weapons, in the course of which an unspecified number of Chinese officials in the Central Chancellery was cashiered.[68]

The peculiar timing of the rebellious demonstrations, coming about a year after the inauguration of his new policies, certainly convinced Bayan that they were not coincidental but were positive and menacing signs of intransigent Chinese opposition. When from far-off Ning-hsia came reports of a plot against his life, Bayan was provoked into anger and vindictiveness.[69] His fear of assassination became known to the population at large, among whom a tale was current that Bayan especially hated the Southern Chinese because his personal augur had predicted that he would die at the hands of one, and thus he prohibited weapons and forbade the Chinese to retaliate if struck by a Mongol or a *se-mu*.[70] Other stories had it that Bayan was prohibiting the use of iron farm tools in South China in order to rid the area of possible weapons for use in rebellion, and that he was forbidding all performances of opera and storytelling, probably in order to stop political satire and frustrate opportunities for clandestine organization.[71] Another rumor spread and caused panic: the officials were going to seize all of the unmarried boys and girls in the empire.[72] Wildest of all was the report that Bayan intended to kill everyone with the five surnames of Chang, Wang, Liu, Li, and Chao—a major percentage of the Chinese population.[73] Horror was compounded with ridicule; a popular jinglet heard in the capital went: "He deceives the ruler above, and oppresses the people below, while leaning on the Grand Empress Dowager." Indeed, he was said to be visiting her secretly at night.[74] Thus fear grew and rumors multiplied on both sides, the specter of a total conspiracy of the Chinese people in the mind of Bayan neatly balancing the vision of a monstrous and irrational official terrorism in the minds of the people. A Confucian might have noted that the soothing effects of *chiao-hua* were not in evidence.

Owing in part to the structure of the Yüan Confucian movement, however, the nightmarish prospect of a total Sino-Mongol confrontation never developed into a reality; for Bayan's policies also landed him in serious difficulty with sections of the Mongol and *se-mu* population in China, among whom Confucianism was a flourishing and growing movement. In fact, it is beyond doubt that the institution of the Confucian examination system had a greater impact upon the Mongols and *se-mu* than it did upon the Chinese. The arrangement of the examinations favored the chances of the non-Chinese candidates, not only because they could take a simpler test, but also because while Mongols and *se-mu* combined constituted only about 3 percent of all registered households in China, they occupied 30 percent of the positions in the regular bureaucracy.[75] If it is assumed that the Northern and Southern Chinese easily filled their total quota of fifty *chin-shih* at each triennial examination, one can then perceive a steadily increasing number of successful non-Chinese candidates from 1315 to 1333, for the combined totals run as follows: 56 (1315), 50 (1318), 64 (1321), 86 (1324), 86 (1327), 97 (1330), and 100 (1333).[76] This process would seem to have produced by 1333 a total of around 189 Mongol and *se-mu* holders of the *chin-shih* degree.

This alternative career program fell short of Confucianizing the non-Chinese bureaucracy as a whole. In about the year 1300, there were 6,782 non-Chinese in the Yüan bureaucracy.[77] Assuming that this number remained constant, *chin-shih* degree holders would by 1333 have constituted about 3 percent of the total, and degree holders of all kinds about 18 percent. No non-Chinese degree holder is known to have held an important position at court in Bayan's time.[78] At stake, however, was more than a small, albeit growing, body of actual Confucian degree holders among the Mongols and the *se-mu*. By all indications, there was a large number of non-Chinese, particularly those domiciled in the provinces, who were attracted to the program and placed their career hopes in it.[79] Involved too was the patronage of Confucian studies by a number of Mongol and *se-mu* clans of high status which did not actually have degree holders among their own members.[80] It was consequently inevitable that Bayan's anti-Confucianism would provoke powerful opposition form within the ranks of the Mongols and *se-mu*, as well as the Chinese.

The Mongol and *se-mu* opposition to Bayan in fact stemmed from two separate but closely related issues. The Confucian issue was intimately bound up with widespread bitterness and resentment against Bayan's destruction of the restoration order of 1328, a program which began in July, 1335, with the liquidation of the Qipchaqs and which was still in progress at the time the examinations were abolished. One by one, Bayan and his agents ferreted out and purged the Mongol and *se-mu* supporters of the restoration order, both Confucian and non-Confucian.

A relatively mild case concerned the Jalair viceroy Dorji, born in the famous Southern Chinese city of Hang-chou. Dorji, it is said, "served his mother with extreme filial piety; he liked reading books, but rather than waste his time with textual pedantry, he devoted his mind to the study of how in antiquity rulers and ministers carried out affairs, how loyalty was given the ruler and solicitude bestowed upon the people."[81] He was admired by a number of Chinese Confucians, and succeeded to the viceregal title in 1329. In 1338, however, Bayan divested him of the title and gave it to Naimantai, a distant cousin of Dorji's, whose career had begun under Qaishan in the steppe wars and whose subsequent experiences had not brought him into any close contact with Chinese or Confucians.[82]

More serious was the abrupt and unexplained disappearance of the Uighur Arigh Qaya, prominent on Tugh Temür's side in 1328, who "favored the classics" and was pleased to endow a Confucian temple school attached to a guards unit which he commanded.[83] An obstreperous opponent of Bayan's, the Tangut Irinjinbal, was sent into exile and his son executed.[84] Treason charges were pressed against members of the family of the Prince of Chia Qonqor Temür, a descendant of Qubilai's elder brother Möngke (r. 1251-59). Qongqor Temür himself, accused of having been the imperial candidate of the Qipchaqs, had committed suicide at the time of the Qipchaq defeat in 1335.[85]

Yang Yü tells us that the people of the capital were much aggrieved at the executions of the Prince of T'an Chechegtü and the ex-*iduq-qut* and Prince of Kao-ch'ang Temür Buqa.[86] Temür Buqa, whose own kingdom of Qaraqojo had passed out of existence, made his career in China and was one of the most prominent of Tugh Temür's partisans in 1328. He was also a patron of aspiring Confucians.[87] The case of Chechegtü, also a descendant of Möngke, is difficult to fathom because the prince had collaborated closely with Bayan in the destruction of the Qipchaqs, and as late as April, 1337, was the recipient of a grant of land in the Yangtze delta. An unofficial source has it that Bayan was originally a "family slave" of the prince, an embarrassment now that he was prime minister, and that Bayan executed him and several of his sons in 1337 on the grounds of treason.[88] Later allegation relates that when Chechegtü was executed, his family and property were confiscated, and in the course of the prosecution against him "countless numbers of El Temür's clan clique *(tsung-tang)* were killed."[89] The true facts of the case seem to be buried in mystery.

At the time of Bayan's downfall in early 1340, he was in the midst of carrying out three more prosecutions. Two concerned the Prince of Wei-shun Köncheg Buqa and his brother, the Prince of Hsüan-jang Temür Buqa, grandsons of Qubilai through his eleventh son Toghon. Twice, apparently, in 1336 and again in 1339, Bayan summoned the two princes from their residences in Central China. Both had been closely associated with Tugh Temür since before his enthronement in 1328, but their supposed crimes were unstated, the charges against them unpublished.[90] The third case, the Fan Meng incident, was more clear-cut and more dangerous, not only because of the possibilities of bureaucratic mutiny which it revealed, but also because of the reckless way in which the case was handled. An extant account describing this incident appears to be closely based upon documentary evidence. Briefly, what occurred was a sudden takeover of the Honan provincial capital of Pien-liang by a low-ranking Chinese clerk named Fan Meng. While he was on duty in provincial government headquarters, Fan had an accomplice act as an imperial messenger bearing an imperial edict. One by one, nine of the chief Mongol and *se-mu* provincial officials were summoned from the banquet table to hear the edict, only to be slaughtered by attack from behind with an iron club as they came out. Appointed "Commander-in-Chief of Honan" by the spurious edict, Fan then called up troops to await orders, took over the whole city, and for a length of time which is not precisely known he was able to seal off one of the main lines of communication between North and South. The danger in this incident lay first of all in its brazenness—Pien-liang was, after all, Bayan's old bailiwick—but even more in its demonstration of the ease with which the Chinese could shift their loyalties away from the dynasty to the first practitioner of strongarm methods who came along. A retired Yüan official and a private citizen who had earlier refused a high Yüan appointment were two prominent Chinese who were made to obey Fan Meng and to serve him in an official capacity. Kuei Ch'ang, a *chin-shih* of 1330 and a native of Pien-liang, gained fame and renown as the only such official or potential official who refused to join in. At length another Chinese clerk, discovering that the edict was false and Fan Meng an imposter, insinuated himself into his confidence and then murdered him.[91]

Bayan and his men reacted savagely to the incident, and apparently tried to implicate as many men as they could. Rumored estimates of the number of guilty Chinese officials involved differed widely: thirty men according to one source, three hundred according to another, and "hundreds and thousands" according to a third.[92] The Jalair Dorji, Chancellor of the Left of Honan province, eager to restrict the scope of the prosecutions to the few ringleaders, was openly accused by Bayan's chief prosecutor Narin of "favoring the Chinese."[93] Bayan made the same accusation against his nephew Toghto, who was Censor-in-Chief.[94]

By now, matters had gone too far. Bayan's last-ditch attempt to save himself by turning the ethnic groups against each other could not succeed. The young emperor was furious at the prosecutions going on against the two princes, and too many highly placed Mongols and *se-mu* were repelled and frightened by Bayan's increasingly murderous activities. Bayan's position within the ruling class was unstable, and he was as a result forced into the unenviable position of having to persecute his opposition without the help of any widely acceptable ideological justification in so doing. His badly articulated appeal to Qubilai in the end fell on deaf ears. His attack upon Confucianism obliged him to persecute the Mongols and *se-mu* who for the sake of self-advancement had come to some understanding with that doctrine and who resented on conservative grounds both his naked rise to power and the brutal means he used to defend himself.

In 1328 it happened that both the non-Confucian leadership of the restoration and the Confucian movement in the bureaucracy had something to gain by the *coup d'état* that took place. Indeed, so generally content were the Confucians with the liquidation of their enemies that they ignored the assassination of Qoshila and never sought to make a cause of it.[95] A secure dictatorship such as that of El Temür could control the Confucians. It could establish an academy such as the K'uei-chang-ko, appoint to it scholars of conflicting ideological tendencies, and thus confuse its goals. It could keep the literati occupied with literary projects, such as compiling the huge *Ching-shih ta-tien* encyclopedia, or writing inscriptions and epitaphs in honor of the leading restoration figures. It could isolate important Confucian leaders such as Yü Chi in high-ranking but meaningless positions. Bayan's dictatorship, however, was not a secure one. While there had been no Confucian drive to block Bayan's takeover of government, his position was vulnerable in that his bloody rise to power had profited the Confucians nothing. This awkward state of affairs Bayan surely sensed correctly, and rather than passively await the inevitable development of Confucian intransigeance and counter-activity, he decided to act first and deliver a crippling blow to the apparently monolithic prestige the Confucians enjoyed within the bureaucracy—a prestige which had been built up for the most part after the death of Qubilai. The tragedy was that the basic insecurity of Bayan's position grew rather than diminished; each defensive act demanded another that was more defensive, more repulsive, more murderous.

Bayan's removal was authorized by the emperor Toghon Temür and engineered by his own nephew, Toghto. On March 14, 1340, as Bayan was returning from a hunt with El Tegüs, he found the capital gates locked against him. Toghto read aloud the edict of dismissal, and Bayan's imperial guards, bribed beforehand, deserted him without incident. Bayan was first exiled to Honan province, then soon afterwards he was banished to the far south. In April, 1340, he died on the way there.[96]

Toghto had earlier sensed the impending political doom of his uncle, and realized that unless something were done his uncle's fall would also mean the elimination or destruction of the entire Merkid clan. To a certain degree, Toghto was in the same political position as his uncle, for he had participated in Bayan's bloody overthrow of the Qipchaqs. But Toghto had certain important connections that Bayan lacked. When Toghto was a young boy, his father Majartai had hired a southern Chinese by the name of Wu Chih-fang to tutor him in Confucian learning. Through Wu Chih-fang, Toghto was later put in contact with a number of other men, who as Confucians were opposed to Bayan and his policies. By 1340, when he was a Censor-in-Chief, Toghto not only had high political standing within Bayan's administration and entree to the emperor; he also enjoyed a somewhat covert relationship with the Confucian opposition. On Wu Chih-fang's urging, he decided to put himself at the head of all the opposition forces and strike down his uncle in the name of Confucian righteousness.

Bayan's attack on Confucianism proved to be ideologically unjustifiable and in the end self-defeating. Toghto's attack on Bayan was ideologically supportable, but only on Confucian grounds. There was no other way to rally and unify support from the bureaucracy. There was no other cause, no alternative principle, no competing movement that could serve to bind the ethnic classes together and permit the Yüan bureaucracy to function normally once again.

The failure of Bayan's attack on Confucianism was the best proof of its strength and resiliency. As the leading movement within the bureaucracy, it could neither be ignored nor eliminated, except at the price of dynastic collapse. The Confucian movement threatened to demand as the price of its suppression both racial war within the bureaucracy and mass popular rebellion against the state itself. With the removal of Bayan, the way was finally prepared for the triumph of Confucian politics at the highest levels of power.

Chapter IV
The Triumph of Confucian Politics

Toghto's timely action spared the Merkid clan the fate of the Qipchaqs. Not only did Toghto contrive the overthrow of his uncle, but he went on to sponsor a major shift in the political direction of the Yüan state. The pending prosecutions were called off and the examination system was at once restored. Bayan's mainstay, the grand empress dowager Budashiri, was exiled; the heir apparent El Tegüs was quietly murdered; and Tugh Temür was posthumously vilified and his tablet removed from the imperial ancestral temple. The imperial succession was again confined to one legitimate line, that of Qoshila. The seventh year of Chih-yüan was changed to the first year of Chih-cheng (1341), and with that the Bayan era was officially closed and a new period begun.[1]

Confucian parlance designated the dismissal and exile of Bayan and the cancellation of his policies as *keng-hua*—a shift *(keng)* in the direction of Confucian suasion, or transformation *(hua)*.[2] The signs of Toghto's *keng-hua* in government can be seen in a number of areas, one of which was the matter of official appointments. Hsü Yu-jen, *chin-shih* of 1315, several times humiliated by Bayan, returned to court in 1340 at the invitation of Toghto and his group and later resumed his former chancellery position of Assistant Administrator.[3] Hsü arrived with three other Chinese who had held prominent chancellery positions under El Temür and who were now offered gifts in token of their political sufferings under Bayan.[4] The list of Toghto's appointees to the Central Chancellery in 1341 shows a definite Confucian bias, at least insofar as the identities of the men can be traced. In 1341 Toghto himself was Chancellor of the Right; his Chancellor of the Left was one Temür Buqa, a descendant of Chinggis Qan's half-brother Belgütei, about whom little is known.[5] The Chief Administrators were Berke Buqa, an Eljigid Mongol, admirer of Chinese literature, and a former Imperial University student, of whom more will be heard; Toghon, a Jalair Mongol, with Confucian sympathies; Toghto's younger brother Esen Temür; and the Qangli Temür Tash, son of the Qangli Toghto, and an avid Confucian.[6] As Vice Administrator of the Right there was Arugh, possibly the same Arugh who as an intimate of the emperor's had worked closely in the plot against Bayan.[7] Hsü Yu-jen was promoted to Vice Administrator of the Left; and as Assistant Administrators there were Ting-chu, a former ally of Bayan's, a Qangli with no known Confucian connections, and a certain Wu Qudu Buqa, who is unidentified.[8] Back to the Han-lin Academy came the great Confucian leaders of the era: Chieh Hsi-ssu of Kiangsi, who under Bayan had left court on the excuse of illness; Huang Chin of Kiangche, also in the provinces during Bayan's ascendancy; back too came Ou-yang Hsüan of Kiangsi, and Chang Ch'i-yen of North China, all of them *chin-shih* of 1315.[9]

There were other signs of *keng-hua*. The *Ching-yen*, or "Classics Mat," suspended by Bayan, was reopened as an avenue of Confucian approach to the emperor. The Classics Mat was a kind of imperial seminar, a highly contrived and formalized meeting held at periodic intervals at which Confucianists expounded doctrine directly to the emperor; its ideological justification lay in the ancient and familiar proposition that the correct ordering of the empire must begin with the rectification of the ruler. As Chancellor, Toghto took over the ex-officio chairmanship of the sessions, but he left other arrangements, such as the procurement of Confucian lecturers and interpreters, to the Han-lin Academy.[10] The institution constituted an important link between the court and Confucian circles in the provinces, particularly in South China.[11]

Southern Chinese political activists of an obscure sort had taken a prominent part in staging the anti-Bayan coup and in advising Toghto on the proper means of winning Confucian support for his cause.[12] Throughout the planning and execution of the coup, Toghto was in frequent consultation with his mentor Wu Chih-fang, a Southern Chinese, concerning problems of both strategy and ideology. Wu Chih-fang's skill in Confucian casuistry helped to transform Toghto's removal of his own uncle from an act of gross impiety to an undertaking of supreme righteousness.[13] When Toghto cast out his uncle in March, 1340, it was probably Wu who advised him not to assume the position of Chancellor of the Right immediately, but for the time being filially to cede the position to his father. This Toghto did. As a patron of aspiring Chinese Confucian officials, Toghto's father Majartai was well known, and as a Chancellor eager for favorable Confucian opinion, his actions were conspicuous and unconcealed.[14] Thus in a gesture unthinkable for either El Temür or Bayan, in May, 1340, Majartai openly declined the designation of *darqan* and enfeoffment as prince of the first class. So well received was this refusal and so indicative was it of a new mood of modesty in government that the Censorate urged the emperor to issue an announcement about it to the empire "in order to encourage probity and deference."[15] A struggle of long standing among the various ethnic groups in Yüan China concerning the right officially to impose the marriage, mourning, and burial customs of one group upon another was resolved at least temporarily by Majartai in favor of the Chinese Confucians and their allies when he forbade the *se-mu* from marrying their maternal aunts.[16]

There appears to have been little doubt in any quarter that Toghto was the real power behind the change in government and Majartai merely a front put up in obedience to the Confucian principle of filial respect. On November 12, 1340, Majartai resigned as Chancellor of the Right on the excuse of illness, and Toghto, up to this time serving as head of the Chief Military Commission, stepped into his place.[17] An unofficial source has it that Majartai had taken advantage of his position to invest heavily in wine and grain shops and in salt distribution, and that Toghto considered his father's evident greed a sufficient reason to approach the emperor and ask him to allow Majartai to resign if he so requested.[18] There are grounds for suspecting that Majartai's resignation was, if not forced, at least strongly urged by Toghto. In its response to this action, Confucian opinion appears to have been sharply divided.[19]

Toghto's assumption of the highest ministerial post in the realm as a champion of *keng-hua* did not signify any qualitative change in the power or perquisites of the chancellorship itself. Although Majartai had abolished certain revenue-producing agencies that his brother Bayan had controlled, Toghto managed to acquire his own sources of wealth.[20] He derived his income from salt wells in Szechwan as well as from a number of landed estates in Huai-an and Sung-chiang.[21] Like El Temür and Bayan, he held concurrent positions of command over several elite guards units.[22] He controlled the inner palace agency known as the *Chao-kung wan-hu-fu;* and he extended his own power through the use of close relatives. As Bayan had once used him, he used his younger brother Esen Temür in the vitally important post of Censor-in-Chief.[23] In securing offices and private revenues, Toghto was more restrained than El Temür or Bayan had been, and less inclined to flaunt his personal wealth and power, yet the nature of his position was much the same. One can detect a strong institutional continuity in the highest ministerial position, even though Toghto did not formally seek to do away with the Chancellorship of the Left as El Temür and Bayan had done. After 1349, he simply left the position unfilled.

It is above all Toghto's new direction in public policy that stands out as the hallmark of his first incumbency. Since 1328 the dynasty had really done little in a positive way. Except for El Temür's sponsorship of the compilation of the *Ching-shih ta-tien* encyclopedia, suggestions for radical new official schemes went unheeded.[24] Under Bayan's administration, it appears that governmental activity was actually lessened in scale. Toghto was, by contrast, receptive to ideas for official involvement in various sorts of projects. The compilation of the Liao, Chin, and Sung dynastic histories, which had lapsed for some time partly owing to a lack of funds, was taken up again in 1343 with Toghto himself as honorary general editor. The clerks and secretaries in the Central Chancellery and in the Han-lin Academy showed him that funds could be made available by borrowing from the cash and grain stored in South China and ordinarily used to defray expenses involved in operating the examination system.[25] Participation in the final editing of the three official histories was a significant and prestigious item in the career records of the officials involved. It was also a means of indulging the desire of the great Confucian scholars to impose their judgments upon the accomplishments of governments and the talents and moral worth of men.[26]

The construction of the forty-mile-long Chin-k'ou canal, which Toghto began in 1342, was another such postponed project. Earlier in the Yüan period, and also during the preceding Chin Dynasty (1115-1234), attempts had been made to tap the Yung-ting River flowing eastward out of the Shensi highlands and join it by a canal through the capital with the Pei-ho at T'ung-chou, about thirteen miles to the east, in order that the annual maritime grain shipments from the Yangtze delta might reach Ta-tu directly by an all-water route. As it was, the grain boats were obliged to unload at T'ung-chou, from which point the grain was hauled by carters at some difficulty and expense the remainder of the distance to the capital. It was also surmised that such a canal might make it possible to ship Shensi coal by water directly into the capital, and put an end to the city's need for its swarms of fagot-sellers.[27]

The launching of the canal project, however, exposed a side of Toghto which many of his Confucian admirers had not fully anticipated. His restoration of the examinations, his relaxation of prohibitions, lowering of the salt quotas, and cancellation of back taxes, and his commitment of the emperor to a full program of imperial sacrifices were all policies that won Confucian support—so much so that, as the *Yüan shih* historiographers put it, "those inside and outside the government hailed him as a 'worthy minister.' "[28] But with the initiation of the canal project, many Confucians were discovering to their dismay that Toghto's *keng-hua* was not a pure substance, but an alloy compounded with *kung-li*, the "merit and profit" of the ancient Legalist Shang Yang and the controversial Sung Confucian Wang An-shih. Against the project it was forcefully argued, especially by the Confucian Hsü Yu-jen, that the rapid rate of flow of the Yung-ting

River would put the capital in danger of inundation during the summer and fall rains if it were diverted and brought right into the city itself, while even under normal conditions the high silt content of the water sitting behind the locks would soon impede navigation in any case. "Since this discussion has been going on," said Hsü, "news about it has leaked outside. Opinions are unanimous that the project cannot be carried out. If it is carried out simply as a means of gaining personal achievement, and if people's opinions are not consulted and their advice is ignored, then we are back to Shang Yang and Wang An-shih and *their* methods. This is not the kind of discussion we ought to have now."[29]

Toghto brushed aside all such objections and went ahead with his plans. In four months, he had the new waterway dug. But as soon as the canal was opened, he was obliged to close it down owing to a storm of protest. It was asserted that the flow was too rapid, mud and silt clogged the canal, people's homes and graves were wrecked during the digging, hordes of laborers had been killed or wounded, the expenses were incalculable, and no accomplishment was gained from it after all. Toghto himself was verbally criticized for the fiasco. The censors impeached two men whom they found responsible for submitting the original proposal, and Toghto signaled his renunciation of the project by allowing them to be executed.[30]

Two years after the abortive canal affair, in June, 1344, Toghto resigned his position as Chancellor of the Right, a move which seems to have been prompted by a number of other events of ill omen. During 1341 and 1342 risings broke out on the far southern fringes of the Yüan empire; there were tribal troubles on the Yunnan frontier, in Kwangsi, as well as in the southern part of present-day Hunan province, where the rebels rallied behind a "King Who Obeys Heaven."[31] These were followed in 1343 by more frontier disturbances: in March a tribal uprising in upper Manchuria, and during the summer new troubles along the Szechwan-Tibet frontier and among the Moslems in southwestern Shansi.[32] In the interior of China, the annals report widespread banditry in Shantung and Hopei; in August, 1343, bandits managed to plunder and burn the Shantung city of Yen-chou.[33]

There was also important political opposition from within the Central Chancellery. The Eljigid Mongol Berke Buqa, who had risen to the Chancellorship of the Left, was indirectly attacking Toghto through denunciations of his father Majartai.[34] Bowing to Heaven's warnings and submitting to the demands of filial respect, Toghto stepped down. In so doing, he left the impression that his political behavior was under the ultimate control of Confucian norms.

Toghto remained out of government for five years. He lived, however, in the capital where he could exert influence behind the scenes until the summer of 1347 when he accompanied his father into exile. In 1344 he named as his replacement the Arulad Mongol Arughtu, a man of impeccable lineage, being a descendant of Boghorchu, a childhood friend of Chinggis Qan, and one of his "Four Heroes."[35] Arughtu was, however, a compromise choice and a political nonentity who lacked previous administrative experience. As Chancellor, he suffered excruciating loss of face before the emperor. On the occasion of the completion of the Liao, Chin, and Sung dynastic histories and their presentation to the throne in 1345, he confessed that he could not read them and did not know what their purpose was; whereupon the emperor, in a curious reversal of roles, delivered a short Confucian lecture to him on the value of history as a mirror for present action.[36]

Berke Buqa, who had been instrumental in bringing about the resignation of Toghto, maneuvered to force his way against Arughtu. Upon failing to enlist Arughtu's support against Toghto, Berke Buqa had a censor denounce him on the grounds of incompetence, and in February of 1347 he resigned.[37] Arughtu was succeeded as Chancellor of the Right by Berke Buqa himself.

Berke Buqa's term in the dynasty's highest ministerial position was a short one, lasting only from February, 1347, until his dismissal in July, but it was really he who controlled policy from Toghto's departure in 1344 until his return in 1349.

He was strongly opposed to Toghto, a point which he made clear when, after taking office, he exiled Majartai from the capital to the far west and impeached Toghto's old mentor, Wu Chih-fang.[38]

Under Berke Buqa's protection, some of Bayan's old adherents and their relatives returned to positions at court.[39] Yet there was no question of Berke Buqa's reviving Bayan's policies and leading an anti-Confucian movement against Toghto. The events of 1340 had ensured that all future politics could henceforth be conducted only in Confucian terms. The important political split that developed between Toghto and Berke Buqa was one in which, for the first time in Yüan history, Confucian ideology predominated on both sides. By 1347, it can definitely be stated, Confucian political ideology had at last become a controlling force in Yüan government.

Since Berke Buqa could not oppose Toghto by falling back upon anti-Confucian policies, he opposed him by appealing to a more "conservative" Confucianism than that represented by Toghto. The conservative variety of Confucianism which Berke Buqa championed tended to value individual morality over public policy, and voluntary consensus over political or factional organization. According to this brand of Confucian ideology, good government was ultimately a matter of good local government, with good and upright men using moral suasion (*chiao-hua*) to control and soothe the population. Unlike Toghto, Berke Buqa had had first-hand experience in the problems of regional and local administration, not only in China proper, but also in the western and southern frontier regions. His biography tells us that he enjoyed extraordinary success in his endeavors in these fields, and that his sympathetic and compassionate measures invariably won public gratitude.[39] Since he was, moreover, a Mongol, his leadership of the conservative Confucian opposition to Toghto was on all counts an appropriate one.

As an official in the Central Chancellery, Berke Buqa's primary political concerns had all along reflected his conservative Confucian approach. He had been sufficiently alarmed by the increase over the last several years in the incidence of floods, famines, plague, and banditry in the center as well as on the frontiers of the empire to turn his attention almost exclusively to problems of local government. It was probably Berke Buqa—certainly it was not Arughtu—who had conceived the idea of an empire-wide investigating commission in November, 1345, for the express purpose of rectifying abuses in the provincial and local administrations. Berke Buqa was Chancellor of the Left at the time. For the investigating commission, he formed two-man teams, each consisting of one Mongol or *se-mu* and one Chinese, and dispatched them to each of the twelve censorial circuits in the realm. They were authorized to examine into the people's distress, dismiss corrupt officials and promote those who deserved it, and relieve onerous tax and corvee burdens. They were permitted to do anything they saw fit to correct local injustices.[40]

The dispatch of the commission was followed by other measures which showed much the same general concern. The *a'urugh*, or camps for the dependents of the Mongol military, which Hsü Yu-jen had vigorously denounced for oppressing local peasants, were ordered abolished in the fall of 1345.[41] In August, 1346, men were directed to be specially picked from the imperial guards to serve as *darughachi*, i.e. non-Chinese representatives of the imperial authority, at levels of local administration, replacing the old and corrupt incumbents with men personally known to the emperor.[42] In April, 1347, students in the Imperial University were examined and chosen for positions as directors of Confucian studies in the local governments and in the elite guards units.[43] Even the clerks attached to the Central Chancellery were ordered to study the classics and histories in the afternoons.[44] As part of the new emphasis upon improving local government, it was proposed by a censor that rather than have the Board of Civil Office at the capital select the magistrates of the lowest grade counties, it would be easier to get better men appointed if the provinces themselves handled the matter.[45]

The government's new concern with local administration derived from its discovery of the importance of *chiao-hua* to the security of the dynasty. Yet despite this concern, social disorder showed definite signs of increase throughout the country, especially after the Yellow River flooded and shifted its course in the summer of 1344. The investigating commission sent out in 1345 met with indifferent success in its effort to rectify matters. It was welcomed with enthusiasm in some quarters, but in the North China area it began to carry out its work so thoroughly that the entrenched bureaucracy, threatened with mass impeachment, had to apply pressure upon the central government and have the leading investigator dismissed.[46] In the Kiangsi-Fukien circuit, the local population, utterly cynical, watched the commission come and go.[47] In the southern part of Hukuang province, a long-simmering tribal disturbance achieved a degree of organization and by 1346 was causing widespread destruction.[48] Members of the scholar gentry, noting this, grew increasingly apprehensive about the likelihood of popular rebellion in Central and South China.[49] On July 2, 1347, the emperor called attention to the lack of official harmony and the frequent observation of adverse portents and on those grounds dismissed Berke Buqa from the Chancellorship of the Right.[50]

Though dismissed, Berke Buqa remained in the capital with the honorary designation of Grand Guardian *(t'ai-pao)*, a title which afforded him access to the emperor and allowed him to operate behind the scenes as a kind of *de facto* prime minister. His administrative machine in the Central Chancellery remained essentially intact. For six months the office of Chancellor of the Right remained vacant; the Qangli Confucian Temür Tash, however, continued in his position as Chancellor of the Left until his death in October, 1347.[51] Temür Tash made further refinements upon Berke Buqa's policies. Among other measures, he set up a system whereby officials might be rotated on a regular basis between court and provincial positions, and he brought the emperor more intimately into the appointive process by requiring all court officials assigned to outside posts to pay their respects to the throne upon their departure in order that the emperor might personally exhort them to achieve good results in local administration.[52] After Temür Tash's death, the Jalair Dorji, an equally avid Confucian, was appointed to replace him. Dorji, however, insisted that he could not serve without his friend Ho Wei-i as a close colleague. In conformity with his wishes, the emperor made Dorji Chancellor of the Right in January, 1348, with Ho Wei-i to assist him as Chancellor of the Left.[53] Berke Buqa remained as Grand Guardian, in ultimate control of policy.

That Ho Wei-i, a Northern Chinese, should occupy so high a position as Chancellor of the Left was of course extraordinary. For anything like an equivalent case, one must go back to the formative years of the dynasty, before 1262, when Qubilai began phasing the Chinese out of the higher positions in the bureaucracy.[54] As the ethnic class system of rule solidified through the years, it became customary for the Central Chancellery to bar Southern Chinese altogether, and to restrict the Northern Chinese to the positions of Chief Administrator or below. Since the restoration of 1328 the Northern Chinese were generally further restricted to the position of Vice Administrator of the Left or below, until under Toghto's aegis Ho Wei-i became Chief Administrator in 1344.[55]

For four generations, however, the Ho family, whose origins were military, had been in the good graces of the Mongol rulers. Around 1253, when Qubilai as prince was undertaking his invasion of Szechwan and Yunnan, Ho Wei-i's great-grandfather visited his camp and presented the conqueror with 5,000 ounces of white gold. Since then the sons of the Ho family had entree to the Imperial Guards, hereditary command of an elite guards unit, and hereditary control of the office of commandant *(liu-shou)* in the imperial summer capital of Shang-tu. Since 1320, when Ho Wei-i's father was executed by the financier Temüder, the Ho family was also highly regarded by the Confucian movement.[56] Ho Wei-i profited politically from what was widely considered to be the righteous martyrdom of his father. From his inherited position, Ho worked his way up through the bureaucracy, holding various positions in the capital and outside. As a censorial official, he resigned in protest early in Bayan's administration and did not return to office until Toghto brought him back in 1342. In October, 1345, while Arughtu was Chancellor of the Right, Ho was elevated to the position of Censor-in-Chief, a post hitherto barred to Chinese. In preparation for this unprecedented occasion, the emperor had conferred upon him the Mongol name of T'ai-p'ing, and thus symbolically adopted him into the Mongol nation.[57]

The government of Dorji and Ho Wei-i lasted from January, 1348, until the Merkid Toghto's return to power in August, 1349. During that time the conservative Confucian administrative program was brought to something of a peak of fulfillment, both in the capital and in the provinces. As Chancellor of the Right, the Confucianist Dorji chose to place himself above politics as symbol of the over-all Confucian tone of the administration. He devoted his attentions to the *ta-t'i*—the over-all polity, the immanent order of things, as contrasted to the more practical aspects of administration *(yung)* that Ho Wei-i handled. As his biography tells us, Dorji examined the ritual canons and revived some of the ancient practices for use at court. He asked that, as a means of honoring Confucianism, the participants in the Classics Mat be permitted to seat themselves in the imperial presence. He had renowned and upright officials study the classical precedents and propose appropriate methods for achieving good rule and order. He defrocked supernumerary Buddhist clerics, and recommended neglected Confucian worthies to the court.[58]

On a more practical level, the government continued to act upon its basic commitment to the improvement of local administration. In January, 1348, it selected sixteen well-known officials from the Censorate and the literary academies of the capital and placed them in local government positions, with the right to memorialize the throne directly on problems of popular affairs.[59] Special efforts were made to honor and reward outstanding local functionaries.[60] The government also tried to revitalize the *she* system of local control.[61] On two occasions high-ranking officials were ordered yearly to recommend men of their acquaintance for local positions, and care was taken to appoint only experienced and qualified Mongols or *se-mu* to local *darughachi* positions. Once more it was vowed that assignments to these positions would not be used as a convenient means for providing relief to needy guards troops.[62]

Despite its well-meaning gestures, the conservative Confucianist government of Berke Buqa, Dorji, and Ho Wei-i found itself in serious political trouble. Popular distress and social disorder, stemming from deep-rooted causes over which the government really had no control, continued to make their presence felt. In the north, the Yellow River was still causing damage. In June and July of 1344, swollen by heavy rains, it had gone on one of its rampages, bursting its dykes in two places east of Pien-liang, and flooding an area of about 6,000 square miles in the lowland triangle west of the Shantung massif. Seventeen walled cities were inundated.[63] The flood set off a migration of refugees, and an upsurge in bandit activity in the area immediately surrounding the scene of the disaster.[64] Since Toghto retired from office just as the Yellow River was beginning to get out of hand, it was left to Berke Buqa to devise some remedy for the catastrophe. But Berke Buqa did not have a ready-made programmatic approach which he could apply to a problem of such magnitude, and what remedies he did devise were minimal. A court discussion of the Yellow River problem held in December, 1344, resulted in a decision simply to make dyke repairs here and there, and to set up water control bureaus along the lower course of the river to inspect and make suggestions.[65] These measures were clearly insufficient. The Yellow River breached its dykes at least three more times and, what was worse, it began to shift its course.[66] It had hitherto flowed eastward as far as Pien-liang, where it veered toward the southeast and added its water to the tributaries of the Huai River system.[67] After the 1344 flood, however, the Yellow River began gradually to shift its course northward. Part of it began flowing along the north side of the Shantung peninsula and into the sea. Another part began to pour into the Grand Canal and up the North China plain toward Ho-chien, where it threatened to wreck one of the government salt works. As a result, the Grand Canal was put out of commission, and the government was in danger of losing the million ingots of cash that the Ho-chien works provided yearly.[68] This loss it could scarcely afford.[69]

At sea there were more difficulties. The annual maritime

grain shipments from the Yangtze delta region to the capital had peaked at 3,340,306 piculs in 1329. Owing to piracy, official corruption, and acts of nature the shipments fell by almost 25 percent to 2,800,000 piculs in 1341 and 2,600,000 in 1342.[70] During the year 1348, moreover, piracy along the Kiangche coast began to assume serious proportions and put even this reduced movement of grain in jeopardy. It was usually the responsibility of the local officials to deal with this maritime banditry, which was common enough along the coast in the 1340s.[71] The local authorities, however, were in many cases hesitant to take to sea, preferring instead to purchase protection for the government grain boats by paying subsidies to the pirates. This policy made piracy a rather rewarding occupation, and had the effect of encouraging some of the coastal people, who might otherwise have been useful in suppressing the trouble, to put to sea themselves and join the number of pirates already there. It was in these circumstances that a certain Fang Kuo-chen from Huang-yen rose to prominence in 1348, when he seized a government grain boat together with the chiliarch who was in charge of it. The act was brazen enough to engage the attention of the Kiangche provincial authorities; the Administration Vice Commissioner of the province set out with a fleet of boats in pursuit of Fang, but instead of arresting him, he miscalculated his chances and fell into the pirate's hands. Fang then pressured him into submitting to the court a demand for honorary titles for himself and his brothers.[72]

After receiving the Administration Vice Commissioner, together with Fang's personal envoy, the Berke Buqa court decided, after some argument, not to punish the luckless official. It was pointed out that, since his troops were northern infantry and cavalry and untrained in naval warfare, punishment would be meaningless. The court also permitted Fang to "surrender" in return for official recognition, even though Fang surrendered from a position of strength and was in fact bullying the court. The court was, in the words of a policy opponent, "interested in expedients."[73] Since, moreover, the court in its concern for the problems of local government tended to emphasize conciliation and moral suasion rather than coercion, it dismissed a proposal to set up a naval commandery at Ch'ing-yüan (Ning-po) when it was reported that the local elders were opposed to the idea.[74] Thus by 1348 the security of the maritime grain shipments was mortgaged to the pirate Fang Kuo-chen; and the Grand Canal, the only alternative grain transport route, was out of service because of the Yellow River floods.[75]

These manifold difficulties which troubled the Yüan realm in the late 1340s demanded some sort of radical action for solution. The Berke Buqa government, confined by its philosophy to the uttering of soft Confucian noises, could offer no adequate solutions and consequently suffered an increasing loss of confidence. The ex-Chancellor Toghto, eager to seize an opportunity to return to power, began to attack the incumbent administration from the sidelines. The incumbents, as a regime with pretensions to Confucian rectitude, were poorly equipped to hold themselves together against such a partisan attack; although Berke Buqa needed at this point a closely knit faction to defend himself, conservative Confucian theory condemned the idea of faction out of hand.

Conservative theory held that bureaucrats should never organize themselves into cliques based upon the principle of common material interest, but should instead form random associations based upon moral and ideological likemindedness. The conservative persuasion desired to achieve for Confucianism a permanent dominance in government, and would appear to have calculated that the greater the atomization of its individual members, the greater the chances for the survival of the movement as a whole. Cliques were all too fragile and vulnerable in the long run. Nevertheless, Berke Buqa's government, at a loss to give adequate answer to Toghto's attacks, unable to deflate or repudiate his charges, made a desperate but unavailing effort to organize factionally to save itself. Under pressure of attack from Toghto, Berke Buqa tried to use personal persuasion to secure support from such figures as Arughtu and the Tangut Irinjinbal, but they refused his advances. He eventually went so far as to swear an oath of brotherhood with ten of his colleagues, including

Ho Wei-i and the Tangut Han-chia-nu.[76] In the end, nevertheless, he was unable to insist upon an unthinking partisan devotion among the higher figures in his administration.

The struggle between Toghto and Berke Buqa for the control of government was fought out, not with weapons in the field, but with words in the Censorate, couched in Confucian terms. With troubles mounting within the empire, the Shensi Branch Censorate initiated the first attack in December, 1347, impeaching the Grand Guardian Berke Buqa for being the son of a "rebellious minister."[77] In order to quell this outburst, Berke Buqa's sworn brother Han-chia-nu was dispatched to act as Censor-in-Chief of the Shensi Branch Censorate.[78]

The struggle, however, continued. It happened that Toghto's father Majartai, living in exile in Kansu since the summer of 1347, died there in December. Ho Wei-i, oblivious of the interests of faction, argued that Toghto must be permitted to return to the capital in order to arrange for his father's burial there. Ho argued that, since Toghto had shown loyalty to the imperial house, it would be remiss now to prevent him from exercising his duties as a filial son. Ho's argument carried. The regime conscious of its Confucian commitments could not easily afford the imputation of obstructing the way of filial piety, and Toghto was permitted to return from exile. In the spring of 1348 the emperor conferred upon him the title of Grand Tutor *(t'ai-fu)*, a degree higher than Berke Buqa's title of Grand Guardian. With Toghto nearby, the attack against Berke Buqa then shifted from the Shensi Branch Censorate to the Censorate proper.[79]

In 1348 the Censorate denounced Berke Buqa for the inability of his regime to deal effectively with the rising problems of banditry and piracy, and for his protection of former Bayan partisans.[80] The first charge was sound enough, but the second was less so. The paths of Berke Buqa and Toghto appear to have crossed for the first time in 1339, when both served as concurrent Censors-in-Chief under Bayan. In the wake of the Fan Meng incident, Bayan ordered the Censorate to draft a demand that all Chinese be removed from the leading positions in the provincial Surveillance Offices.[81] Berke

Buqa, who was fearful of Bayan's increasing recklessness, did not at all want to send this demand up to the emperor. Toghto, instead of joining him in a common stand against Bayan, left it to him to take the demand up while he approached the emperor indirectly and persuaded him to reject it.[82] As a result of Toghto's sly maneuvering, Bayan was thwarted and Berke Buqa placed in a politically damaging position. The affair not only turned Berke Buqa against Toghto, but it also made him the natural protector of a number of smaller bureaucrats whom Toghto threw out of office for purely partisan reasons after Bayan's ouster.[83] Urged on by Toghto, the Censorate now tried to use this fact to pin the Bayan label upon Berke Buqa, and impugn the genuineness of his Confucianism.

The attack was unscrupulous, and Berke Buqa tried to persuade the Censor-in-Chief Irinjinbal not to forward the impeachment to the emperor. Irinjinbal, whose son had been executed by Bayan, would not be dissuaded, and sent the statement up. The emperor was faced with the choice between endorsing the impeachment and dismissing the regime and rejecting it and provoking an uproar in the Censorate. He decided to reject it. He removed Irinjinbal from his position and sent him off to the provinces. The emperor's action was an expression of no confidence in the Censorate.

The Censorate, an increasingly restless institution since the death of Tugh Temür, was a rather special organ of government. It demanded strong institutional loyalty from its membership, and it insisted upon its right to speak out freely at any time. It was an organ in which Confucianism was firmly established. Unless it was ruled over by a strong partisan hand, it tended to become obstreperous and unruly. The emperor's rejection of its impeachment of Berke Buqa caused it a damaging loss of institutional prestige. It had to attack back, and since it could not attack the emperor directly, it did so indirectly. The Jalair Dorjibal, a distant cousin of the Chancellor of the Right Dorji, and as avid a Confucian as he, resubmitted the impeachment to the emperor, threatening the total collapse of the Censorate as an institution if it was rejected again.[84] The censor Li Chi laid the blame for the first rejection upon the inner palace functionary Ko Yong-bok, whom he impeached for presuming upon favor, impeding government, usurping authority, and conniving with the chief ministers of the Central Chancellery. Since the departure of Irinjinbal left as sole Censor-in-Chief the Tangut Narin, a man associated with Bayan and Berke Buqa, Li Chi further demanded that the censors be allowed to memorialize the throne directly, without the prior approval of the Censor-in-Chief. The emperor accepted the impeachment of Ko Yong-bok, and sent him back to his native Korea, but he rejected the other demands of the Censorate. Thereupon Dorjibal and a number of other censors resigned *en bloc* from the Censorate, and the attack against Berke Buqa was once again taken up by the outside censorial organs.[85]

At the height of the struggle, Berke Buqa made the mistake of ridiculing the Censorate, a *faux pas* which aroused Confucian resentment and only helped to damage his cause.[86] The Censor-in-Chief Narin, apparently sensing Berke Buqa's hopeless impasse, attempted an attack upon a member of the Central Chancellery, but he was himself impeached by a censor and dismissed in March, 1348.[87] Berke Buqa's sworn brother Han-chia-nu, who replaced Narin as Censor-in-Chief, organized a retaliatory attack upon presumed Toghto partisans in the inner palace and succeeded in getting the emperor to dismiss and exile them in July, 1349.[88]

The enhanced power of the monarchy, evident throughout these censorial convulsions, was a conspicuous result of recent political change. Toghto's strategy for the overthrow of Bayan had centered about the participation of the emperor not as a symbol, but as a free political agent. After the eradication of the rival imperial line of Tugh Temür, the imperial institution remained relatively free of outside manipulation. Toghon Temür's principal empress, the Qunggirad Bayan Qudu, was quiet and self-effacing.[89] She was upstaged by Toghon Temür's second empress Öljei Qudu, nee Ki, a Korean. Bayan had prevented the emperor from elevating Öljei Qudu to the rank of empress on the grounds of her nationality; but after Bayan's overthrow, Toghon Temür got his way and finally obtained a consort who had no clan behind her powerful enough to interfere in imperial affairs. After 1340 Toghon Temür carefully exploited the opportunities for improving the monarchical position which events and circumstances had placed before him. While he was no statesman after the pattern of Qubilai, he enjoyed his role as the sponsor of *keng-hua,* and he used cautiously and consistently in the monarchical interest his power as final arbiter over the struggle going on in the leading organs of government. On August 16, 1349, he finally decided that the Berke Buqa government had had enough. He reappointed Toghto Chancellor of the Right.

That Yüan politics had become Confucianized is evident from the fact that after 1340 political division at the highest levels of power in the state had come to express itself in terms of the conservative and reformist tendencies within Neo-Confucian ideology. As political leaders at court, both Toghto and Berke Buqa were obliged to couch their differences, justify their political activities, and formulate their ideas for the use of power in Confucian language. Each attacked the other by questioning the validity and honesty of his opponent's Confucianism. Toghto was attacked as a Legalist, Berke Buqa as a protector of Bayan men.

Toghto emerged at the top of the political hierarchy in 1340 as a Confucian hero, a sponsor of *keng-hua,* savior of the emperor, restorer of the examination system, and much else. In 1344 he capped this reputation by gracefully retiring from political life, a Confucian act and an untypical one for Yüan chancellors. Such previous chancellors as Bayan, El Temür, and Daula-shah had been removed only by death or violence.

Toghto proved to have a special affinity for the reform variety of Confucianism, an ideological tendency specially notable among certain Southern Chinese from Kiangsi, the old home province of the Sung reformer Wang An-shih, An idea originally conceived by Yü Chi of Kiangsi (d. 1348) to eliminate the maritime grain shipments by large-scale agricultural development in North China was in fact carried out by Toghto in 1352. The Kiangsi Confucians Chieh Hsi-ssu (d. 1344) and Ou-yang Hsüan (d. 1358) were friendly with Toghto and may have served as the original source for some of his governmental ideas. Certainly the new institutional use of the Han-lin Academy as a kind of training base for prospective Confucian appointees to the Central Chancellery was strongly urged upon Toghto as an idea by Chieh Hsi-ssu.[90]

When Toghto returned to office in 1349, conservative Confucianism had proved ineffective as a means of assuaging the troubled conditions of the time. China's *feng-su* was not responding to Berke Buqa's increased applications of *chiao-hua.* In these circumstances, Toghto's reformist Confucian approach held promise. Reform Confucianism was less hostile to the idea of clique, and Toghto needed a tightly knit personal machine to carry out the large-scale projects he had in mind.

The reform Confucian approach was often called the doctrine of "merit and profit" *(kung-li)* by its critics. Used with *li,* meaning opportunism or profiteering, *kung* implies unbridled activism and reputation-seeking by individuals or bureaucratic administrations. In what his opponents would term the pursuit of "merit and profit," Toghto would emerge as financial reformer, rechanneler of the Yellow River, and conqueror of the Red Turban rebels. He would come very near to settling the worst of the empire's problems and establishing the Yüan Dynasty on an entirely new basis.

Chapter V
In Pursuit of "Merit and Profit"

In August, 1349, Toghto and his men returned to power in a spirit of partisan vengeance. The Chancellor of the Right Dorji resumed his viceroyship and returned to his home in Manchuria. The Censorate attacked Ho Wei-i for his administrative deficiencies and his son Ho Chün for having married a girl of the imperial house, and both departed in exile to Shensi. An adherent suggested to Ho Wei-i that he dramatize through suicide the injustice that was being done him. Ho dismissed the suggestion and decided instead to pass his days studiously absorbed in the histories and classics. Toghto succeeded Dorji as Chancellor of the Right; the post of Chancellor of the Left remained unfilled throughout Toghto's second ministry (1349-55), a reversal in fact if not entirely in name to the sole chancellorships of El Temür and Bayan. Han-chia-nu and Tümender, both sworn brothers of Berke Buqa, were impeached on various charges of crime and corruption. The former was deported to the mouth of the Amur River, where he died; and the latter was murdered en route to a post in the provinces. Berke Buqa himself was removed to Shantung, and he died there in 1350.[1]

Toghto's overthrow of the opposition was difficult to justify on Confucian moral grounds. He was careful to leave the visible performance of the more unpleasant aspects of the task to the lower-level personal operatives he assigned to advisory positions in the Central Chancellery.[2] Toghto's removal of the Berke Buqa leadership was unlike El Temür's removal twenty year before, of Daula-shah—minion of the usurper Yesün Temür, and a Moslem, to whom any real or fancied criminality could be believably imputed. Toghto was aware of the difference, and refrained from posthumously vilifying his victims. His coup against his uncle Bayan in 1340, his revival of the examination system, and his timely retirement in 1344 were apparently still sufficient to secure his own Confucian credentials, or at least to make widely acceptable his reentry into government. At any rate he had gained the support of the Censorate by posing as the champion of its institutional integrity, and that was most important.

In comparing the staff of Toghto's new Central Chancellery with his appointees of 1341, however, one notices above all the absence of any Mongols or *se-mu* with known Confucian leanings. The Qangli Temür Tash was dead, and several other Confucianist Mongols and *se-mu* who served in the Chancellery between 1343 and 1346 were now branded as members of the opposition and removed from office. The Qunggirad Tai Buqa and the Qangli Ting-chu, both non-Confucians, conveniently switched sides and joined Toghto; they retained their Chief Administrator positions.[3] The other Chief Administrators were the Kashmiri Bayan and the Kereid Mongol Chösgem.[4] The Qangli Üch Qurtuqa came in as Vice Administrator of the Right, and Han Yüan-shan, a graduate of the Imperial University, as Vice Administrator of the Left.[5] Han Yung (no relation), a *chin-shih* of 1318, was made an Administration Vice Commissioner.[6]

During his first ministry of 1340-44, Toghto had given an indication of his activist political tendencies. His canal project encountered vociferous opposition, however, and had to be scuttled. This time, Toghto succeeded in discrediting beforehand the main sources of conservative Confucian opposition to the activist approach by his timely and successful attack on the Berke Buqa administration. In addition, the Central Chancellery was now more fully under his own personal control than it had been earlier. The Censorate was in his debt. On all sides, the way was open for a new thrust of policy, a vigorous and imaginative response to the grave problems that were threatening the existence of the dynasty. Writing unofficially, the chroncler Ch'üan Heng ascribed this vision to Toghto: "He was of a mind to inititate policies, for he believed that nothing would be remembered of the former prime ministers because they were indifferent to ceremony, to literary celebration, and to institutional measures. He wanted actively to display his power and brilliance to the empire, surpass the old norms of the ancestors, and make his name immortal in the historical records."[7]

As a step preparatory to his further plans, Toghto needed to offer some compensation to the conservative Confucians for their loss of a controlling voice in the inner councils of government. In November, 1349, he accordingly established the Tuan-pen-t'ang, a palace school of Confucian learning, for the education of the heir presumptive Ayushiridara. Son of Toghon Temür by his Korean consort, Ayushiridara was now about eleven years of age. Since it was likely that he would be named heir apparent, and one day become emperor, the conservatives' pedagogical instinct was aroused, and their concerns in part transferred from the immediate present to the future.[8]

Although it would appear that Toghto already had some idea of the kinds of projects he wanted to carry out, he preferred that ideas and suggestions should come up from below. The government announced that it would welcome project proposals, and in October, 1349, it set up a special staff to sift through the responses and report the more practical ones to the Central Chancellery.[9] Since it was anticipated that the new projects would demand large sums of money, the first major proposal to be taken up was one submitted in May, 1350, by Wu Ch'i, a minor official in the Board of Revenue, urging that the government expand the money supply and increase its rate of circulation.[10] It had evidently been the policy of the Bayan and Berke Buqa administrations to cut governmental expenditures and to restrict the issuance of paper currency. In 1348, however, there was some court sentiment favoring an immediate issue of 5,000,000 ingots in paper cash in order to rectify the tight money situation. It was to be put into circulation through the merchants, who would obtain it by surrendering silver bullion to the government. The idea was opposed by the *chin-shih* Kuei Ch'ang on the grounds that such a policy would enrich the merchants but not benefit the people.[11] The court then apparently dropped the idea, for by 1349 there was still a severe money shortage, compensated for in part by the continued circulation of worn notes and an increase in counterfeiting. In November, 1350, the Uighur Hsieh Che-tu, a *chin-shih* and President of the Board of Civil Office, further proposed a currency reform along the lines laid down by Wu Ch'i, adding the suggestion that the government also mint and circulate subsidiary copper coins.[12]

A general court conference was then called by Toghto to discuss and make a decision upon the matter of revitalizing the monetary system. Despite conservative objections, Toghto decided to mint copper coins and to print and issue a new variety of paper currency to circulate alongside the old and at twice its face value. On December 17, 1350, the emperor announced the new currency system to the empire, and by October, 1351, twelve issuing offices were established in various parts of the realm.[13] During 1351 the government issued a total of 2,000,000 ingots in new paper currency.[14]

The government, however, wanted to do more than simply increase the amount of money in circulation. Had that been its main purpose in reforming the currency, it would probably have issued the new notes through the merchants as was proposed in 1348; and it would probably have taken care that the new note issue be to some extent backed by precious metal reserves.[15] But the new issue was not so backed, and it was put into circulation through government payments for materials and labor. It was Toghto's real but unstated aim to use the new issue of currency to pay for the larger official projects that lay in the offing.[16]

By 1350 there was probably no way to raise funds other than through currency manipulation. It was out of the question to raise the household land tax rates, or even to collect the full amounts due under the regular rates; that had been tried before with disastrous results, for the landlord gentry had made it clear that they would rebel rather than pay.[17] Nor was it any longer feasible to raise the salt production quotas and sell more salt, or to force increased salt prices upon the population. During the late Yüan period, the profits received from the production and sale of monopoly salt provided the government with about 7,661,000 ingots of paper currency annually, or 82 percent of the income necessary to meet official expenses.[18] Prices and production quotas in the Yüan period had been revised steadily and drastically upward through the reigns of Qaishan and Ayurbarwada; they remained relatively stable from then until 1335, when Bayan found it necessary to revise the production quotas downward. After 1335 the salt production quotas continued to be revised downward, owing to a decline in the salt-producing households, increasing impoverishment on the part of the population, and mounting backlogs of unsellable government salt.[19] Since the population could no longer afford to purchase larger quantities of government salt at the artificially high prices that were charged, Toghto could not attempt to derive extra income for his projects from this otherwise lucrative source.

With the question of finance settled by currency expansion, Toghto went ahead to act upon the more attractive of the other project proposals that were being submitted to the government. In 1351 the government spent "several myriad" ingots of paper money to recruit 10,000 laborers and clear the silt out of the Chih-ku River southeast of Ta-tu.[20] This project, however, was hardly one of great moment. There was another problem for which proposals were solicited: one which, if solved, would indeed credit the Yüan Dynasty and the Toghto administration with the historically significant accomplishment it was looking for. This problem was the Yellow River.

As was discussed in the previous chapter, the Yellow River as a governmental responsibility was politically and economically related to the rise of piracy along the China coast. Since in 1348 the government's maritime grain transport system had fallen under the protection of the pirate Fang Kuo-chen, it could not regain control of the grain shipments until it either put down Fang Kuo-chen, or else outflanked him by opening the alternative Grand Canal transport route. Until the Yellow River was somehow put back under control, the Grand Canal would remain inoperative.

Toghto made an attempt to suppress Fang Kuo-chen. When Toghto came to power in the summer of 1349, it was of course axiomatic that whatever agreements had been struck between Fang and the Berke Buqa leadership would have to be renegotiated. It was therefore incumbent upon Fang to make a new demonstration of his power for the enlightenment of Toghto's government. In the spring of 1350 he therefore made a raid at T'ai-ts'ang, one of the major ports of embarkation for the maritime grain boats.[21] Early in 1351 he also attacked Wen-chou and other coastal cities south of the Yangtze delta.[22]

Toghto responded cautiously to these provocations, one reason being that the local gentry were clearly of two minds about Fang Kuo-chen. Some hated the pirate for personal reasons, and some ambitious local men were eager to pounce upon Fang and thus make their mark in Yüan service. In this they had the full backing of local Confucian opinion, which was quick to point out that the prestige and integrity of the empire were at stake in this matter, and that immediate retaliatory measures against Fang were necessary. But other local notables felt that there was little likelihood of reward for their cooperation against Fang, and that Fang was really the government's problem, not theirs.[23] In the winter of 1350-51, however, Toghto had the Qangli Dash Temür set up a naval commandery in the Yangtze delta and recruit local men who were accustomed to seafaring to protect the grain shipments.[24] At the same time he sent out the Baya'ud Mongol *chin-shih* Tai Buqa to head a naval expedition from Wen-chou against Fang. But Fang captured Tai Buqa's chief aide, and in repetition of the earlier incident, the captured aide had to memorialize the court on Fang's behalf. As a result, the court decided once again to raise the ranks of Fang and his brothers and to cancel the expedition.[25]

Toghto had earlier attacked the Berke Buqa regime for pursuing the very same policy of appeasement toward Fang. Toghto had, however, an alternative plan. He knew that he lacked the immediate naval capability to ensure victory, and so he withdrew his expedition as soon as it appeared that it might be humiliatingly defeated. He hoped to confine Fang Kuo-chen to the coast south of the Yangtze delta, and eventually, perhaps, slough him off as a purely local problem. Most important in the present connection, however, is the fact that because of Fang Kuo-chen the regulation of the Yellow River and the restoration of the Grand Canal became matters of pressing need, since it was clear enough that the Yüan government no longer had control of the sea. And rather than go to war at sea, Toghto preferred to bypass the dangers inherent in that choice by the more peaceful, more profitable, and more traditional plan of restoring the inland water transport system.

Shortly after the 1344 flood of the Yellow River, the emperor, personally distressed by the catastrophe, had officials inspect the scene and recommend plans for repairing the damage. His personal appointee as chief of the Branch Directorate of Water Control *(Hsing tu-shui-chien)*, a non-Confucian Chinese by the name of Chia Lu, was sent to make a tour of the lower course of the Yellow River.[26] He mapped the topography, and suggested two alternative plans for regulating the river. The simpler plan proposed leaving the river in its new northern bed, and dyking it along its north bank. The more ambitious plan called for the digging of another bed south of the Shantung peninsula and the diversion of the Yellow River into it. When Toghto returned to power in 1349, he was apparently convinced that the more ambitious proposal was the best one, and he pressed for its adoption. With the approval of the emperor, Toghto called together a court conference for a discussion of the matter. "The emperor is just now worrying about the common people," insisted Toghto. "We who fill the high offices ought to share his concern. The matter is hard to manage, and perhaps it will be impossible to repair it, since from ancient times Yellow River problems have been extremely difficult to deal with. But he definitely wants us to go ahead and clear up the trouble."[27]

But the court was reluctant to rubber-stamp Toghto's proposal. Some officials were strongly of the opinion that the simpler and less expensive plan would suffice. In the spring of 1351 this group secured imperial permission to send out a team of its own, headed by the *chin-shih* and President of the Board of Works Ch'eng Tsun together with the Grand

Minister of Agriculture *(Ta ssu-nung)* Tughlugh, to investigate the Yellow River for itself. After carrying out an engineering survey, checking into the historical records, and soliciting the opinions of outsiders, the team concluded that the river could not be rechanneled as Toghto proposed.[28] By the time the team returned, however, Toghto had already obtained the emperor's approval for the rechanneling project and was determined to move ahead with it. Ch'eng Tsun and his colleague brought Toghto face to face with the conservative Confucian objection to large programmatic schemes: their inherent tendency to produce popular disorder. "The area in question has had successive years of famine and the people cannot survive," they argued. "If you gather 200,000 men here, there will be an even worse disaster than the flood." Toghto, reportedly, continued the argument for his detractors. "Are you saying that the people will rebel?" he retorted.[29]

The possibility of popular disorder was not out of the question. Banditry continued to disturb Shantung. In Honan province the situation was not too different. Famine there in 1344 and plague in the following year caused widespread death. The court's plea to the richer households to contribute cash and grain to relieve the destitute received a good response, but when the harvest improved a little the year following, relief measures were stopped, leaving the basic problem of overgrown fields and shortages in oxen and farm tools unsolved.[30] Bandits troubled the Honan city of Nan-yang; more bandits raided merchant boats on the Huai section of the Grand Canal.[31] The western Huai area was overtaxed and impoverished.[32] Throughout the 1340s famines were recurrent in North China. In December, 1347, the Board of Revenue reported a widespread harvest failure due to drought; and in January, 1348, it was noted that the successive droughts had driven many people out of farming.[33] The Berka Buqa administration had been concerned enough with these conditions to begin setting up temporary military agencies in an effort to control the gangs of refugees and bandits.[34] Toghto carried this program further. In November, 1350, he established four Foot and Horse Commanderies

(*Ping-ma chih-hui-ssu*), each with a full supporting staff of officials and clerks, in the general area of west Shantung. This was in response not only to banditry, but also to what the government called the "prophetic miasma" (*yao-ch'i*), by which it presumably meant secret society activities.[35] In the spring of 1351 the government set up two commanderies on the Shantung coast to check piracy, and it opened a military-agricultural colony on the Grand Canal south of Shantung.[36] It was apparently in Shantung that the government anticipated trouble, for most of its new military agencies were concentrated there. Toghto did not provide special protection for the Huai region, where Chinese sectarian rioting broke out in May.

The Yellow River project was officially announced on April 29, 1351, with the engineer Chia Lu in immediate charge. Local men of standing were given official titles and quantities of paper currency, and were sent out to the towns and cities to assemble laborers and purchase supplies.[37] Altogether 150,000 commoners from nearby towns and 20,000 troops from the Huai region were called up to supply the labor.[38] Work began on May 17, and continued throughout the summer and fall until its completion in December.[39] A sum of 1,845,636 ingots in new currency was spent on official salaries, food and clothing for the troops and commoners, wages (*kung-ch'ien*), medicines, sacrifices, relief, horses and post stations, together with payments (*yung-tzu*) to the lumber carriers, boatmen, pile-drivers, and workers in stone, iron, wood, and rope, and compensations to families whose properties were condemned by the project.[40] Toghto's desire to accomplish something of genuine historical significance was realized. The rerouting of the Yellow River was one of the greatest hydraulic projects ever undertaken in China in premodern times.[41]

Trouble, however, darkened the luster of success. As Toghto's conservative opposition had warned, popular rebellion did break out. On May 28, barely a week after the laborers were assembled for work, a small disturbance broke out, not in Shantung, as anticipated, but in the Huai city of Ying-chou (Fou-yang, Anhwei), which lay about 100 miles south of the Yellow River. The rebels, incited by the White Lotus Society and its messianic propaganda, were still only clandestinely organizing when local officials learned of their activities and arrested the White Lotus leader. The other rebels then decided that they either had to act at once or be captured themselves, whereupon they moved in and openly seized the city of Ying-chou.[42] This was the first action in a rebellion soon to involve almost all of China. During the summer and fall of 1351 the rebels, known as Red Turbans, captured a large bloc of territory lying generally west of Ying-chou along the upper reaches of the Huai and its tributaries, comprising some half-dozen cities and about 50,000 square miles of land. In August and September another group of rebels seized the city of Hsü-chou on the Grand Canal near the eastern terminus of the rechanneling project. Beginning late in the year 1351, another group of Red Turbans from the mid-Yangtze initiated a series of riots which by 1353 affected some 200,000 square miles of South China from the modern province of Hunan east to the sea. Early in 1353 a former salt-smuggler by the name of Chang Shih-ch'eng took the city of Kao-yu, about 150 miles southeast of Hsü-chou, and thus cut off the Grand Canal entirely.[43]

In the face of conservative opposition, Toghto had launched the immense Yellow River project and had succeeded with it. But as the conservatives predicted, popular insurrections had broken out. Sectarian rioters, bandits, and rebels of various sorts were in temporary occupation of enormous stretches of territory in Central and South China. Local government was overwhelmed and in many places had ceased to function. The Grand Canal, under rebel control at Hsü-chou and Kao-yu, was still unusable as an alternative grain transport route. Popular opinion tended to affix the blame for all the disorders upon Toghto and his innovative programs.[44] For a brief moment, Toghto allowed himself to fall victim, as Bayan had done, to the undiscriminating fear that the entire Chinese population was rising up against him.[45] When, however, it turned out that the rebels were only a minority of the Chinese population, and that they were in rebellion not only against the local officials of the dynasty but against the Chinese landlord gentry as well, Toghto recovered his composure. He decided that the suppression of the disorders, far from compelling him to alter drastically his programmatic *kung-li* approach to the problems of the realm, could in fact best be handled through intensified bureaucratic and programmatic means. Rather than conclude that his search for "merit and profit" had itself helped to incite the rebellions, and was therefore discredited, Toghto eventually came to the view that his previous methods alone afforded the best means for putting down the rebels. His response indicated that he came to see the rebellions as a problem requiring organized governmental action on a scale similar to that necessitated by the Yellow River project.

The unexpected rising at Ying-chou caught the court unprepared. Since the emperor was then vacationing at Shang-tu, and could not be reached rapidly to authorize the movement of troops, some of the officials at Ta-tu hesitantly decided on their own authority to send out a force of 500 Imperial Guards.[46] Not until June 18, almost three weeks after the onset of the rebellion, did the emperor finally authorize the dispatch of more forces.[47] These were still not enough, for the rebel movement continued to spread through the upper Huai region during the summer and fall of 1351.

Toghto's first recourse was to the regularly constituted military forces of the dynasty. These troops campaigned in the Huai region of central and western Honan, the main center of rebel activity in 1351 and 1352, and suffered some unfortunate reverses there. According to the unofficial chronicler Ch'üan Heng, the Red Turban rebels put to rout the mixed Chinese and Alan forces led by Tughchi, Vice Commissioner in Chief of the Chief Military Commission, whom the court had sent out on June 18. In Ch'üan Heng's view, this happened not because the "green-eyed Christian Alans" were timid or unskilled, but because they were undisciplined, disease-ridden, unused to the watery topography of the Huai area, and were, moreover, mobbed by a great horde of Red Turbans. The story of their rout became a much-repeated joke in the Huai region.[48] Ch'üan Heng also has it that the Chief Administrator *Gongbubal, who commanded the main forces in Honan after Tughchi's reverse, was kidnaped and butchered by Red Turbans while his army of 10,000 nomad tribesmen and Chinese was drunk and asleep.[49]

Late in October, 1351, in the wake of these setbacks, Toghto put his younger brother Esen Temür, and Köncheg, who was Prince of Wei and a head of the Chief Military Commission, in over-all command of the pacification effort in Honan. Their troops, said to have numbered 100,000 men, seem to have consisted largely of elite guards.[50] These forces campaigned from the fall of 1351 through the spring of 1352. They registered a few triumphs. In November a commander who was an imperial prince was rewarded for his recapture of two county seats southeast of Hsü-chou.[51] In January, 1352, Esen Temür was credited with the recovery of a county seat and the capture of several rebel leaders.[52] Following this victory, however, Esen Temür withdrew his forces and made camp on the banks of the Sha River. One night during the spring of 1352 the enemy stole into his camp and by some means succeeded in striking terror among his entire army. Esen Temür then made a frantic retreat north towards the city of Pien-liang, abandoning his weapons and supplies to the rebels as he went.[53]

Serious as these three successive routs were, they proved to be less than catastrophic in their effects. Elsewhere in North China, the imperial forces did better against the rebels; the Qunggirad Tai Buqa, for example, rapidly retook a half-dozen cities of the western Huai region.[54] What the Red Turbans gained from their daring and provocative actions was an important but momentary psychological victory. They bolstered their morale, and gained perhaps an undue reputation for invincibility among the populace. There is no doubt that their example directly encouraged the spread of rebel activity to other parts. But their essentially psychological victories were no real test of the fighting capacities of the Yüan Dynasty.

Toghto protected the commanders whom the Red Turbans had initially discredited.[55] He was able to save his younger brother Essen Temür from impeachment. The Shensi Branch

Censorate, led by the Jalair Dorjibal, submitted to the central government a formal impeachment of Esen Temür for "losing the army and shaming the state." The impeachment was, however, only a gesture; the branch censors knew well enough beforehand that they would only be demoted and transferred for their temerity. As he had anticipated, Dorjibal was shifted to a non-censorial position in Hukuang province.[56] The Tangut Irinjinbal, now one of the heads of the Chief Military Commission, met with Toghto informally and tried to urge upon him the necessity of punishing those responsible for the defeats. In response to this unsolicited and unwelcome advice, apparently, Toghto transferred Irinjinbal to Kiangsi province.[57] If the conservative opposition was trying to break Toghto's power by pressuring him into dismissing his unsuccessful military commanders, their efforts were in vain.

In other parts of China the anti-rebel effort of 1351-52 showed signs of succeeding. Before his transfer in May or June, 1352, the Shensi Branch Censor-in-Chief Dorjibal provided for the defense of the far west by enlisting into Yüan service the famous local militia outfit known as the "Hairy Gourds."[58] The Honan provincial capital of Pien-liang was successfully defended against rebel attack.[59] Tung T'uan-hsiao, chief official in Tsi-ning (Shantung), organized a military-agricultural colony and a militia group and helped his superior, the Kiangche Chief Administrator Chiao-hua, recover the Huai city of An-feng.[60] In the upper Han River area, the Salji'ud Mongol Dash Badulugh, recalled with 3,000 of his *tamachi* troops from the Yünnan frontier, aided the Szechwan Chief Administrator Yao-chu in the recovery of the important town of Hsiang-yang in January, 1353.[61] In South China, too, the rebel onslaught was turned back and the poorly organized and poorly trained rebel movements crushed. The provincial authorities in Lung-hsing (Nanch'ang), the Kiangsi provincial capital, were unprepared for a rebel attack, but they rallied sufficiently to save the city itself from being overrun.[62] The Kiangche provincial capital of Hang-chou, seized by Red Turbans during 1352, was retaken in January, 1353, by Chiao-hua and Tung T'uan-hsiao, who had moved their forces down from the Huai region.[63] Numerous other southern administrative centers were recovered from the rebels during 1353-54.

In order that the preponderance of military power might be kept in its own hands, and not be transferred by default to provincial or other outside agencies, the central government itself led the largest military contingents and directly carried out the annihilation of the more ominous rebel concentrations. Especially important in the view of the court was the eastern Huai city of Hsü-chou, situated where the Grand Canal intersected the recently rechanneled Yellow River, and occupied by rebels since August, 1351. It had to be retaken, and Toghto decided to lead the expedition against it in person. During the first half of 1352 Toghto busied himself amassing the necessary military forces. Aside from one contingent of elite guards, the bulk of the forces came to consist of newly recruited Chinese. Early in 1352 Toghto sent the Huai-nan Pacification Commissioner Lu Lu-tseng to the eastern Huai area to assemble and lead 5,000 Chinese salt workers for the Hsü-chou expedition, on the grounds that the regular government troops were unaccustomed to the climate. Eventually, these *ad hoc* recruits—salt workers, river project laborers, and various market place youth—came to number 20,000 men. They were generally styled the "Yellow Army" after the color of their uniforms.[64]

On February 29 the rebels in and around Hsü-chou were issued an ultimatum giving them twenty days in which to disperse and return to their homes. On August 28, the ultimatum having gone unheeded, Toghto received the emperor's permission to command the expedition against the city. On October 5 he departed Ta-tu; marching about 22 miles per day he reached Hsü-chou on October 23. Six days later the city was in his hands. This was a major victory for the government side.[65] The rest of the Huai area, with the exception of the single town of Po-chou (Po-hsien, Anhwei), was soon after recovered from the rebels.

By 1354 the mass outbreaks known as the Red Turban rebellions were finished. In both North and South China, the chief administrative centers had either been successfully defended against the rebels, or were recovered after a brief period of rebel occupation. The Huai-area Red Turbans lost all of their previous conquests and were thrown back upon Po-chou, their last redoubt. The Red Turbans of South China were pushed out of the cities, the river valleys, and the main population centers, and into the wooded hill country between the provinces of Kiangsi and Hukuang. Yüan forces overran the southern Red Turban rebel center in 1353 and captured four hundred men there.[66] By 1354 the Yüan authorities in South China were undertaking the work of peaceful reconstruction—canceling summer and fall taxes, resettling refugees, and giving work relief to the impoverished.[67] There remained, by 1354, only Fang Kuo-chen and Chang Shih-ch'eng still in open defiance of the Yüan government. Fang had not been able to take advantage of the mass rebellions of 1351-52 to establish himself on land, and was still confined to the sea. The former salt-smuggler Chang Shih-ch'eng, who had seized the Grand Canal city of Kao-yu, and occupied an arc of territory around the Huainan provincial capital of Yang-chou, was the last remaining land-based rebel of any importance. Toghto decided to lead personally the campaign against him, hoping thus to bring the suppression effort to a glorious and emphatic conclusion.

It is a measure of Toghto's ability as a statesman that he was able to put down the rebellions. Even more remarkable, however, was his success in maintaining central control of the entire pacification effort. That pacification, nearly complete by 1354, had of course been a major new undertaking for the Yüan state. It had never before been obliged to handle mass insurrection on so immense a scale. The task was accomplished only by effecting major changes in bureaucratic and administrative routine, changes which had important implications for the distribution of political power within the Yüan state.

Rebel pacification did not, however, lead to any immediate change in the balance of power between state and society, even though the early ineffectiveness of the regular armies perhaps pointed to the likelihood of such a change, with real power and initiative descending into the hands of gentry-led militia. However, between the years 1351 and 1354, a shift indeed took place in the composition of the Yüan military forces. For the first time in recent Yüan history, the bulk of the troops used to suppress the rebels was made up of Chinese recruits. The shift seems clearest in the case of the main body of central forces: as the leadership of these passed from Tughchi to *Gongbubal to Esen Temür to Toghto, Chinese troops became more and more prominent. Toghto used the largely Chinese "Yellow Army" to deliver the first really crushing blow against the rebels at Hsü-chou. In other parts of China, Chinese militia troops appear to have predominated in the Yüan forces from the very beginning. There were, to be sure, a few exceptions. The commander 'Abd ar-Rahman led the Lung-chen Guards, an elite unit of Alans and Qipchaqs, with some measure of success in Hukuang in 1352. Miao tribal forces, commanded by the Hukuang provincial official Alqui in 1353, saw service also.[67] The 3,000 *tamachi* troops led by the Salji'ud Dash Badulugh at Hsiang-yang could have been partly Chinese in composition; in any event, the 20,000 extra men he used in taking the city were locally recruited Chinese militia.[68] Yet the fact that the Yüan had come to depend largely upon Chinese troops in suppressing the rebellions was a simple product of the expansion of rebel activity beyond what the regular forces could handle. Much the same sort of process had occurred when the Mongols undertook their vast world conquests of the previous century; the Mongols were accustomed to the use of conquered peoples as troops, especially in those days. In itself, the mere process of recruiting Chinese troops could not lead to any immediate drift of power and initiative away from the state as long as Mongols and *se-mu* continued as they did to monopolize military command. The Chinese landlord gentry, often instrumental in recruiting militia forces, especially in the South, were on the whole content enough to cooperate with the Yüan government and not to demand independent military power for themselves. Only through such cooperation could their common enemy, the Red Turbans, be put down. In the circumstances, it was unnecessary for the state to deliver the Yüan armies to outside Chinese control.

The massive recruitment, supply, and command of troops that had to be undertaken, however, did force changes on a different level of power. The need to supply the forces in the field, to concentrate anti-rebel efforts, and to provide the official machinery necessary to deal with stricken or vulnerable areas dictated certain temporary changes in the Yüan central administrative structure. In view of the geography of the rebellions—the fact that they were almost empire-wide in extent and spread rapidly from one region to another—the central government could not hope to direct every aspect of the pacification from a supreme command located in the capital. Authority had to be delegated to lower echelons, and certain regional officials had to be allowed to "act at convenience" *(pien-i hsing-shih)* and make the command decisions they judged necessary without seeking the prior approval of the central government. Yet, while the central government was obliged to surrender some of its decision-making powers to regional authorities, it did so with great caution. Through 1354 it was able to pit imperial princes, provincial officials, and censorial personnel against each other in such a way as to inhibit the creation of any unitary regional force strong enough to constitute a power challenge to the capital.

The problem of military supply, for example, was met in a number of ways, although the same care was always taken that supply and command were never handled by the same men. In the metropolitan *(Chung-shu)* province of North China, administrations "detached" from the Central Chancellery *(Chung-shu fen-sheng)* were set up in Tsi-ning and in Chang-te in 1351 and 1352. Their purpose was to interdict the upward flow of grain taxes and divert the proceeds directly to the armies in the field.[69] In view of the heavy demand for military rations in 1352, the government further issued special orders to the local officials in Honan and Shensi, urging them to ensure that the peasants cultivated all available land to the fullest extent, and that the military commanders kept their armies from trampling and destroying the grain fields.[70] Extra efforts were also made to extract the maximum in tax revenues. In 1351, in spite of all difficulties, the salt tax was collected on schedule.[71] In 1352 Chinese Confucian officials were sent out to various parts of North China to plead with the local elders and urge the necessity of prompt tax payments.[72] The government, however, rejected a proposal to carry out a complete resurvey of the fields of North China.[73]

In South China supply was the primary responsibility of the provincial governments. Rations procurement often involved the cooperation of two or more provinces, a situation which may have served as a check upon too much provincial independence. As Chief Administrator of Hukuang province, the Jalair Dorjibal amassed grain supplies by purchasing them in the neighboring provinces of Szechwan and Honan, and by awarding official positions to local people who contributed grain voluntarily.[74] Ch'eng Tsun, magistrate in the Hukuang provincial capital of Wu-ch'ang, purchased grain in Honan and Kiangche provinces.[75] Kiangsi province obtained salt and grain from Kiangche.[76]

Food was also needed in the capital. The Grand Canal was blocked at Kao-yu by Chang Shih-ch'eng, and the pirate Fang Kuo-chen still remained at liberty on the sea. The Yüan government made still further attempts both to coax Fang into submission and to attack him outright—all to no avail. In June, 1352, the government decided temporarily to suspend all maritime grain shipments from the Yangtze delta to the capital, and in consequence no grain at all arrived by the sea route in 1352.[77] The food situation was serious. The government purchased 500,000 piculs of grain and beans in Liaoyang in November, but that was not enough.[78] Late in 1352, Toghto conceived the grand idea of solving the problem by opening state farms on a broad scale in North China near the capital. An area of about 150,000 square miles, bounded by the Great Wall in the north, Shan-hai-kuan in the east, Pao-ting and Ho-chien in the south, and the Western Hills in the west was thrown open to government-sponsored colonization. Peasants were brought in from the Shantung area to augment the indigenous population. It was decided to emphasize the cultivation of rice, since an earlier experiment had shown that sufficient water was available and that rice could in fact be grown in the area. Since the northern peasants were ignorant of the techniques of rice cultivation,

Toghto arranged to import from the Yangtze delta region two thousand experienced rice farmers to serve a year's term as agricultural teachers. The project was costly; 5,000,000 ingots were allotted to cover all expenses. Yet it appears doubtful whether Toghto actually got the million-picul harvests that he anticipated.[79] The Grand Ministry of Agriculture, which had over-all charge of the operation, was headed by two men, both of whom held concurrent positions in the Central Chancellery. In view of Toghto's general desire to inhibit the concentration of power in single hands, the arrangement seems typical.

Besides keeping rations procurement out of the hands of the commanders, Toghto went further in his efforts to prevent successful generals and provincial officials from developing into warlords or regional satraps. In almost all the major anti-rebel campaigns the Yüan carried out, special exertions were made to keep military commands divided. In the Hsiang-yang campaign of 1352-53, for example, the commanders Dash Badulugh and Yao-chu both held high positions in the Szechwan provincial government, although the major battles they engaged in took place not there, but in Honan province. Nor were they left free to monopolize the direction of military operations. The government sent out one force under the control of the local Pacification Commissioner, and another, consisting of Uighur troops, led by the son of the *iduq qut*.[80] To these were added yet other men commanded by the Prince of Hsi-ning Yaghan-shah.[81] Despite these precautions, Dash Badulugh managed, during the course of the long campaign in the Hsiang-yang region, to appoint his own local civilian magistrates in an effort to gather more food supplies. At the conclusion of the campaigns in the early summer of 1354, however, Dash Badulugh was replaced and was transferred together with his army to the upper Huai region.[82] Clearly the court was eager to remove Dash Badulugh from the local power base that he had begun to build.

Roughly the same pattern of divided commands can be seen in the Yüan government's Yangtze River campaigns against the main center of southern Red Turban power. In 1352, over-all control of the suppression effort in the three southern provinces of Kiangche, Kiangsi, and Hukuang was given to the Censor-in-Chief of the Kiangnan Censorate, the Tangut Narin, whose headquarters were in Nanking.[83] It is not clear, however, what degree of control he exercised over the campaign against the rebel center, especially in view of the fact that he was closely concerned with military operations in the immediate vicinity of Nanking itself at the time. In any event, the suppression of the rebel center was at length accomplished by the joint action of several commanders, including Manzi Qaya, who as Vice Censor-in-Chief of the Kiangnan Censorate was an immediate subordinate of Narin's. The other major commanders included the Kiangsi Chief Administrator Shinggi—until his death in November, 1352; the Hukuang Chief Administrator Esen Temür; the Hukuang Vice Administrator of the Left Bayan Buqa; the Szechwan Assistant Administrator Qarimtu; the Prince of Hsi-ning Yaghan-shah; the Prince of Wei-shun Köncheg Buqa; and above all the Kiangche Chief Administrator Buyan Temür, known familiarly as "the Chief Administrator with the piebald horse." Buyan Temür, apparently a popular figure, was the real driving spirit behind the success of the campaign. As soon as their joint forces overran the rebel capital, however, Toghto broke up the coalition and assigned new stations to the various commanders.[84] This dismemberment was the more easily carried out precisely because the commanders were assembled from a half-dozen separate administrative agencies and princely establishments, and had not been permitted to integrate themselves and their men into a single organization.

In the Huai region north of the Yangtze, the Yüan government made a major administrative change in May, 1352, when it detached from Honan province the whole area between the Yangtze and the Huai Rivers and created from it the new province of Huainan, with its capital at Yangchou.[85] Huainan was a sort of "war-zone" province, embracing all the territory in Honan where the rebels were especially active. Its establishment facilitated the coordination of the anti-rebel effort, inasmuch as the Honan provincial capital of Pien-liang in the north was too far removed from the scene to provide sufficiently close supervision. But Huainan province with its official staff of twenty-five men was obliged to tolerate the existence of a parallel agency in Yang-chou—the princely establishment of the Prince of Chen-nan Bolod Buqa, which had its own Pacification Office, and which conducted its own military campaigns.[86] Nor was that all; the writ of the Kiangnan Branch Censorate extended into the Yangtze River, where it constituted yet a third authority. Under these circumstances, we find the commander Naṣr ad-Dīn obeying all three authorities during 1352. First, the princely Pacification Office ordered him to build defense works, then the Huainan provincial authorities had him patrol the Yangtze, and finally the Kiangnan Censorate had him come to the aid of the town of Wu-hu on the south shore of the Yangtze.[87] Of the Huainan provincial officials, the Chief Administrator Qonqor Buqa, previously a member of the Han-lin Academy, was also given a concurrent position within the Prince of Chen-nan's establishment.[88] This device probably provided some coordination between the two agencies, at the same time that it discouraged either from becoming too independent. The sources name, besides Qonqor Buqa, five other men appointed to the top provincial positions in Huainan, two of them Chinese and three non-Chinese. Of the five, three had previously held censorial positions elsewhere, one had held provincial position in Hukuang, and one was appointed from the military hierarchy. From this, two things seem clear: first, that the mixed official backgrounds of the new appointees would inhibit their forming a tight clique; and second, that Honan province was afforded no means of control over its former Huainan territory.

The above evidence should suffice to cast doubt upon the widespread impression that the Yüan Dynasty collapsed because its armies had grown too decadent and soft to give effective opposition to the Red Turban rebels.[89] It would appear that, far from collapsing outright, the Yüan Dynasty rallied in short order through the copious use of mixed auxiliary forces—Chinese, Miao, and Mongols and *se-mu*. The dynasty not only halted the rebel advance, but almost destroyed the whole rebel movement. Whatever inadequacies the Yüan military arm may have shown in 1351 and 1352, it proved more than equal to the challenge by 1353 and 1354.

In effecting this suppression, the Chancellor of the Right Toghto saw to it that no semi-independent regional machine should arise to challenge the powers of the central government, and that the chief military and civilian positions should remain, as always, in the hands of Mongols and *se-mu*. Despite the new and massive military and bureaucratic effort which the suppression of the rebellions demanded, the central government proved capable of exercising a significant degree of control over the entire operation. Large military concentrations were generally composed of mutually independent units which the central government could easily split apart after the completion of a campaign. Rations procurement and the command of troops were kept as separate and distinct functions. The civilian jurisdictions which oversaw local operations overlapped and conflicted. So much for the atomization of power in the provinces.

At court, an opposite tendency can be detected. The singular and stark concentration of power there stood in complete and perhaps invidious contrast with the situation at the provincial level. It would appear that the Chancellor of the Right Toghto alone saw his personal power and prestige grow in proportion to the enormous increase in new governmental activity which the rebellions, and his new programs, occasioned.

Far from suffering the rebellions as a political defeat, as his court opponents might have expected, the Chancellor of the Right was actually profiting from them. The pacification of the rebels turned out to be simply one more program of merit and profit for Toghto and his administration. Exactly as in the case of some of the other projects, the pacification program demanded that the government recruit, supply, and direct large numbers of men, and this the government was competent and eager to do. The career of the engineer Chia Lu would appear to illustrate the fundamental equivalence of river rechanneling and rebel pacification in the eyes of the government. Like his master Toghto, Chia Lu easily shifted from manager of hydraulic operations to commander of troops in the field.[90] Even though the earlier warning of the court opposition that the Yellow River project might bring on popular rebellion had come true, the Toghto administration proved its competence to handle both, and remained in power, stronger than ever.

As Toghto's various operations each came to a successful conclusion, his personal wealth and honors increased. When the Yellow River project ended late in 1351, a censor disregarded the Red Turban rebellion which was by then raging in the Huai region and proposed "extraordinary rewards" for Toghto's successful sponsorship of the project. In response to this, the emperor awarded Toghto the hereditary title of *darqan*, granted him an income fief *(shih-i)* in Huai-an, permitted him to appoint personally the local officials in that place, and commissioned the erection of a commemorative stela whereon a detailed account of the Yellow River project was inscribed.[91] In June, 1352, an office *(tsung-kuan-fu)* was established for Toghto at his Huai-an estates for the purpose of managing the hunter, falconer, artisan, and other revenue-producing households allotted to him.[92] Toghto's proposed campaign on Hsü-chou in 1352 elicited a joint and friendly protest from the presidents of the Six Boards; the government, they said, could not possibly function without his presence.[93] Toghto went anyway. On October 17, twelve days after Toghto had left for Hsü-chou, a concerted effort on the part of the court censors and various military and censorial officials in Honan and Shensi succeeded in clearing the name of the Censor-in-Chief Esen Temür, and securing a reward for him besides.[94] On top of Toghto's victory at Hsü-chou came another spate of honors and rewards. In November, 1352, Toghto was elevated from Grand Tutor *(t'ai-fu)* to Grand Preceptor *(t'ai-shih)*.[95] In December the Central Chancellery received imperial authorization to erect a stela in commemoration of Toghto's victory; even more, the grant of a princely fief was requested for Toghto. This honor Toghto apparently declined.[96] In March, 1353, the elders of Hsü-chou received imperial permission to erect another stela in Toghto's honor, and to build a temple *(shen-tz'u)* for him as well.[97]

One can only speculate what further honors and rewards Toghto's elimination of Chang Shih-ch'eng at Kao-yu might have brought him. The emperor, perhaps, asked himself the same question. Had Toghto succeeded in his campaign against Chang Shih-ch'eng, as was entirely likely, the pacification program would have been completed and his position as Chancellor of the Right strengthened yet more. The one power relationship that Toghto's pursuit of "merit and profit" *(kung-li)* affected above all others was that between himself and the emperor. As the power of the Chancellor grew, that of the monarchy had to decline. Perhaps the emperor, who owed his political emancipation to Toghto and the events of 1340, pendered that matter as his Chancellor of the Right prepared for the Kao-yu campaign.

Chapter VI
The Growth of Yüan Regionalism

*It was not Toghto's original plan to or*ganize a campaign against Kao-yu, or to lead such a campaign personally. Before he decided to use force against the former salt smuggler Chang Shih-ch'eng, Toghto made four fruitless attempts to urge him to surrender peacefully in return for an official appointment.[1] When it became clear that Chang would not negotiate, Toghto decided to use force. In 1353 or 1354 he ordered the *chin-shih* Shih P'u, a Chinese subordinate official in the Chief Military Commission, to recruit 10,000 militiamen in Shantung and to command these men "at convenience" *(pien-i hsing-shih)* against Kao-yu. While Shih P'u was marching toward Kao-yu with his army, however, one of Toghto's aides rescinded the earlier order allowing Shih P'u to act at convenience. Shih P'u was instead placed under the administrative jurisdiction of Huainan province, and half his troops were taken away from him. In these reduced circumstances Shih P'u continued his expedition. When he arrived at Kao-yu, he let a Mongol cavalry unit attack first in order to let it have the merit of breaching the city defenses. But Chang's men beat off the attack, and routed Shih P'u's forces.[2] It would appear that at the last minute Toghto decided, or was persuaded, that Kao-yu was too choice a rebel target to let fall to anyone but himself. The expedition, led by a Chinese, was apparently deliberately sabotaged.

During 1354 the Yüan government laid long and careful plans for Toghto's coming attack on Kao-yu. Arrangements were made for supplies of clothing, weapons, rations, and fuel to be shipped from the southern province of Kiangche by both land and water routes to the staging area of the attack. During June and July, 1354, an agreement was made with

Korea for the procurement of troops and weapons, for which purpose 60,000 ingots in paper cash was paid to the Korean Government. The date of August 28 was fixed for the Korean expeditionary force of around 23,000 men to assemble at the Yüan capital. The Yüan government also assembled "Hairy Gourd" militiamen from Shensi, troops from Central Asia and Tibet, in addition to provincial regulars and men under the command of various Mongol princes. A formal edict of September 19 put Toghto in supreme command of all forces with the authority to give rewards and promotions at will. The provincial governments, censorates, and the Chief Military Commission were allowed to select officials to accompany the expedition. Toghto probably left Ta-tu, the Yüan capital, late in October. On the way south, he sent envoys to offer sacrifices to Confucius and Mencius at their respective shrines.[3]

After Toghto's expedition arrived at Kao-yu, it skirmished with Chang Shih-ch'eng's men outside the city walls for about two weeks, from November 28 to December 12. Various military units jockeyed among themselves for the honor of leading the assault on the city walls. After December 12 fighting appears to have ceased. One source says that Toghto wanted to rest his troops before the final onslaught.[4] Kao-yu, however, was completely surrounded and its destruction a matter of certainty on any day that Toghto might care to select. It is possible that he decided to starve the city into surrender rather than take it by storm.[5]

Whatever the reasons for it, Toghto's delay at Kao-yu was a fatal political mistake, for it provided the emperor with a convenient pretext for ordering Toghto's dismissal. Traditional historiography places the blame for Toghto's fall upon a certain Qama, an intrigue-loving courtier of Qangli origin, and ostensibly a member of Toghto's own political clique. The sources have it that sometime between February, 1353, and September, 1354, Qama was temporarily removed from his position as Chief Administrator, owing to a complaint made against him by Ju Chung-po, one of Toghto's close aides. Although Qama had returned to his position by the time Toghto departed the capital for Kao-yu, he remained under suspicion. While Toghto was out on campaign, his younger brother, the Censor-in-Chief Esen Temür, fell sick and absented himself from court. Qama took advantage of this opportunity to avenge himself upon the Merkid brothers. He made contact with a censor who agreed to submit directly to the emperor a memorial of impeachment against Toghto and Esen Temür. The memorial imputed various derelictions to Esen Temür, and accused Toghto of the crime of deliberately delaying his advance on Kao-yu and wasting the state's resources in the process. It went on to add, gratuitously, that half of the court officials were personal followers of Toghto. The emperor accepted the impeachment upon its third submission to him. He ordered the dismissal of Esen Temür on December 23, 1354, and of Toghto himself on the following day.[6]

Qama had taken care to forewarn many of the officials participating in the Kao-yu campaign about Toghto's coming dismissal, and to threaten them with the extirpation of themselves and their clans if they attempted to rally behind Toghto. By the time he received the letter of edict, on the night of January 7, 1355, Toghto was aware of what it contained. Some of his followers urged him to conquer Kao-yu first and open the edict afterwards. Others proposed that he back the Prince of Chen-nan Bolod Buqa and set up an opposition southern dynasty. Toghto's own reported response was fully Confucian, yet vengeful. According to his biography, Toghto spoke as follows: "If the emperor orders me and I do not obey, that would be to oppose the emperor. Where then would be the righteousness between sovereign and minister?" Then he bowed his head, and continued: "Stupid as I am, I received the emperor's favor. He entrusted me with the great military responsibilities of state. Day and night I trembled, unable to bear them. Now he has relieved me of this great burden. Great indeed is the mercy of the emperor."[7]

An official stepped forward. In dramatic but vain protest against Toghto's decision to obey the emperor, he pulled out his sword and committed suicide on the spot.

The emperor divided Toghto's forces up among three commanders. Various units, however, mutinied and turned outlaw, and the attack on Kao-yu was in fact never pressed further. Toghto's agricultural program in North China was abolished, and the bureaus issuing the new currency closed down. The Merkid family properties were confiscated; Esen Temür's property went to Qama. Esen Temür was banished to Szechwan, where he apparently died. Toghto's two sons were exiled to Kansu. Toghto himself was first exiled to his estates in Huai-an; later he was removed to Etsin-gol, and finally he was transported to the Yunnan frontier, where on January 10, 1356, he was poisoned by Qama's agents. He was forty-two years of age at the time.[8]

The dismissal of Toghto had utterly disastrous political consequences for the future of the Yüan as a dynasty ruling in China. What these consequences were will be discussed below. It is necessary to try to answer a deceptively simple question first: why it was that the emperor dismissed Toghto. A number of possible reasons suggest themselves, but no single explanation is completely satisfactory. The answer rather lies in a combination of factors.

Five years of Toghto and his managerial bureaucratic programs, his monopolization of power, and the supremacy of reform ideology had produced astounding and beneficial results within the Yüan empire. The Yellow River had been tamed in one of the greatest hydraulic enterprises ever organized; North China agriculture had been revolutionized; the Red Turban rebellions had been crushed. But five years of Toghto had also produced a feeling of suffocation and a mood of restlessness in the bureaucracy. The Censorate and the provincial administrations were beginning to chafe and grow rebellious under the continuing need to toe the political line. The conservative Confucians were growing impatient with the administration's constant refusal to listen to them, especially now that Toghto's programs seemed to be drawing to a close. Within the monarchy, there was apprehension as to what Toghto might attempt to do next.

By making himself appear as the true defender of the censorial prerogatives, Toghto had been able to compel Berke Buqa's overthrow in 1349 and win the gratitude of that organ.

In the six years since then, however, the Censorate had been under the firm partisan control of Toghto's younger brother Esen Temür. In 1352, nevertheless, Toghto had been obliged to quell an incipient revolt in the Censorate. It was apparently on the verge of joining the Shensi Branch Censorate in its impeachment of Esen Temür until Toghto revised the ethnic qualifications for office-holding, appointed three Southern Chinese as censors, and used them to lead the counterattack against Esen Temür's Shensi detractors.[9] In 1354 Qama seems to have made common cause with the lower censorial opposition when he leagued with a censor by the name of Yüan Sain Buqa, of whom practically nothing is known, in order to arrange the impeachment of the two Merkid brothers. It would appear that by 1354 many lower censors felt they had been docile long enough, and were eager to speak out once again against those in power.

There are also indications that Toghto had enemies among the provincial officials who were succeeding so well in putting down the Red Turban disturbances. It is not unlikely that many of them were impatient with the Chancellor's determination to restrict their fields of operation and frustrate their creation of personal power bases. What lends credence to such a supposition is that sometime after 1352, and before Toghto's dismissal, one Wang Ssu-ch'eng, Expositor-in-Waiting in the Chi-hsien Academy and concurrent Rector of the Imperial University, presented a seven-point memorial to the emperor. His very first point was a plea to reactivate the positions of Chancellor of the Right and Chancellor of the Left in the provincial governments, and to permit the holders of such offices to take exclusive charge of all matters within their respective jurisdictions.[10] Toghto ordinarily assigned no provincial posts higher than that of Chief Administrator, since it was precisely the growth of this kind of concentrated provincial power that he always tried to inhibit. The fact that the provincial chancellorships were revived immediately after Toghto's ouster makes it seem certain that Wang Ssu-ch'eng was under strong pressure earlier to make such a plea to the emperor.

That there was strong conservative opposition to Toghto

is evident, but difficult to prove. The conservatives declined on ideological grounds to consider themselves a faction, and they did not behave as a faction either before or after the dismissal. There is no evidence that they organized a movement against Toghto, and no evidence that they made a concerted grab for the spoils of office after Toghto was gone. Some of the old conservatives were dead. Berke Buqa died in 1350. The former Chancellor of the Right, the Jalair Dorji, commanded troops and voluntarily participated in Toghto's campaign on Kao-yu. He died in his army at Yang-chou in 1355.[11] The former Chancellor of the Left Ho Wei-i was recalled from retirement in 1355, but was made Chancellor of the Right of Huainan province. In 1357, however, he did resume his old position in the Central Chancellery.[12] Hsü Yu-jen, an old policy opponent of Toghto's (it was he who put the *kung-li* label on Toghto's enterprises), had served under Toghto since 1353 as Vice Administrator of the Left for Honan province. In 1355 he too was recalled to the capital for position there.[13] Though some conservatives certainly benefited politically from Toghto's overthrow, they had no visible machine and no real leader.

The ideological justification for Toghto's dismissal had, however, a definitely conservative ring. Conservative ideology tended to support the censorial right to speak out against anyone in power. Against Toghto's political centralization, it stressed the necessity of some regional autonomy. Good local officials should be able to feed the starving, supply the troops, and attack rebels and bandits without constant interference and politically imposed restriction from above. Even more, the premium the conservatives placed upon selecting morally good men for office seems especially to have disposed them to the opposite task of rooting out the bad and the ineffectual, a matter which called for the full exercise of the powers of the Censorate. A case in point, of course, was the Shensi Branch Censorate's attempted impeachment of Esen Temür for allowing his army to be terrorized and dispersed by Red Turbans in 1352. In addition, it was no doubt his awareness, perhaps even his support, of conservative opinion that led the Tangut Irinjinbal to urge Toghto to punish his unsuccessful military commanders, a measure which Toghto refused to take. When Toghto was dismissed, the charge laid against him was deliberate delay and military failure.[14] After Toghto's dismissal, the conservatives could continue to demand, and obtain, exemplary punishments of unsuccessful Yüan commanders.[15]

There is, finally, the question of Toghto's relationship to the monarchy, and the possibility that as the all-powerful Chancellor of the Right he constituted some sort of danger to the imperial house. Certainly Qama tried to point to the existence of such a danger. He had earlier approached Toghon Temür's Korean empress and laid before her the charge that the Merkid brothers were responsible for delaying the formal investiture of her son Ayushiridara as heir apparent. Although it would not appear that Toghto was in any way opposed to Ayushiridara, there were some irregularities in Ayushiridara's position that proved troublesome to Toghto. His mother was Korean, and there was sentiment against her on these grounds. She was, in addition, only a second-ranking empress. The principal empress was Bayan Qudu, whose Qunggirad clan enjoyed traditional marriage ties to the imperial house. Sometime around 1353 Bayan Qudu gave birth to a son. Under these circumstances, when Qama first approached Toghto with a view to conferring the patent of investiture upon Ayushiridara as heir apparent, Toghto procrastinated.[16] He apparently did so not because he opposed Ayushiridara, but rather because the birth of this new baby seriously complicated the question of the imperial succession.[17] The matter required careful deliberation.

Toghto's hesitancy on the succession question understandably prejudiced his relationships with Ayushiridara and his ambitious mother. By his very silence, Toghto was casting doubt upon Ayushiridara's legitimacy. Ayushiridara was about sixteen years of age at the time of Toghto's dismissal. The indications are that unlike his father he possessed considerable if undeveloped executive talent, and that he was eager to take an active part in the administration of the realm.[18] We have it that he strongly disapproved of his father's passivity, his pleasurable diversions, and his coterie of palace playmates.[19] It was likely that sooner or later Ayushiridara would come to an open confrontation with Toghto.

Through intermediaries such as Qama the restlessness and frustration of the bureaucracy and its desire for Toghto's removal were being channeled up to the emperor. Since his Korean empress and his son Ayushiridara were interpreting Toghto's evasiveness on the succession question as a sign of his opposition, the emperor was under pressure from within the monarchical establishment to remove the Chancellor of the Right. The emperor also had possible personal reasons for resenting Toghto. Under the conservative administration of Berke Buqa, his visible presence had been demanded by the bureaucracy. He was permitted a hortatory role; he participated in the making of official appointments; and his solicitude for the people was prominently advertised through such devices as sending special delegations to honor and reward popular local officials. This role the emperor seemed to enjoy. Under Toghto, however, there was nothing for him to do but pass his time in idle diversions in the palace and let Toghto run everything. For this his own son was beginning to criticize him.

Although it was not one but probably all of these factors that influenced the emperor's decision to remove Toghto, the pressure was no doubt strongest within the monarchy itself. One simply could not tell what Toghto planned to do with the monarchy. Through his machine, Toghto completely controlled the state. There were no higher positions to promote him to, no honors and rewards that he did not possess already. What possible leverage did the imperial house still retain over Toghto? Early in the previous century the Merkids had been rivals to Chinggis Qan. Chinggis, in his vindictive fury, pronounced anathemas upon the Merkids and all but destroyed them. What were Toghto's feelings on this matter? Was it by accident that he bore the same name as the last great leader of the Merkids, whom Chinggis killed in 1208?[20] How loyal, ultimately, was Toghto to the house of Chinggis Qan? What concrete facts could not prove, imagination could easily invent. There can be no doubt that the imperial house felt itself to be in danger from Toghto, a danger that it could not quite define. There were too many questions about him that begged an answer.

Hence the emperor's edict of December 24, 1354, dismissing Toghto. The rebel Chang Shih-ch'eng, trapped inside the walls of Kao-yu, must have watched in disbelief as Toghto's forces, so near to annihilating him, suddenly and unaccountably fell to pieces.

As for Toghto's immediate and complete act of obedience to the emperor's edict, one may perhaps interpret it as the most extreme form of revenge he could possibly have chosen. One can imagine that to prove the point that the integrity of the dynasty rested upon him and upon him alone, he decided simply to scuttle it then and there, and let whoever pleased pick up the pieces. He would permit his entire machine to collapse at once, and abandon his men, his officials, and his generals to the mercies of the opposition.[21] The restless censors, the provincial autonomists, and the frustrated conservatives could inherit the empire, or what was left of it. Whatever they did would make no difference, for the inheritance of Chinggis Qan and Qubilai in China was at an end; the Yüan Dynasty was, in all essential respects, finished.

The dismissal of Toghto constitutes a major turning point in late Yüan history. It marks the end of Yüan territorial and administrative centralization and the rise of regionalism in both North and South China. In North China and along the China coast the regionalists were nominally loyal to the Yüan. In the interior of South China grew the movements that would culminate in the founding of the Ming Dynasty in 1368.

Along the South China coast, regional warlords came into power not long after Toghto's dismissal. A clear case in point is that of Chang Shih-ch'eng, Toghto's intended victim at Kao-yu. Having given unmistakable sign that it was afraid of its own apparatus of pacification, the Yüan court then proceeded to rearrange its priorities and place conciliation ahead of suppression. It is true that Toghto himself had attempted to negotiate with Chang before leading the campaign against him, but Toghto at the time negotiated from a position of strength, and had the necessary military power in reserve when the former salt-smuggler refused to surrender peacefully. After Toghto's downfall, the Yüan court turned once again to negotiation and sent envoys to Kao-yu to persuade Chang to surrender voluntarily in return for an official position. This time, however, the court held no serious military force in reserve and was obliged to let Chang impose his own terms.[22] The court could not prevent Chang's migration south from the Huai area in 1356 and his forcible seizure and occupation of the Yangtze delta region, the chief rice-growing and salt-producing part of the empire.[23] It stood by helplessly while Chang proceeded to create his own system of central and local government with its capital at P'ing-chiang (Soochow).[24] Having thus consolidated his position, with direct and complete administrative control over his own territory, Chang Shih-ch'eng considered himself secure and under these circumstances opened negotiations with the Yüan court. In 1357 he agreed to abolish the Great Chou, i.e., the outward trappings of independence, and accept from the Yüan court the title of Grand Commandant (*t'ai-wei*). The Great Chou dynasty was renamed the Kiangtung Branch Province (*fen-sheng*); Chang's adherents all accepted positions as Yüan officials, and from 1359 Chang began to send token amounts of tribute grain to the Yüan capital.[25]

Chang's surrender was only nominal and the voluntary incorporation of his regime into the Yüan Dynasty a fiction. He stayed complete master in his own house, maintained personal diplomatic relations with Korea, and in 1363, when the situation seemed to warrant it, he threw off the Yüan cloak and declared his independence once again.

The court's policy toward Chang Shih-ch'eng was paralleled by similar arrangements with other regionalists along the China coast. The pirate Fang Kuo-chen, whose emergence in 1348 seemed to set the trend for the future, remained at liberty on the sea. From 1352 to 1354 Toghto had wavered between conciliation and warfare in his policy toward the pirate, but Toghto's negotiating terms were harsh; he would allow Fang to surrender only in return for an official appointment somewhere away from the coast where his power lay, and that only on the condition that Fang first turn in his boats and disperse his followers.[26] At the time of Toghto's dismissal, the official policy toward Fang Kuo-chen was one of hostility. This situation changed radically in 1356, for by this time Fang had moved ashore and seized the coastal cities of T'ai-chou, Ch'ing-yüan (Ning-po), Yü-yao, and Wen-chou. In 1356 Fang was approached by Yüan officials who hoped to enlist his aid against Chang Shih-ch'eng.[27] In return for a sea attack upon Chang, which Fang undertook, though without enthusiasm and without success, the Yüan court appointed him myriarch in charge of maritime grain shipments and at the same time myriarch in charge of the protection of the shipments.[28] These were substantive appointments; Fang's power base at sea was legitimized and recognized. The court went yet further in 1357, when it also appointed him Assistant Administrator of Kiangche province, and thus recognized his territorial power as well.[29] Like Chang Shih-ch'eng, Fang controlled his own regional administration. He was able to obtain successively higher provincial posts for himself and his adherents down to the end of the dynasty.[30]

The autonomous coastal warlords for the most part preferred to act as Yüan loyalists, but their loyalty was purely voluntary, and was intended in part as a means of gaining legitimacy in the eyes of the local landlord gentry, who had learned from the Red Turban troubles to associate anti-dynastic rebellion with the massacre of their own kind. In the interior of South China the situation was rather different. The leadership that emerged there after Toghto's downfall consisted of rebels who had formerly been involved in the messianic Red Turban movements of 1351 and after, and who on the whole continued to maintain an attitude of hostility toward the Yüan Dynasty. While the warlords on the China coast were largely content to exercise authority on a purely regional basis, and to mask their actual independence by submitting nominally to the Yüan government, the rebels of the interior, although regionally based at the initial stages, very early made clear their claim to the Mandate of Heaven and their desire eventually to rule not simply a province or an area, but all of China.[31]

The strategic realities favored such a development. In North China the rebels who initiated the riots of 1351, and were subsequently crushed, emerged again in 1355 and established a "Sung" dynasty with a central government in the northern Huai town of Po-chou. In their earlier religious phase, the rebels had attempted nothing of this sort. This time their messianic propaganda was muted and their dynastic pretensions more serious. From 1355 to 1360 the Sung regime acted the part of a traditional government, imposing a system of taxation and instituting its own coinage. At the same time it made alliances with remnant rebel groups in various parts of Central and North China, and sent these reconstituted forces out on campaign against the Yüan Dynasty in various directions at once. In 1358 the Sung regime moved its capital northwest to Pien-liang (K'ai-feng). Lacking sufficient food supplies, and occupying an undefendable plains region, the rebel dynasty made a heroic but unsuccessful effort to seize the grain-growing valleys of Shensi and Shansi, and even to storm the Yüan capital itself. By 1360 the Sung forces were spent. Yet the historical role of the rebel Sung regime was a crucial one. It forced the Yüan Dynasty to permit the creation of an outside military machine under the loyalist Chaghan Temür in order to put it down. This matter will de dealt with more fully below. In addition, the existence of the Sung movement in the north effectively prevented the Yüan court from interfering in any direct way in the situation in South China.[32]

Between North China and South China lay the Huai region, earlier the seedbed of the Red Turban risings, but increasingly after 1355 a no man's land, exhausted and ravaged, and unable to support either provincial loyalists or rebels with dynastic ambitions. The Huai area was gradually evacuated, its major occupiers either migrating northwest like the Sung regime, or south across the Yangtze like Chang Shih-ch'eng. The Huai region thus came to constitute a kind of buffer zone which, together with the Sung movement raging north of it, effectively sealed off the interior of South China from any landward interference on the part of the Yüan. Until Chaghan Temür's partial reunification of North China in 1361 the Yüan court could confront the developing rebel regimes of Ch'en Yu-liang and the future Ming founder Chu Yüan-chang only through the cooperation of the loyalist coastal warlords, who were not eager to undertake major campaigns inland. Consequently, rebels such as Ch'en and Chu could build their incipient imperial regimes relatively unhindered.

In these circumstances, it is not surprising that Yüan provincial and local authority south of the Yangtze should have begun disintegrating after 1355. Many of the high-ranking bureaucrats who had performed so successfully under Toghto's direction in putting down the Red Turbans in 1352 and 1353 were gone. One of the earliest to die was the Tangut Shinggi, Chief Administrator of Kiangche, who was captured and killed in November, 1352.[33] The Tangut Buyan Temür, the commander who led the successful attack on the southern Red Turban capital in 1353, died in November or December, 1356, in the Yangtze city of Ch'ih-chou (Kuei-ch'ih, Anhwei).[34] The Jalair Dorjibal, Chief Administrator of Hukuang, died in the former rebel-held city of Huang-chou at some undetermined date.[35] The Dörben (Mongol) Örüg Temür, Chief Administrator of Kiangche, died of illness in his army at Hui-chou (She-hsien, Anhwei) in the late summer of 1352.[36] The Tangut Irinjinbal, Chancellor of the Left of Kiangsi, died in office there in the late summer of 1354.[37] These men were important figures; they had enjoyed the confidence of the administration above and the allegiance of the local gentry and their militias below, and although they were by training civilian bureaucrats, they had commanded personally the pacification effort at the highest provincial levels.

A few veterans of the earlier pacification campaigns were still alive and serving in office after 1355, but they were unable to cope with the new rebel power that emerged after Toghto's removal. This second rebel advance was militarily better organized than the first. In addition, the rebels were employing an entirely new strategy: instead of fomenting popular riots against the landlord gentry as they had done earlier, they began making an overt bid for landlord gentry support. By so doing, they split the phalanx of gentry-led militia that had rallied to the Yüan officials earlier, and left the Yüan officials with little of their former role as champions of the existing social order to play. By the early 1360s, the regimes of Ch'en Yu-liang and Chu Yüan-chang had grown to such an extent, thanks to gentry support, that the remaining loyalist gentry could only submit to one or the other. Between them, Ch'en and Chu overpowered the isolated loyalist walled cities one by one, and brought a complete end to Yüan rule in the interior regions of the South. Some of the Yüan local officials perished along with the fall of their cities, as Confucian duty required. For this, they were posthumously honored by Ch'en and Chu.[38] After 1355 Southern Chinese history is no longer really Yüan history, but fits more properly into the history of Chu Yüan-chang's foundation of the Ming Dynasty (1368-1644).

More pertinent to the history of the dying Yüan Dynasty was the slow and intricate process which led to the formation of semi-independent regional machines in North China, and the concomitant reduction in the scope of Yüan central authority to little more than the capital city itself. It was the rise of the rebel Sung regime in North China after Toghto's dismissal that provoked and justified the growth of semi-independent loyalist power. The Yüan court either had to allow its growth, or be overrun by the Sung rebels.

The chief architect of this new regional organization was Chaghan Temür. He was the great-grandson of one Kökötei, who as a *tamachi,* or non-Mongol soldier under Mongol command, participated in the conquest of Honan province during the reign of the *qaghan* Ögödei (r. 1229-41). Kökötei was a Naiman Turk, whose home was in Pei-t'ing (Beshbaliq) in Uighur territory.[39] His son Naimantai and grandson Arghun, however, settled in Honan province as landowners, registering their family in the county of Shen-ch'iu. Arghun did not hold office and evidently had no powerful connections at the Yüan court. If he had, one might expect that so robust and capable a young man as his son Chaghan Temür would have gained entry into the Imperial Guards. Instead, like many other provincial Mongols and *se-mu,* Chaghan Temür prepared himself for the official examinations, which he passed at the *chü-jen* level sometime before the Red Turban rebellions of 1351. He occasionally used a Chinese surname, Li, and is sometimes referred to, *more sinico,* as Li Ch'a-han. He apparently had no sons of his own. His sister was married to a Chinese named Wang, and Chaghan Temür adopted a son of theirs named Wang Pao-pao, later known as Kökö Temür.[40]

Although he may have been "earnest in study," as his biography in the *Yüan shih* flatteringly asserts, he was widely known in his part of Honan for rather different qualities. These one may infer from the accounts written about some of his friends and adherents. The epitaph of one such adherent, named Kuan-kuan, describes not a literary or Confucian type, but a muscular bravo. "In his youth," begins the epitaph, "he was fierce, talented, and brave. He was fond of hunting and was practiced in riding and shooting. He lived in Shen-ch'iu, and in his travels . . . he became familiar with the locally powerful people (*hao-chieh*). He was at one with them in his temperament and in his ideas."[41] Like Chaghan Temür, Kuan-kuan had a Chinese polite name, or *tzu.* From this it may be presumed that like Chaghan he had a Chinese teacher and had studied for the examinations also. Kuan-kuan's ethnic origin is unknown. However, he was clearly not Chinese, since he lacked a surname (*hsing*).

Another friend of Chaghan Temür's was an equally unlikely companion for an earnest Confucian. He was Li Ssu-ch'i, a Chinese police chief and tax clerk (*tien-shih*) in his home county of Lo-shan further south. Li had no pretensions whatever to Confucian learning.[42] Over Kuan-kuan and Li and others like them, Chaghan Temür appears to have assumed a kind of leadership, or exerted some sort of informal dominance. Chaghan Temür's biography portrays his personality simply by noting that he had bushy eyebrows and three hairs on his left cheek which stuck out straight when he was angry.[43]

The county of Shen-ch'iu, located in the upper Huai region, lay about thirty miles west of Ying-chou where the Red Turban rebellion first broke out in 1351. The uprising was a matter which closely concerned Chaghan Temür as a member of a landowning family, for some of the rebels were attacking and threatening landlords in addition to burning the cities and killing the local officials. In 1352 Chaghan raised a militia (*i-ping*) of "several hundred" men from among the sons and younger brothers of Shen-ch'iu. With these troops he defended his home area, and later aided Li Ssu-ch'i in recovering the city of Lo-shan, which had come under Red Turban occupation. In this he was aided by Kuan-kuan, who recruited a number of militia braves (*i-yung*) and came to join him.[44]

The anti-rebel merits of Chaghan and his allies were made known to the imperial authorities at Ta-tu, and generous rewards were forthcoming. Chaghan was made *darughachi* and Li Ssu-ch'i magistrate of the prefecture of Ju-ning, and Kuan-kuan received the military post of centurion.[45] These positions, however, appear to have been purely honorary. Chaghan and Li actually remained with their troops at Shen-ch'iu, and from time to time engaged in local skirmishes against the Red Turbans, apparently on higher orders.[46]

Nothing further is heard of Chaghan and the militia of Shen-ch'iu until 1355, when Toghto was dismissed, and as Chaghan's biography puts it, "the bandit forces spread." In 1355 aboriginal Miao forces, originally sent north as loyalists to protect the city of Pien-liang, mutinied and went on rampage, seizing four county seats to the south and west. Apparently on higher orders, Chaghan moved his forces northwest and annihilated the mutineers on the north bank of the Yellow River, where the armies of the Szechwan Chief Administrator Dash Badulugh and the Honan Chancellor of the Left Tai Buqa had driven them. For his merit in this, the court promoted Chaghan to the honorary position of Vice Minister in the Board of Punishments.[47]

During the same year Chaghan had another and better opportunity to prove himself. After his victory over the Miao mutineers, he moved his forces to Chung-mou, about twenty-five miles west of Pien-liang, and there pitched camp alongside the army of the Salji'ud Dash Badulugh. In July Dash Badulugh received a new appointment as Chief Administrator of Honan, and was put in charge of the bulk of the Honan forces, which included the troops of the Mongol princes and fresh levies of Miao from the south. He had court permission to "act at convenience." The Qunggirad Tai Buqa had been impeached by the censors and removed from his position in June for failing to move rapidly against the rebel forces and for oppressing the people. As punishment, he and his troops were also put under Dash Badulugh's command. Chaghan Temür too must have been under the command of Dash Badulugh, although there is no direct evidence of this.[48]

In July and August, 1355, the rebel Sung forces marched westward in strength and resoundingly defeated Dash Badulugh at Ch'ang-ko, about thirty miles south of Chung-mou. Dash Badulugh's defeat was a little surprising; he had been eminently successful against the Red Turbans in 1352-53, and thus received the rapid promotions which led to his present high position in Honan. The rebels he had defeated earlier, however, were a loosely organized mob. Evidently he was not prepared for the better organized Sung armies. He was no better prepared in October and November, when the Sung forces directly attacked his camp at Chung-mou and plundered his stores. Chaghan Temür, however, took advantage of a sandstorm to lead an attack on the main section of the enemy forces, and he succeeded in driving them back. For this, he was promoted honorarily to President of the Board of War.[49]

Early in 1356 the loyalist forces rallied further and put the Sung temporarily on the defensive. The court had meantime sent an official from the Chief Military Commission down to Dash Badulugh's camp in order to oversee operations. Whether his visit was responsible for the greater effectiveness of the loyalist army is unknown. In any event, Dash Badulugh finally managed in January, 1356, to crush the Sung army near T'ai-k'ang, about sixty-five miles southeast of Chung-mou. After that, he continued eastward and besieged the rebel capital of Po-chou, and forced the Sung court to evacuate and reestablish itself further south.[50] For this endeavor, Dash Badulugh was promoted to Chancellor of the Left of Honan. He retained his previous concurrent position as head of the Branch Military Commission. His sons Hsi-li-mu and Bolod Temür were given lesser posts in Yunnan and Szechwan provinces, although they were actually fighting in Honan.[51]

Chaghan Temür, meanwhile, was busy elsewhere. Dash Badulugh had sent him and Li Ssu-ch'i westward to stop the Sung forces at Han-ku Pass and prevent their invading Shensi and Shansi. This Chaghan failed to do, but he found some of the rebel forces occupying the walled city of Ling-pao just south of the Yellow River, and with the aid of a smoke screen produced by burning horse dung he was able to drive them out. Some of the enemy then crossed the Yellow River for plunder. Chaghan eventually followed them and after a confrontation lasting several months he was able to stop them, partly by using heavy iron-clad cavalry. For this, the court promoted Chaghan to a post in the Branch Military Commission. Kuan-kuan participated in this campaign, too, and was promoted to myriarch. The disgraced Qunggirad Tai Buqa, since restored to his former position as Chancellor of the Left of Honan, contributed to the total pacification effort by bringing the Nan-yang area in western Honan under control. The emperor was sufficiently heartened by the loyalist successes in Honan in 1356 to issue a special edict of amnesty in celebration.[52]

It may be noticed at this point that even though the Sung thrust had been blunted, temporarily so as it turned out, provincial autonomy in Honan was as yet only weakly developed. The court, dominated by conservative Confucian ideology after Toghto's overthrow, was still able to maintain some leverage over the forces in the field. Certain typical patterns had, nevertheless, already begun to emerge. There were two kinds of military forces operating in Honan. There were semi-independent forces controlled by Dash Badulugh and Chaghan Temür; and there were government forces under the command of Tai Buqa. The central government treated each quite differently. For the semi-autonomous forces, led by men who had no stake at court and no reputation to preserve there, the government employed an exceedingly complex system of promotions through official ranks which to a surprising extent were not even remotely connected with the operations the commanders were engaged in. On the other hand, there was no system of punishments for them. No attempt was made to impeach Dash Badulugh for his early reverses at the hands of the rebels. For Tai Buqa, however, who wanted court position, and who was not at all happy commanding troops in the field, the system was different. Tai Buqa was fair game for censorial attack as an unsuccessful general. This pattern held generally true in the coming years. While the censors lacerated the various central government commanders, absolutely no attack was made upon those men whose personal interests were tied to a growth in regional power.[53]

Although regionalism was still weak, the beginnings were in evidence by 1356. Dash Badulugh had begun to accumulate those powers which Toghto always attempted to keep in separate hands. In June, 1355, after Tai Buqa's impeachment, he came to exert over-all military power in the province for the first time. In July he was shifted from Chief Administrator of Szechwan to Chief Administrator of Honan, and thus for the first time came to hold office in the province in which his own troops were campaigning. Although he became Chancellor of the Left of Honan after his defeat of the rebels in 1356, the Qunggirad Tai Buqa also held this position at the same time; moreover, Dash Badulugh was shifted back to Szechwan in May, 1357, again as Chancellor of the Left. Even though he remained in Honan, his official position there was not entirely secure.[54] There was danger, however, in the fact that Dash Badulugh arranged for his own supplies.[55] Yet, despite his possessing the rudiments of an independent power base, Dash Badulugh was not overwhelmingly successful in his battles with the rebels. Probably for this reason, the court was able to keep a certain amount of leverage over him. It was, for example, able to compel him to relocate his camp so that better protection might be given the Honan provincial capital of Pienliang.[56]

The revival of the Sung rebel movement after 1356 was directly responsible for the further development of regional autonomy under Chaghan Temür. The great Sung expeditions of 1357-58 took them through Honan into Shensi and Shansi; they took Pien-liang and made it their capital, and nearly succeeded in storming Ta-tu itself.[57]

It was in Shensi that Chaghan Temür took advantage of the Sung thrust to lay the foundations of his independence. Early in 1357 the rebels regrouped themselves in the mountains southeast of the Shensi provincial capital of Feng-yüan (Sian), and put the province in danger of imminent invasion.[58] Since the Red Turban disorders of 1352 the Shensi bureaucracy had ceased observing the regulations, which in the interest of dynastic security, had imposed a policy of mutual nonfraternization and noncooperation between the provincial administration and the Shensi Branch Censorate.[59] In emergency situations, both bodies now met in the presence of Aradnashiri, the Prince of Yü.[60] This new arrangement the court on several occasions pointedly authorized.[61] It was at such a meeting in the spring of 1357 that the Secretarial Censor Wang Ssu-ch'eng, a conservative, successfully argued in favor of inviting Chaghan Temür and his army into Shensi to bolster the defenses, even though the local government commanders feared they would be overwhelmed, and even though it was actually illegal for any but the court itself to permit the passage of troops across provincial boundaries.[62]

As it turned out, the decision had grave consequences for the integrity of the central administration. Upon receiving the joint request of the Shensi authorities for aid, Chaghan and Li Ssu-ch'i at once set out with 5,000 light-armed troops from their camp near the Shensi border. They succeeded in driving back the rebels, who had begun to invade the Wei River valley.[63] Chaghan's superiors in Honan, greatly concerned over this irregular and unauthorized venture, made a complaint about it to the court. At the time, however, the court was devoting all of its attention to a rapidly deteriorating situation in east China. Rather than discipline Chaghan and the Shensi authorities, it decided to recognize a *fait accompli.* It appointed Chaghan Vice Administrator of the Left for Shensi, and Li Ssu-ch'i to the same position in Szechwan.[64]

The presence of Chaghan Temür and his armies led to

civil war in Shensi. The Prince of Yü and the regular Shensi officials campaigned against the rebels for the last time in January, 1358; in that action the rebels were defeated, but for that the main credit went to Chaghan and Li, for the preponderance of military power in Shensi lay definitely with the imported Honan armies.[65] The Yüan court was aware of what was happening and apparently tried to lend support to the regular provincial authorities. In March, 1358, the court ordered Chaghan and Li to separate their armies. In order to allow the regular provincial administration to increase its power, the court ordered it to begin printing its own paper money to facilitate the purchase of military supplies.[66] The court also authorized the establishment of bureaus for military organization, control, and agriculture in Feng-yüan, Yen-an, and Kung-ch'ang.[67]

In retaliation against the attempt of the Shensi officials to strengthen themselves, Chaghan and Li began appointing their own local officials in order to assure the delivery of supplies. In the summer of 1358, immediately after defeating the rebels, Li Ssu-ch'i moved against two pro-government commanders, eliminated them, and incorporated their troops into his own army.[68] In 1359 the conflict grew sharper. By this time, the officials who had invited Li and Chaghan into Shensi had been transferred; the Prince of Yü, for reasons unknown, was removed, possibly exiled, from the province in November, 1358.[69] In September, 1359, the court appointed one Teri Temür Chancellor of the Left of Shensi, with permission to "act at convenience."[70] Teri Temür was determined to make war upon the armies of Chaghan and Li in spite of strong opposition from the Branch Censorate. The censors argued that Chaghan and Li already had enough power to seize the provincial capital; all they needed was a good excuse upon which to act. Teri Temür, however, ignored the censorial counsel and lost Feng-yüan to Chaghan and Li sometime during the winter of 1359-60.[71]

By 1360, however, the power of Chaghan had already spread far beyond Shensi. Li Ssu-ch'i settled in western Shensi as a warlord and ally of Chaghan; although Chaghan kept a contingent of troops in that province, he was seldom there himself. Late in 1357 the rebels made an initial attempt to seize the Fen River valley of Shansi to the northeast. Chaghan's men beat off the attack, and were appointed to positions in the local Pacification Office.[72] In 1358, however, the rebels appeared in greater strength and invaded the Fen valley. Again Chaghan's men proved effective. They put continual pressure upon the invading forces and prevented them from permanently occupying any part of Shansi. One rebel contingent was obliged to leave the valley at its north end.[73] Other defeated remnants straggled back south through the valley and attempted an exit at the lower end, but Chaghan was waiting for them there and crushed them as they came out.[74] As a result of these actions, Chaghan Temür's power grew to include Shansi as well as Shensi and Honan. By the end of 1358 he was Vice Commissioner of the Honan Branch Military Commission, Chief Administrator and Secretarial Censor in Shensi, with orders to hold and defend Shansi and act at convenience there.[75] His generals occupied key districts in Shansi, and the chief magistrate in the important city of Ki-ning (T'ai-yüan) was his appointee, not the court's.[76]

The rebels had tried to seize the agriculturally important river valleys of Shensi and Shansi because Honan province was ravaged. Honan suffered a general famine in 1357, and it is clear from official reports that the cumulative effects of six years of riot and war had seriously affected its agricultural capacity and hence its power to sustain a rebel regime.[77] But when the rebels failed in their attempts to take Shansi and Shensi, they in effect delivered these areas and their grain-growing capacities into the hands of Chaghan Temür. The Yüan court could do little to prohibit or impede this development, since it was more directly concerned in 1358 with a rebel attack upon Ta-tu itself.[78] By the time it had thrown back this attack, Chaghan's position in the west was secure.

After the events of 1358 it remained for Chaghan Temür to move his armies eastward and annihilate the faltering rebel regime. While preparing his forces, he took care to secure court permission to arrange for the holding of provincial-level examinations in Honan in the fall of 1359. The examination stalls were to be set up in Shan-chou, a city under his occupation; refugee scholars from outside the province were to be admitted under the regular Honan quota for the *chü-jen* degree.[79] The measure was in a way a counterchallenge to the legitimist values inherent in the rebel Sung restoration movement, which itself, however, made no known attempt to institute the Confucian examination system. More important, arranging the examinations allowed Chaghan to serve as an intermediary between the aspiring provincial elite and the Yüan government. Chaghan's intercession was highly irregular and outside the normal bureaucratic channels for arranging examinations. It was a good sign that the Honan provincial bureaucracy was no longer functioning.[80] In the circumstances, Chaghan must have controlled all those parts of Honan not occupied by the rebels.

The annihilation of the Sung regime was therefore a matter of personal concern to Chaghan Temür, who could reasonably expect to gain complete control of Honan province at the same time that he eliminated an implacable enemy of the Yüan Dynasty. His first thrust was not slow in coming. In May and June of 1359 he moved his Shensi and Shansi forces and Miao auxiliaries eastward and surrounded the Sung capital, formerly the Honan provincial capital of Pien-liang.[81] By September the defenders were out of food, and Chaghan's men forced their way into the city on the tenth of that month. The Sung "emperor" fled through the east gate with his close officials and several hundred cavalry and retreated, once again, to the Huai town of An-feng. To Chaghan Temür fell the rebel empress, 5,000 rebel officials with their wives and children, together with all of the imperial treasury and official paraphernalia. The 200,000 inhabitants of the city were spared; once inside the city, Chaghan's troops were careful to cause only a minimum of disorder. The court immediately awarded Chaghan a suit of imperial clothes and a seven-jewel belt, and appointed him Chief Administrator of Honan province, chief of the Honan Branch Military Commission, and Vice Censor-in-Chief of the Shensi Branch Censorate, with permission to act at convenience.[82]

Immediately after Chaghan's crushing victory over the

rebel Sung regime, however, the Yüan court began to take steps to contain him. It cannot have been accidental that Teri Temür was made Chancellor of the Left in Shensi just two weeks after Chaghan's victory at Pien-liang. It must be assumed that Teri Temür's anti-Chaghan policy had court endorsement. The court was also determined to curtail Chaghan's power in Shansi, which in the Yüan period was part of the metropolitan (Chung-shu) province. Significantly, the court was obliged to bypass the regular bureaucratic machinery entirely in its effort to contain Chaghan there. It made no attempt to punish Chaghan by having the Censorate impeach him. Rather, it chose to support against Chaghan Temür in Shansi another aspiring regionalist. This other regionalist was Bolod Temür, son of Chaghan Temür's former superior, Dash Badulugh. Bolod Temür had earlier been sent by his father to command troops in Hopei; he was there in February, 1358, when his father died and the court ordered him to succeed to the command of his father's army.[83] During 1358, when the rebels were campaigning in various parts of North China, Bolod Temür and his men held the main cities east of Shansi, where the T'ai-hang Mountains drop down to the Hopei plain. Early in 1359, however, the court moved him and part of his army to the extreme north of Shansi and there put him in charge of a newly established system of military-agricultural colonies.[84] Bolod Temür spent the year 1359 crushing rebel remnants in north Shansi, at the same time that Chaghan was busy with his attack on Pien-liang.

Conflict between Chaghan and Bolod in Shansi broke out within a few months after the conclusion of Chaghan's campaign in Honan. In the course of chasing rebels and rounding up leaderless and rampaging government troops, Bolod's generals had penetrated into the area north of Ki-ning, which was part of Chaghan Temür's unofficial personal domain.[85] Once there, Bolod was intent upon staying in order to take advantage of its grain supplies. According to Chaghan Temür himself, the Ki-ning area was so productive a grain-growing region that for the past several years it had supplied almost all of his military needs.[86] Bolod had a better claim to it—and indeed to all of Shansi—than did Chaghan, for the court had appointed him a Chief Administrator in the Central Chancellery.[87] Chaghan at this time held no post legitimizing his occupation of any part of the Shansi region.

The court wavered in its position on the fighting that broke out between Bolod and Chaghan over Ki-ning. Until November, 1360, it sent envoys to urge both sides to cease fighting and recognize the Shih-ling Pass (about thirty-five miles north of Ki-ning) as their common boundary. On November 9, however, the court changed its mind and officially awarded Ki-ning to Bolod Temür.[88]

For Chaghan, this was a most critical juncture. The court was compelling him to make an uncomfortable choice between ceding Ki-ning and its grain to his rival, or openly flouting an explicit imperial directive at the expense of the loyalist pose he has so carefully cultivated thus far. Chaghan decided to disobey the imperial directive.

Despite Chaghan's assertion, it is difficult to believe that the Ki-ning grain was all that vital to his army. He had occupied Ki-ning since the early summer of 1358, and in February, 1359, he sent 20,000 troops there, presumably to grow grain for him.[89] Thus he probably had the benefit of only one crop, and that would have been harvested in the fall of 1359, too late to feed the troops who were then attacking Pien-liang, 250 miles away in the southeast. Grain could be grown in the whole rest of the Fen valley south of Ki-ning; moreover, in January, 1360, Chaghan received court permission to establish a military-agricultural colony in Honan.[90] It seems clear that the loss of Ki-ning could not have had any catastrophic effect upon Chaghan's ability to continue the fight against the remaining Sung rebels on behalf of the Yüan Dynasty. The surrender of Ki-ning could have seriously damaged only his position against Bolod Temür. In these circumstances, Chaghan's real choice becomes apparent. It was to postpone his campaign against the Sung remnants in east China, and to risk the consequences of defying the emperor, in order to protect an entirely personal power base over which he had no officially recognized jurisdiction. The choice was clear and decisive; for the sake of regional independence, the loyalist mask could be sacrificed.

Against Chaghan's breach of loyalty, there were no institutional sanctions that the court could apply. It could not lightly declare him a rebel, for there was a remote possibility that Chaghan might then defect to the rebel side.[91] The court attempted first to use personal pressure. A certain Li Shih-chan, who knew Chaghan Temür rather well, having visited him as an envoy of the government on an earlier occasion, wrote Chaghan a personal letter of advice. Li offered a little cajolery, a little flattery, and a few threats. In a transparently specious interpretation of court policy, Li stated that Bolod's occupation of Ki-ning was only a temporary measure designed to "bring a little peace to the Shansi area, and calm the minds of his troops." As soon as the area quieted down, the court would begin shipping all Ki-ning grain to the capital, and then Bolod and Chaghan could leave Shansi altogether and make a joint attack on the remaining Sung rebels. Li followed this cajolery with flattery. "That young boy," wrote Li, referring to Bolod, "sooner or later will bring himself to ruin. How can he be considered a match for you?" After this flattery came the threat. Li suggested that Chaghan's behavior was being widely interpreted as treason, and that someone might under these circumstances try to make a righteous name for himself by assassinating him. Li ended by listing as models the good and evil regionalists of Chinese history, leaving it for Chaghan to determine where he would take his stand.[92]

As if to draw the two sides even more clearly, Bolod Temür managed dutifully to ship 50,000 piculs of grain to the capital to relieve a shortage there.[93] Chaghan, however, refused to be moved either by the letter or by Bolod's example. He sent no grain. Not only that; he continued to fight Bolod Temür even after the court in February, 1361, finally changed its mind again and gave Ki-ning back to him.[94] Late in the spring of 1361 Bolod Temür gave up the struggle in Shansi and turned his attention to Shensi. Only then did Chaghan Temür send tribute grain to the court and begin organizing his long-postponed attack on the remaining rebels in east

China.[95] Only with his personal power base secure did he resume the loyalist pose and once again court the good opinion of the central government. It was absolutely clear that in Chaghan's personal order of priorities, his own interests came first, and loyalist considerations second.

In the summer of 1361 Chaghan's legions marched down from the Shansi highlands in several columns to put an end to the remaining Sung rebels. Three local militarists of western Shantung, who had surrendered to the Sung rebels in 1357-58, switched their allegiances and joined Chaghan Temür soon after his forces entered their territories.[96] Those more firmly committed to the rebel movement retreated to the Shan-tung city of I-tu, determined to resist until the end. Chaghan pacified the remaining territory of Shantung, and then proceeded to bring I-tu down by siege. In October, he sent a subordinate to offer sacrifice at Confucius's shrine at Ch'ü-fou, and respectfully announce the coming reunification of the Yuan empire to the Master's shade.[97] In November the court shifted his position as Chief Administrator from Honan to the metropolitan province of Chung-shu, of which Shantung was a part. He retained his former posts in the Honan Branch Military Commission and in the Shensi Branch Censorate.[98]

This, as it turned out, was as far as Chaghan Temür ever got. I-tu continued to hold out, and Chaghan appeared to be in no hurry to take it. Instead, he began to capitalize upon the power and prestige his recent campaign had given him to intervene diplomatically in the warlord struggle in South China, and at the same time to support his old ally Li Ssu-ch'i in his wars against Bolod Temür's adherents in Shensi.[99] It was in the midst of these activities that on July 7, 1362, Chaghan Temür was assassinated by two warlords, T'ien Feng and Wang Shih-ch'eng, who had surrendered to him the year before. Chaghan, they felt, was no loyalist, no "leader of a Yüan restoration" (*Yüan-ch'ao chung-hsing jen-wu*) at all, but a warlord and a bandit like themselves.[100] The assassination, apparently carried out in a spirit of pure righteousness, strikingly confirmed the seriousness of Li Shih-chan's threat of a few years earlier.

If the assassination of Chaghan Temür was a blow struck in the name of political righteousness, the Yüan court was unable to capitalize upon the act and dismantle Chaghan's regional machine. After the assassination some of Chaghan's former companions were definitely in a mood to make his adopted son Kökö Temür their ruler and rebel against the Yüan Dynasty altogether. But the Yüan court stepped in very quickly to recognize and confirm Kökö Temür in the succession to his father's command, and to award Chaghan Temür the highest of posthumous honors.[101] In so doing, however, the Yüan court gave clear and final recognition to the fact that it could no longer hope to control the provinces of North China. It recognized the autonomous regional machine as a permanent institution, and conceded the point that its own direct power hardly extended further than the walls of the capital.

Epilogue
The Last Days of the Yüan Court in China

*The story of court politics after the dis*missal of Toghto in January, 1355, seems to be properly epilogue. After 1355 the central government directly controlled little more than the capital city and its immediate environs. Most of the rest of North China was surrendered by default to autonomous regional machines. The true center of history-making activity shifted to South China, where between 1355 and 1363 Chu Yüan-chang, harboring imperial ambitions of his own, emerged as the very likely founder of a successor dynasty.

Yüan court history from 1355 to 1368 has features of interest, if hardly of great moment. Even in its death agonies, however, it continued to act upon the assumption that somehow, with the right men in charge, it could revive and restore itself. An air of unreality infected the court; it knew its cause was lost, yet it refused to act upon that assumption.

Ayushiridara was fully invested as heir apparent on April 20, 1355.[1] Toghto's immediate successor as Chancellor of the Right was the Qangli Ting-chu, who was appointed to that post on May 29. Ting-chu objected strongly to the continued presence of the Qangli Qama, organizer of the overthrow of Toghto, whom the emperor had appointed Chancellor of the Left. For his part, Qama hoped to bring about the retirement of Toghon Temür as emperor, and his replacement by the erratic but more energetic Ayushiridara. After a long struggle, Ting-chu gained the support of both the emperor and the Censorate against Qama; Qama was impeached and shortly afterwards flogged to death.[2]

In June, 1357, Ting-chu was followed as Chancellor of the Right by the Kereid Mongol Chösgem, scion of a distinguished ministerial family, who as Censor-in-Chief earlier had led the attack against Qama. Ho Wei-i returned to court life, and was appointed Chancellor of the Left. By this time, however, the Central Chancellery and the Censorate were clearly beginning to split into two equally conservative yet irreconcilable alignments. One alignment supported the emperor against the ambitions of his son, and for outside support attached itself to the warlord Bolod Temür. The other alignment supported Ayushiridara against the ineffectual Toghon Temür, and for outside support looked to the warlord Kökö Temür, the adopted son and after 1362 the successor of Chaghan Temür.

These tensions eventually forced a rift between Chösgem and Ho Wei-i. In 1358 Ho gave no support to the Censorate when it impeached Chösgem on the charge that a younger brother of one of his concubines was heading a counterfeiting ring in the capital.[3] When after this impeachment Chösgem returned as Chancellor of the Right in 1360, with the support of Ayushiridara and Kökö Temür, Ho Wei-i refused to cooperate. He demonstrated his support for the opposing factional alignment, and in so doing helped to exacerbate the split that widened further as time went on.[4]

In 1363 the Censorate supported its Censor-in-Chief Lao-ti-sha in a vigorous impeachment of the Chancellor of the Right Chösgem. Ayushiridara, however, exercising his power of review *(ch'i)*, blocked the memorial of impeachment and refused to pass it up to the emperor. The censors vehemently protested this act. The Censorate, they insisted, was not expressing its private views, it was expressing the public opinion of the whole empire, and that only after having carefully examined the case. The censor Ch'en Tsu-jen, a *chin-shih* of 1342, managed to make contact with the emperor and scold him for his weakness and his failure to take a strong stand in the matter. Ayushiridara, however, won out and dismissed all of the opposition censors; Lao-ti-sha, in fear for his life, fled to Bolod Temür's camp in north Shansi for protection. A new corps of censors more favorable to the heir apparent then impeached Ho Wei-i, charging him with treason and other crimes. Ho Wei-i, dismissed, committed suicide.[5]

The conflict then escalated. The emperor's faction, crushed

at court, looked to the outside warlord Bolod Temür for support. Since 1362 Bolod Temür had been engaged in a military confrontation with Kökö Temür, who had succeeded to his foster-father's command and destroyed the last remaining rebels in Shantung. Along a front that stretched about six hundred miles from Shensi in the west to Hopei in the east, the rival armies of Bolod and Kökö faced each other. By late 1363 it was evident that Bolod was losing this match. He was successful in the east, but had difficulty in the west, and he lost an important battle to Kökö at Ki-ning (T'ai-yüan), which demoralized his army.[6] It was therefore probably desperation that prompted Bolod's decision first to threaten and then to occupy the capital city of Ta-tu in 1364. However, what more immediately provoked Bolod Temür was Ayushiridara's rash and unenforceable order relieving him of command in retaliation for the protection he was giving to Lao-ti-sha, the fugitive Censor-in-Chief. Bolod decided that it was time to impose radical personnel changes in the capital. In May, 1364, he marched his army to the gates of Ta-tu, but withdrew after receiving the emperor's promise to remove and punish Chösgem. In August, when it turned out that the promise was not kept, and that Ayushiridara was ordering Kökö Temür to increase his military pressure, Bolod Temür marched into the capital and seized it. He then proceeded on his own to root out the opposition faction on the emperor's behalf. Ayushiridara fled from the capital to Kökö Temür's camp in Ki-ning. Chösgem and others were executed. Toghon Temür's Korean empress was impeached by the Censorate for meddling in government, and confined to her quarters. In the palace, Bolod ordered that expenses be cut, Buddhist ritual suspended, and the eunuchs and Tibetan monks thrown out. In the bureaucracy, officials considered corrupt were executed.[7]

Bolod Temür was made first Chancellor of the Left, then Chancellor of the Right. The sources, however, make the assertion that, soon after his seizure of the capital, Bolod Temür fell victim to its pleasures, and became swinish and lecherous. Militarily, his position in the east was disintegrating; perhaps Bolod saw the end coming and decided to live his last days to the full. In any event, the party in support of Ayushiridara convinced the emperor that Bolod Temür planned treason. An unemployed scholar by the name of Hsü Shih-pen was taken into the emperor's confidence and allegedly laid the plans for Bolod's murder. In August, 1365, the emperor issued secret orders for the strongman's removal. On August 16, as Bolod Temür was on his way to present a memorial to the emperor, assassins sank an axe into his brain. His head was cut off, boxed, and sent to Ayushiridara as proof that it was now safe for him to return to the capital.[8]

Throughout these vicissitudes, the Yüan court maintained an outward Confucian veneer. Except for the year 1357, when the capital was under rebel attack, the examinations for the *chin-shih* degree continued to be held as ever. Thirty-five candidates were passed in 1360, sixty-two in 1363, and seventy-two in 1366.[9] While he was in power, Ho Wei-i sought throughout the empire, north and south, for worthy talents to come to the aid of the dynasty.[10] The Censorate, besides preparing impeachments, offered hopeful suggestions on how to improve the court's military position.[11] The court was, however, also distracted by other diversions. In 1361 some of the steppe princes, angry with Toghon Temür's weakness and helplessness, began a march south to seize the throne from him. The court managed to defend itself, and put the princes down militarily.[12] Early in 1364 it was not so fortunate; Ayushiridara sent a military expedition to Korea to avenge the king's executions of his mother's clansmen, but when this force reached the Yalu, it was routed and put to flight by the Korean army.[13] Yet the court could still place new emphasis upon the necessity to find and appoint good local officials; the emperor modestly refused to accept birthday congratulations; he blamed himself for the renewed rebel troubles, and pledged himself to a strengthened program of imperial ritual sacrifices.[14]

The elimination of Bolod Temür in 1365 did not heal the terrible divisions in the fast-expiring Yüan Dynasty. Unity lasted only the length of time it took Kökö Temür to escort Ayushiridara back to the capital, for it soon became apparent that the Yüan court and Kökö Temür were pursuing conflicting strategies.

Ayushiridara's strategy called for the redirection of all efforts toward the reconquest of the Huai and Yangtze regions and Szechwan. The emperor agreed with this plan, but decided to let Kökö Temür and not Ayushiridara assume overall direction of it. Toward the end of November, 1365, Kökö Temür was made Prince of Honan, and was permitted to establish a branch government of his own. This government, which numbered 2,610 men in 1367, was said to have been almost as large as the central government itself. The court gave Kökö permission to formulate his own plans, arrange for his own supplies, and appoint and dismiss his men as he saw fit. In addition, most of the other semi-independent warlords of North China were put under his command.[15]

After escorting Ayushiridara back to the capital, Kökö Temür refused to support his designs upon the throne. Unlike Bolod Temür, he had no desire to remain in Ta-tu and dominate the court. The court officials resented his presence, and Kökö, bored with court routine and ceremony, preferred to be with his troops in the field, where he could, as he is supposed to have said, "act without restraint."[16] He was thus not unwilling to leave the capital and take up the charge the emperor placed upon him. Yet once in the field, he was not at all eager to set forth on campaign. His official excuse was that he was still in mourning for his foster-father. Apparently, however, his advisers convinced him that any campaign upon Chu Yüan-chang in the south would have to be a combined effort involving the Shensi warlord armies of Chang Liang-pi, K'ung Hsing, and Törebeg, former followers of Bolod Temür. The emperor had, after all, issued two orders: Kökö Temür was to attack the south, but the Shensi warlords were to submit to Kökö Temür's authority. Therefore it was only reasonable first to put the North China house in order and then proceed with the second part of the instructions.

Kökö may have suspected imperial treachery. Did the emperor send him off to South China so that his position in the North could be undermined? In March, 1366, Kökö from his headquarters in Huai-ch'ing issued orders for the Shensi army of Chang Liang-pi, stationed near Feng-yüan (Sian), to move east. The court had clearly given Kökö Temür command over Chang Liang-pi, but it gave him no such authority over Li Ssu-ch'i, Chaghan's old comrade-in-arms, who was stationed further west at Feng-hsiang. It appears to have been the court's intention that Li Ssu-ch'i should remain independent and take charge of the proposed reconquest of Szechwan, although it did not order this specifically until November, 1366. In any event, Li Ssu-ch'i decided to support Chang Liang-pi's decision to disobey Kökö Temür, and thus laid the foundations for civil war in North China. As Kökö threateningly moved his forces toward Shensi, the four Shensi warlords exchanged hostages among themselves and formed a defensive alliance. In February, 1367, the four met together and elected Li the alliance president *(meng-chu)*. Fighting between Kökö and the Shensi group broke out and continued for over a year.[17]

The Yüan court viewed this civil war with dismay, but repeated orders to both sides to stop the fighting had no effect. In the fall of 1366, however, Kökö ordered Mo Kao and two other commanders to move into Shantung in order to tighten the defenses against Chu Yüan-chang and soothe the anxieties of the court. This action, which Kökö announced as "the plan for purifying the Huai and Yangtze areas," was clearly only perfunctory. The few desultory stabs that Kökö's lieutenants made in the direction of the south only served to provide Chu with pretexts for an attack on the North.[18] In the spring of 1367 Kökö reestablished contact with the beleaguered loyalist warlords of the China coast; an embassy from Chang Shih-ch'eng visited Kökö at Huai-ch'ing in a desperate attempt to get help in breaking Chu Yüan-chang's siege of Soochow, but Kökö explained that there was nothing he could do.[19]

In the summer of 1367 the military fragmentation of North China grew worse. It seemed that the more imminent an invasion from the south by Chu Yüan-chang became, the less the warring northern factions were willing to cooperate to hold the line. Kökö Temür had already received a number of threatening letters from Chu Yuan-chang, but he either considered them bluff or miscalculated the unity and strength of Chu's army. Whatever his calculations were, he decided to reduce his Shantung defenses for the time being in order to throw more men into the war against the Shensi alliance.

This plan was not entirely reckless, since Chu still had the bulk of his forces committed to the siege of Chang Shih-ch'eng's capital, and probably would not be ready to invade North China for some months, at least. But Kökö miscalculated on two different counts: he did not consider the determination of the Yüan court to maintain some vestige of control over the defense of North China, and he misjudged the loyalty of Mo Kao, one of the commanders he pulled out of Shantung. Both these miscalculations acted in conjunction to upset Kökö Temür's plans.

On August 27 the emperor issued an edict which reduced Kökö from Prince of Honan to a mere commander, giving him orders to invade the Huai region, and rendering illegal his plan to attack Shensi. Kökö's over-all command functions were taken over by Ayushiridara, who now headed a supreme military bureau in the capital. In his edict the emperor made it clear that it was Kökö's decision to pull Mo Kao's army out of Shantung that prompted this retaliatory action.[20]

Mo Kao and his men must have been aware of the court's action when just before dawn on August 31 they mutinied against Kökö Temür. Many of the mutineers were former followers of Bolod Temür. They were content to defend Shantung against Chu Yüan-chang on behalf of the Yüan Dynasty, but they refused to act as Kökö's private retainers and fight the Shensi alliance. They therefore repudiated Kökö, elected their commander Mo Kao as Kökö's replacement, sent the court a written impeachment of Kökö, and on their own initiative attacked Huai-ch'ing and Chang-te, Kökö's main campsites.

To the court the Mo Kao mutiny was an opportunity to move further to break up Kökö Temür's power. The new supreme military bureau *(Ta fu-chün-yüan)* was an emergency extra-constitutional body, with command over military operations and local civilian government. One of its first steps was to move new forces under the command of the central commander Yesü into Shantung, and have him set up a branch government there. The court failed, however, in its attempt to remove a local militarist by the name of Wang

Hsin. It was unable to induce him to move out by offering him a branch government of his own elsewhere. Further, on November 1 the court relieved Kökö of all authority whatever, on the grounds of his refusal to attack the Huai region. He was banished to Ho-nan-fu (but he actually chose not to go), and his army was ordered to be divided up among his lieutenants. High honors and titles were then given to Mo Kao.[21]

The court's attempt to provide coordination and unity for the defense of the North had less chance of success than Kökö Temür's, for Kökö had greater military power at his disposal. The court placed false hopes in the prospects for Mo Kao's army; while its mutiny was timely and dramatic, it was too small to challenge Kökö Temür successfully, and having no means of supply, it was forced to resort to plunder. If the court anticipated cooperation from the Shensi warlords, it was disappointed here, too. Li Ssu-ch'i simply ignored the court's orders and directives. The court thus found itself in the same position that Kökö Temür had found himself in, and it took the same path out that it had chastised Kökö for taking. While the court tried to hold the Shantung line as best it could, it went to war on its own dissidents.[22] It went to war upon Kökö Temür by encouraging his lieutenants to desert him. It used these deserters, together with Mo Kao's army and the Shensi forces of K'ung Hsing and Törebeg to try to drive Kökö out of his vital Shansi supply base.

In January, 1368, in order to forestall this move, Kökö begged the court for forgiveness and reinstatement. On the advice of the Censorate, the court decided, for the sake of the dynasty, to reinstate Kökö Temür with the stipulation that he should proceed at once to Shantung to stop the forces of the newly announced Ming Dynasty of Chu Yüan-chang, who had by this time defeated Chang Shih-ch'eng, and was already embarked upon his long-threatened northern expedition. Kökö, however, ignored the stipulation; he was determined to recover his Shansi base first, and so he marched into Ki-ning and murdered the central officials the court had posted there.

With the Ming forces already in Shantung territory, the

Yüan court decided, on the grounds of this latest outrage, to destroy Kökö Temür once and for all. In February, 1368, it in effect declared Kökö to be a rebel and an outlaw. His command of troops and all of his honors and titles were taken away; all of the generals, troops, and officials who deserted him were promised good treatment by the court. Li Ssu-ch'i and Chang Liang-pi were ordered to join Mo Kao and make war upon him.

Li and Chang, however, may have guessed that it was Chu Yüan-chang's intention to march west from Shantung against them before turning northward against the Yüan capital. In any event, they made contact with Kökö and informed him that they did not intend to carry out the court's order. Mo Kao and the others, meanwhile, began moving into Shansi. Kökö Temür bided his time until August, 1368, when he caught Mo Kao and another general off guard and captured them both in a nocturnal surprise-raid. The Yüan court's war upon Kökö Temür thereupon collapsed.

The psychology of the court at about this time may perhaps be discerned in the stories we have, possibly apocryphal, that the shade of Chinggis Qan began appearing in dreams. According to one such story, Chinggis Qan appeared in the dreams of Qarajang, grandson of the one-time Chancellor of the Right Arughtu, a descendant of one of Chinggis's "Four Heroes." Chinggis's message was: get rid of Ayushiridara.

During the spring of 1368 the Ming emperor chased Li Ssu-ch'i and Chang Liang-pi back into Shensi, and then spent the first part of the summer conducting small operations in Honan. On August 15, as the grain harvest was coming in, the Ming forces finally began their march upon the Yüan capital. Meanwhile, the Yüan court, heeding the advice of the Censorate, if not of Chinggis Qan, reversed itself once again and ended its policy of opposition to Kökö Temür. On August 14 Kökö was given permission to execute Mo Kao. On September 1, with the Ming army within 200 miles of the Yüan capital, the court abolished the supreme military *bureau (Ta fu-chü-yüan)*, executing all of the chief officials, and reprimanding its head, Ayushiridara.

Court policy had come full circle since it first gave Kökö

Temür supreme command, three years before. But it was now too late to save the dynasty. On September 10 the emperor and part of the central government fled the capital for Mongolia. Not long afterward, Kökö retreated to the far west.[23]

Summary and Conclusion

Later Yüan political history may be conveniently said to have begun with the restoration of 1328-29. After the date, one is safe in assuming that Yüan history is Chinese history. Before that date, one is never so sure. Before the restoration, it was not entirely impossible that the emperors of the Yüan Dynasty might still under certain circumstances act as *qaghans* of the Mongol world empire. It was still not out of the question that an emperor in China might owe his throne to Mongol support from outside. Not until the assassination of Qoshila in the summer of 1329 was it finally made clear that the Yüan Dynasty in China had become a self-enclosed political entity, impermeable to force or pressure from outside its defined borders. When Qoshila was murdered, the last trace of political pan-Mongolism was destroyed and the political powerlessness of the Mongolian homeland confirmed. Issues of a purely Mongolian nature, unrelated to the problems of China, no longer existed to permit the Yüan emperors to function simultaneously as Mongol *qaghans*. In these circumstances, the conquerors in China fell captive to the forces of Chinese history, inasmuch as the leading problems of the realm were now entirely domestic Chinese problems.

The leaders of the restoration erased from political influence the last remnants of the financial cliques that had controlled the Yüan bureaucracy with few interruptions since early in Qubilai's reign, about seventy years before. The leaders permitted the Confucian movement to emerge from minority opposition status to a position of recognized dominance in the bureaucracy. After 1328 it would no longer be possible for the Yüan emperors to play Confucians and anti-Confucians against each other, as the emperors from Qubilai down to Yesün Temür had done. In addition, because it was not an emperor that sponsored the Confucian triumph, but rather the leaders of the restoration clique, the Yüan monarchy suffered a great decline in its power as a functioning organ of state. After 1328 it was never really able to gain full leverage over the bureaucracy again.

In view of the final secession of the Yüan Dynasty from the Mongol empire, the restoration political order was yet in some ways internally anachronistic. The leaders of the restoration had but weak links with the Confucian movement in the bureaucracy; El Temür and Bayan were not themselves Confucian, nor were they Confucian spokesmen. The only tie that bound the restoration leaders together was their common service as young guardsmen under Prince Qaishan during the final steppe campaigns against Qaidu. When they installed Qaishan's son Tugh Temür as emperor after the *coup d'état* of September, 1328, they installed not an emperor who was expected to function politically as such, but a figure who symbolized their personal association. The restoration order looked back to Qaishan, rather than Qubilai, as its justifying founding father; but it looked upon Qaishan less as an emperor than as an imperial prince and leader of the steppe wars in which the men of the restoration had been involved. Consequently, the restoration did not at all imply a revival of Qaishan's policies as emperor; rather it implied a revival of Qaishan himself in the person of his son. This state of affairs was anachronistic in that it did not precisely conform to current Confucian ideas as to the proper relationship between a sovereign and his ministers, but recalled more the old Mongol ties between the tribal or clan chief *(qan)* and his companions *(nököd)*.

The restoration order of 1328 permitted the eclipse of the monarchy as a ruling institution because Tugh Temür's constitutional prerogatives as emperor were overridden by his concrete function as a tangible symbol of his father and a rallying point for the clique. From this it followed that personal ties and personal loyalty should be the indispensable prerequisites for holding high bureaucratic office. These prerequisites the Censorate honored and upheld in numerous impeachments during Tugh Temür's reign.

The keystone of the entire restoration order was Tugh Temür. With his death in 1332 that keystone was removed and the restoration order collapsed. Bayan allied with the Qunggirad consort clan to outmaneuver and finally destroy El Temür's Qipchaqs and give the throne over to Qoshila's sons. Between them, Bayan and the Qunggirad Grand Empress Dowager managed to keep the monarchy in an institutional limbo down to 1340. The paternity of the young emperor Toghon Temür, officially declared to be spurious while Tugh Temür was alive, remained officially in doubt until Bayan's overthrow in 1340. Thus the institutional debility of the monarchy continued after Tugh Temür's death, but with the important difference that the original justification for that debility no longer applied. The meritorious and unique personal associations that justified the restoration order of 1328 were entirely destroyed by Bayan in his rise to political supremacy after 1332. For Bayan, the figure of Toghon Temür did not serve as any kind of symbol. He was not an irreplaceable individual, for Bayan kept his cousin, Tugh Temür's son, in reserve as his likely successor.

Bayan's revival of the political figure of Qubilai in 1335 was as clear a sign as any that the intensely personal basis of the restoration order had disintegrated, and that Qaishan was no longer of use as a symbol. Even more, Bayan's appeal to Qubilai was to Qubilai not as a person, but as the founder of the dynasty in a purely political and constitutional sense. Bayan needed Qubilai as the authoritative source for the orthodoxy of his attempt to show that the Confucian triumph of 1328 was only temporary, and that under his patronage an anti-Confucian coalition could be restored as an alternative factional group in the bureaucracy. Bayan's real and original aim was not to extirpate Confucianism root and branch, but simply to restore at Confucian expense the two-clique system that had existed in the bureaucracy from Qubilai's time until 1328. The plan was a reasonable one; no chancellor desired to work with a monolithic Confucian bureaucracy, especially when he himself was not its patron or spokesman.

The Confucian bureaucrats, however, interpreted Bayan's maneuvers as something positively sinister, a malevolent attempt to destroy Confucianism altogether. Bayan's appeal to Qubilai as his authority for abolishing the Confucian examination system appeared to have a false ring. The resemblance between Bayan's overt act of abolition and the fact that no examinations had been held under Qubilai was only casual. Bayan's opponents could easily argue that Qubilai always had the intention of instituting the examinations, and "although the matter was never carried out, the system itself was already established."[1] Qubilai had paid sufficient court to Confucianism in his long reign to render dubious any authority-seeking appeal to him as an anti-Confucian. The legacy of Qubilai was a broad one; Bayan seemed to be reviving only parts of it, and misinterpreting those.[2]

Had Bayan not been completely alienated from the Confucian movement, he might possibly have seen that it was really no monolith at all, but was potentially divisible into antagonistic parts. He chose, however, to see it as a monolith that needed balancing off by the creation of a non-Confucian alignment within the bureaucracy. But Bayan miscalculated the very strong commitment among the Mongol and *se-mu* conquerors to the Confucian movement, and he was unprepared for their vehement protest against his desire to limit and contain it. Only when this happened did Bayan, in a desperate defensive measure, make an attempt to equate Confucianism with Chinese nationality, and appeal to the racial solidarity of the Mongols and *se-mu* as conquerors. This step was defensive, and it was also deeply subversive of the entire foundations of the Yüan conquest order. The Yüan system worked precisely because the major bureaucratic factional alignments were supranational in character. Were the ethnic classes to freeze into closed factional groups, and the bureaucracy engage in open ethnic or racial strife, then the whole system would cease to function together as a bureaucracy. One of the main purposes of the ethnic class system was to reserve certain official positions at all ranks in the bureaucracy for the Mongols and *se-mu* as their right by conquest. What made cooperation among the ethnic groups within the bureaucracy possible was that the factions were organized primarily on ideological, not ethnic lines.

The strength of the Confucian movement did not derive

solely from its function as a supranational unifying device within the bureaucracy. The financial cliques had, after all, been equally supranational in their membership. There were certain extra features in the Confucian movement that served to make it widely attractive. For example, it provided a new set of recognized relationships and channels of contact between the monarchy and the higher bureaucracy. After Qaishan, the Yüan emperors were no longer martial figures; and after the passing of Tugh Temür and the restoration order, the higher bureaucrats could no longer openly approach, or dominate, the monarch in the guise of companions *(nököd)* rallying around a symbolic *qan.* Confucian institutions provided new means of approach which were unimpeachably correct in their ostensible purpose. As the Uighur Confucian Nao-nao explained it, Confucians had three regular means of bringing their demands to the ruler's notice. These were through the Central Chancellery itself; failing that, the Censorate; and as a last resort, recourse could be had to the "Classics Mat," private ideological sessions with the emperor during which matters of confidence could be brought to his attention.[3]

The Confucian examination system, moreover, performed a vitally significant political and sociological role within the Mongol and *se-mu* conquest group. The system of ethnic preference provided the conquerors with a grossly disproportionate advantage over the Chinese in access to the examination route to bureaucratic office. While the Mongols and *se-mu* combined constituted only about 3 percent of all registered households in China, they had a combined legal claim to 50 percent of the total quota for all degrees. The degree-takers were largely Mongols and *se-mu* from various provincial garrisons scattered all over China, who had no other ready means of scaling the social and bureaucratic ladder except through success in the examinations. Without the examinations, it would have been difficult for the court to ensure the commitment of these conquest provincials to the idea of a centralized Yüan state. With so many of them intermarrying with the local Chinese gentry, it was not unthinkable that they might at some point divorce their interests from the court entirely. As Toghto's mentor Wu Chih-fang advised him: "When the examination system is in operation, not everyone will be ensured an official post and salary. But even so, it is by means of this that families will have students, and when everyone studies, naturally no one will dare to do wrong things. This has an important bearing upon the process of orderly rule."[4]

This was one crucial arrangement that Bayan's anti-Confucian measures disrupted. The threat of a movement for regional autonomy led by provincial Mongols and *se-mu* did not materialize until after Toghto's removal in 1355; yet the rise of such figures as Dash Badulugh and Chaghan Temür at that time perhaps showed that such a movement could have come into being earlier under the right circumstances.

After Bayan's overthrow in 1340 Confucianism came into its own as the dominant ideological force, not simply in the lower bureaucracy, but in political life on higher levels. The emperor was committed to it, the chancellors were spokesmen for it, and political discourse on all sides was articulated in Confucian language. In 1340 the Confucian movement went beyond its gains of 1328 to enroll the highest ministers of state, the real wielders of power, in its ranks. Confucian ideology and political power finally merged. Yet once again, as in 1328, the monarchy was only tangentially involved in a major Confucian political breakthrough. Once again the real management and guidance of a Confucian forward step was undertaken at the ministerial level. The Confucian movement was not in debt to the monarchy for the political gains it made; rather, its fortunes were tied to the occupant of the office of Chancellor of the Right.

It is true that Toghto's coup against Bayan in 1340 liberated the monarchy from complete captivity. From 1340 it was understood that the emperor had the power to appoint and dismiss chancellors and their administrations. But this was a device of last resort, not a power that the emperor used every day. The emperor himself did not control the bureaucratic forces that now and then pressured him to exercise his prerogative of appointment and dismissal.

When the victorious Confucian ranks split into reform and conservative wings soon after 1340, the question of bureaucratic control became a particularly uncertain one. Bureaucratic leadership appeared to shift at approximately five-year intervals. From 1340 to 1344 Toghto as reform leader controlled the bureaucracy. From 1344 to 1349 the bureaucracy came under the control of Berke Buqa, Dorji, and Ho Wei-i and the conservative wing. In 1349, with popular disturbances and natural disasters getting out of hand, Toghto overthrew the conservative leadership and returned to power as Chancellor of the Right. Finally in 1355, in an especially violent swing of the political pendulum, the conservative opposition overthrew Toghto, and wrecked the political foundations of the state in so doing. The only part the emperor had in all of this was to legalize the overturn of bureaucratic administrations through the issuing of edicts. The monarchy had few defenses against the violent processes of partisan Confucian politics that ended in tearing the Yüan Dynasty to pieces.

Considered as a factional movement, reform Confucianism in late Yüan China possessed an awareness of itself as a special group with specific policy objectives that it had defined and desired to implement. The members were conscious of a need to maintain internal discipline as an indispensable precondition for the realization of their aims. Within the group, power tended to concentrate itself in the hands of the leader, the Chancellor of the Right Toghto, supreme patron and protector of his factional adherents, chief sponsor of the group's programs, and omnipotent coordinator of all governmental activity. Although the process of policy formulation did encourage the free upward flow of ideas and proposals and the open debate of alternatives at court, once policy was decided and defined the group closed ranks and maintained an intolerant attitude toward outside criticism of policies or personnel. In return for its obedience and in recompense for its submission to the reform wing, the bureaucracy as a whole was generously funded, turned loose upon society, and given ample opportunity to occupy itself with the administration of large-scale and expensive official programs.

The Yellow River rechanneling was one typical product of this approach. Reform Confucianism as a factional movement appears to have been in some respects well-suited to the highly centralized official organization of the Yüan state, a structural legacy bequeathed by Qubilai.

Conservative Confucianism in the late Yüan period had a much looser organization. It conceded a large measure of autonomy to such formal bureaucratic agencies as the Censorate and the provincial governments, and showed a strong predilection for adversary relationships within the formal bureaucratic order. Whereas the reformists' desire for definite and tangible material accomplishments demanded the precise definition of a series of policy goals and relied heavily upon factional loyalty and organizational discipline for their implementation, the conservative tendency aimed at the less definite, more diffuse goal of over-all harmony between state and society—a catch-all objective with no particular beginning, no precise ingredients, and no real end—and therefore did not demand tight factional organization for its implementation. In fact, the conservatives consciously rejected the whole idea of factional organization. They pictured themselves organizationally not as a faction *(tang)*, but as a "flock" *(ch'ün)*.[5] Their general goal of societal harmony, unlike the various specific goals of the reformists, stood above factional considerations and, being entirely immune to attack, needed no organized partisan defense. As a "flock," the conservatives considered themselves individually distinct yet ultimately held together by spontaneous ties arising from individual moral exertion and commonly held patterns of thought, not by coercive discipline or the material bonds of profit and self-interest. The smooth working relationship between the chancellors Dorji and Ho Wei-i seems to exemplify this form of voluntary cooperation at its most effective.

Yet the conservatives' leading ideal of harmony tended at times to lose itself in impassioned controversy at the higher levels of government and in embarrassing compromise at the lower. These dysfunctions were related to the conservatives' preferred mode of rule, one in which power in the hands of high bureaucrats above was regulated, even challenged, by the uninterrupted flow of pressure and opinion from below.

At the local level, where official goals and priorities impinged most directly upon the life and activities of society, the contrasting ruling styles of the reformists and conservatives tended to produce different symptoms of dysfunction, and each side used these as political ammunition against the other. The predetermined policy activism of the reformists seems in some cases to have aroused social opposition at the local level, which the reformists themselves, bound to their own internal discipline, could not always easily remedy. In this connection the conservatives consistently used against the reformists the argument that their various plans and projects were not only disruptive of the social order, but, in a much more positive and menacing sense, were outright provocations to social rebellion. For their own part, the conservatives were generally reluctant to undertake anything without first consulting the local gentry and obtaining their advice and consent, for only in that way could they get the gentry to cooperate in the business of applying suasion *(chiao-hua)* and other deterrents to the perennially base drives and disorderly proclivities of the common population, and thus forestall what they saw as the ever-present likelihood of social explosion. As the conservatives saw it, the manpower requirements and other disruptions and impositions demanded by the innovating reform programs tended to frustrate and subvert the existing bonds of authority in local society to the extent that the local officials and gentry became unable, or unwilling, to impose deterrents upon the generally wavering and riot-prone population. A breakdown in dialogue between state and society, such as the reformist tendency threatened, surely prefigured social disaster. This is why the Tangut Confucian Yü Ch'üeh, for example, as a magistrate felt strongly that the empire was a matter of concern to more than just its rulers, that its fortunes affected everyone's lives, and consequently its integrity and well-being depended upon whether the views of a concerned (gentry and local official) public could be made known to the rulers on an unrestricted basis.[6]

In practice, however, the conservatives' concern for the responsiveness of government to local opinion did not always produce harmonious results. The effectiveness of the investigating commission of 1345 was seriously compromised in some areas by gentry ridicule of the personal venality of some of the commissioners, and, moreover, the government did not have the will or the power to enforce many of the indictments that the commissioners made. Even worse, the whole logic of the conservative argument broke down in hopeless self-contradiction when the Berke Buqa administration decided in the face of gentry pressure not to set up a key naval commandery to check a mounting condition of coastal piracy that endangered both the dynasty's food supply and the local social order. Toghto made political capital of this impasse at the time of his return to power in 1349.

At another level, within the central government itself, the preferred working style of the conservatives again had a tendency to produce markedly discordant notes which disfigured and at times even drowned out the guiding theme of harmony. At the central level the high value the conservatives placed upon the unhindered expression of opinion invariably led them, when they were able, to unmuzzle the Censorate, the opinion-expressing organ par excellence, and after 1340 a pivotal element in the overthrow of ruling administrations. The Censorate as an organ usually generated strong institutional loyalties among its personnel, often its lower personnel, and in this connection was most audibly responsible for the production of discordant notes. If the conservatives had a poor sense of themselves as a party or faction, the conservatives who were appointed Censors had an exceptionally keen group sense of themselves as holders of a unique office with a sacrosanct adversary role to play within the formal organizational structure of the state. The Censors periodically refused to submit either to a partisan political line or to the dominant ministerial personalities, and were apt to attack anyone, reformist or conservative, against whom they found charges or grievances to press. In doing this, however, the Censorate had to walk a very thin line—between fulfilling a due need for courageously impartial criticism and impeachment, but without going so far in this direction as to forfeit the basic political order and jeopardize the public tranquillity. As it turned out, the Censorate in the end proved deaf to the guiding theme of harmony, and sacrificed the entire societal order to the assertion of its institutional prerogatives. When it impeached Toghto late in 1354, the Censorate openly crossed the thin line and as an institution took a prominent share in the responsibility for the collapse of government and the renewed rebel activity that resulted from its act. Thereafter, the Censorate continued to devote itself to providing criticism and formulating impeachments, thereby helping to destroy what little public order was left.

Nevertheless, by 1355 it hardly mattered what the Censorate did, for by then the Yüan Dynasty was unsalvageable anyway. The failure of the Yüan expeditionary force under Toghto at Kao-yu had a fatally demoralizing effect upon the army, which was deprived of almost certain victory and its consequent due rewards. The commanders who succeeded to the various parts of this demoralized central army could neither make them fight nor prevent their plunder of the countryside. The Censorate knew very well that the new independent regional armies of Chaghan Temür and Dash Badulugh were the only sure lines of defense against the revived and reorganized rebel movements, and it also realized how much reports of their anti-rebel victories did to lift sagging morale in the capital. Consequently, the Censorate bent over backwards to overlook their occasional failures and to ignore the menace to central power that their growing regional machines posed, and instead spent its moral capital upon the impeachment of unsuccessful central commanders and unpopular or ineffectual chancellors, thus helping to keep the expiring central government in continual upheaval. Yet, thanks in large part to the efforts of the Censorate, the Yüan Dynasty withered and shrank in Confucian style and down to the very end made no overt retreat from its Confucian commitments. When in September, 1368, the newly declared Ming Dynasty of the ex-rebel Chu Yüan-chang forced the Yüan court back to the grasslands whence it had originated, it departed still wearing a recognizably Confucian face.

It would be a gross overstatement to say that extremist Confucian politics alone had "caused" the collapse of the Yüan Dynasty, unless one is prepared to admit basic importance to the mere operations of government, with all of its inherent superficialities and limitations. Yet it is evident that, within the orb of government, one can trace through the late Yüan period a steadily narrowing scope of political choice and maneuver that made a decisive response to crises and emergencies ever more difficult to engineer. As the conquest establishment in Yüan China, represented by such men as El Temür, forced the Yüan emperor to dissociate himself entirely from the Qaghanate and give up his prerogatives as *qaghan*, the monarchy lost all vestige of an important margin of leverage over China that it had held hitherto. The Yüan monarchy, once it fell captive to the conquest establishment in China, could no longer override the preferences of that establishment by using against it the larger Mongol empire, the preserve of the princes and *qans* who were the blood descendants of Chinggis. The conquest establishment, having bound the monarchy to itself and its own particular interests in China, then came to find in turn that it could no longer assume an air of unconcerned detachment toward the country it occupied. Despite the reluctance shown by Bayan, the establishment was obliged to climb down from its eminence and fully involve itself on either side of a Confucian argument that originally had nothing to do with the conquest, but was purely a product of Chinese history. This involvement came at a price, and the price was a painful circumscription of the conquest establishment's freedom of political choice in China. Once involved in the Confucian argument, the establishment had no way of transcending it. Faced with crisis, it could not grope back into the past and find there some ancient ledge of solidarity upon which to cling in safety, while the riot and the controversy swirled harmlessly by. It could no longer act *as* an establishment;

neither could it act together as a *Confucian* establishment, for in adopting Confucianism the conquerors, following their Chinese mentors and teachers, had to swallow the violently irreconcilable divisions that lay within it. When the conquest establishment began to fall into divergent Confucian patterns of behavior and act contrary to its own best interests, the monarchy was already too limited and dependent an institution to rescue it, and could only go down with it. In a crisis, the monarchy could not choose between a Confucianized establishment and some other group; it could only choose one of two Confucianized extremes. The Yüan Dynasty finally collapsed exhausted from its playing too many antagonistic historical parts written in China: monarch against official, reformist official against conservative, central official against regionalist.

The new political movement that in 1368 became the Ming Dynasty began to take shape in 1355, just after Toghto's dismissal demonstrated in a most dramatic way the Yüan Dynasty's capacity for self-destruction. The Ming founders, Chu Yüan-chang and his gentry adherents, read the lessons of the late Yüan political experience very closely and, in resuming the thread of Confucian history, avoided both the institutional anarchism of the Yüan conservatives and the programmatic cliquism of the Yüan reformists. By annulling the Confucian argument, and by increasing enormously the power of the monarchy, they were able to resolve for their own generation many of the theoretical dilemmas and practical impasses that the Mongol conquerors had, in their day in power, amply exposed.

Biographical Notes

ARADNADARA (d. 1332), eldest son of Tugh Temür. He was Tugh Temür's heir apparent until his death in February, 1332.

ARADNASHIRI, Mongol prince, descendant of Qubilai through his eighth son A'urughchi. Aradnashiri held various princely fiefs in Shensi and was an important supporter of the restoration of 1328. He later coordinated the anti-rebel defense of Shensi until Chaghan Temür displaced him in 1358.

ARUGHTU, Mongol of the Arulad tribe. He held the position of Chancellor of the Right from Toghto's resignation in 1344 until Berke Buqa replaced him in 1347.

AYURBARWADA (d. 1320), Yüan emperor, younger son of prince Darmabala, who was the second son of Qubilai's one-time heir apparent Jingim. As the "Chinese" candidate in 1307, he was made heir apparent to his elder brother Qaishan. He succeeded Qaishan and reigned 1311-20. He reinstituted the Confucian examination system in 1315.

AYUSHIRIDARA (d. 1378), son of Toghon Temür by his Korean empress Öljei Qudu, nee Ki. He was invested as heir apparent in 1355, and became Mongol ruler in the steppes upon his father's death in 1370.

BAYAN (d. 1340), Mongol of the Merkid tribe. He was a junior aide to Prince Qaishan during the final phases of the anti-Qaidu wars. He was a leader of the restoration of 1328, and an anti-Confucian chancellor from 1335 to 1340.

BERKE BUQA (d. 1350), Mongol of the Eljigid tribe. His father Aqutai, Chancellor of the Left during Temür's reign, was executed in 1307 for his support of the imperial candidacy of Ananda. Berke Buqa was Chancellor of the Right for a few months in 1347, but remained an important leader of the conservative opposition to Toghto until 1349.

BOLOD TEMÜR (murdered 1365), a son of Dash Badulugh. As the commander of an autonomous regional machine in north China after 1358, he was a rival of both Chaghan Temür and later Kökö Temür.

BUDASHIRI (exiled 1340), Mongol of the Qunggirad tribe, Tugh Temür's empress, and mother of Aradnadara and El Tegüs. She was the ally and supporter of Bayan from 1332 until 1340.

CHAGHAN TEMÜR (assassinated 1361), a Turk of the Naiman tribe, from a landholding family settled in Honan province. After the dismissal of Toghto in 1355, he was the first to create an autonomous regional organization in north China.

CHANG SHIH-CH'ENG (executed 1367), salt-smuggler and anti-Yüan rebel leader. Chang was saved from almost certain annihilation when Toghto's siege of his stronghold at Kao-yu collapsed in January, 1355. Chang later migrated to the Yangtze Delta area, and as a regional warlord professed nominal loyalty to the Yüan until his defeat by the Ming founder Chu Yüan-chang in 1367.

CH'I-T'AI-P'U-CHI (d. 1313), a Tangut. He was a commander and adviser to Prince Qaishan during the anti-Qaidu wars. He was made Chancellor of the Right upon Qaishan's enthronement, and received the princely fief of An-chi, which was later canceled. Yeh-erh-chi-ni and Li-jih were his sons.

*CHONG'UR (d. 1322), a son of Tughtugha. He was a commander and senior aide to Prince Qaishan in the wars against Qaidu. He received the princely fief of Chü-jung in 1309. El Temür was his son.

CHÖSGEM (executed 1364), Mongol of the Kereid tribe. He served as a Chief Administrator during Toghto's second administration. As Censor-in-Chief after Toghto's dismissal, he led a successful censorial attack upon Qama, and became Chancellor of the Right in 1357. He was executed by Bolod Temür at the time of his occupation of the capital.

CHU YÜAN-CHANG (d. 1398), anti-Yüan rebel leader, and founder of the Ming Dynasty in 1368.

DASH BADULUGH (d. 1358), Mongol of the Salji'ud tribe. He led successful anti-rebel campaigns in the Han River area in 1352-53, but achieved indifferent results against the Sung rebels in north China after 1355. His son Bolod Temür inherited his campaign forces, and used them to build a regional machine.

DAULA-SHAH (executed 1328), a Moslem. He was Chancellor of the Right under Yesün Temür and his heir Aragibag, and surrendered to El Temür's restoration forces in November, 1328.

DORJI, Mongol of the Jalair tribe, and a learned Neo-Confucian scholar. He succeeded to the Jalair viceroyship in 1328, but was removed by Bayan in 1338. Later, as Chancellor of the Left of Honan province, he protested Bayan's handling of the

Fan Meng case. As a conservative, he served as Chancellor of the Right in the central government from 1348 to 1349.

DORJIBAL, also a Jalair, and a Neo-Confucian scholar. He led an unsuccessful censorial attack upon the Berke Buqa government in 1349; and in 1352, as chief of the Shensi Branch Censorate, he attempted to impeach Toghto's younger brother Esen Temür for his military failure against the Red Turbans. Dorjibal was an active organizer and coordinator of the anti-rebel effort. He died in south China sometime after 1355.

EL TEGÜS (murdered 1340), second son of Tugh Temür. He was twice bypassed for the succession in favor of Qoshila's sons, but was heir apparent to Toghon Temür during Bayan's administration.

EL TEMÜR (d. *ca.* 1334), Qipchaq Turk, and son of *Chong'ur. During the anti-Qaidu wars, he served as a junior aide to Qaishan. He led the restoration of 1328, and served as Chancellor of the Right throughout the reign of Tugh Temür (1328-32).

ESEN TEMÜR, younger brother of Toghto, and his Censor-in-Chief. His forces were routed by Red Turban rebels in 1352. He was exiled at the time of Toghto's dismissal in 1355.

FANG KUO-CHEN (d. 1374), a Chinese pirate from Huang-yen on the Chekiang (Kiangche) coast. He achieved a position of strength at sea in 1348, and used his power over the maritime grain shipments to blackmail the Yüan court. By 1356 he also established himself on the mainland. He remained nominally loyal to the Yüan until his surrender to Chu Yüan-chang in 1367.

HO WEI-I (suicide, 1363). Northern Chinese, adopted into the Mongol nation with the name T'ai-p'ing in 1345. He served as Dorji's Chancellor of the Left, 1348-49. He returned to official life in 1355, and became Chancellor of the Left again in 1357.

IRINJIBAL (d. 1332), Yüan emperor, younger son of Qoshila. He died in childhood after a reign of two months.

IRINJINBAL (d. 1354), a Tangut. He was an opponent of Bayan's; later as Censor-in-Chief, he tried unsuccessfully to impeach the conservative government of Berke Buqa. He afterwards commanded the anti-rebel effort in Kiangsi province in south China.

KÖKÖ TEMÜR (d. 1375), Chinese, adopted son of Chaghan Temür. He succeeded to the command of Chaghan's regional machine in 1361. After the expulsion of the Yüan Dynasty from China in 1368, he commanded steppe armies in Mongolia.

LI SSU-CH'I (d. 1374). As a friend and ally of Chaghan Temür's,

Li became a semi-independent warlord in Shensi province. In 1369 he surrendered himself to the Ming Dynasty.

LI-JIH (d. *ca.* 1316), a Tangut, and son of Ch'i-t'ai-p'u-chi. During the struggle against Qaidu, he was a commander to Qaishan, and was made Censor-in-Chief upon Qaishan's enthronement. He supported Qoshila's rebellion in Shensi in 1316.

MAJARTAI, brother of Bayan and father of Toghto. A patron of aspiring Confucians, Majartai briefly held the position of Chancellor of the Right after Bayan's overthrow in 1340.

NARIN, a Tangut. As Censor-in-Chief, he attempted an impeachment of the Berke Buqa government in 1349. As Censor-in-Chief of the Kiangnan Branch Censorate, he was responsible for coordinating anti-rebel efforts in south China after 1352.

QAIDU (d. 1301). Grandson of the *qaghan* Ögödei (r. 1229-41), Qaidu rebuilt the Ögödei patrimony in Central Asia, and in alliance with Duwa of the Chaghatai house he directed a powerful Central Asian opposition movement against Qubilai and Temür in Yüan China. Qaidu's son Chapar and his descendants were later granted a princely fief in China, where they came to settle. Qaidu's great-grandson Hula'atai supported the loyalist side during the restoration of 1328.

QAISHAN (d. 1311), Yüan emperor, elder son of Prince Darmabala and elder brother of Ayurbarwada. As the "steppe" candidate in 1307, he succeeded Temür and reigned 1307-11. The restoration of 1328 was carried out in his name.

QAMA, a Turk of the Qangli tribe. A one-time partisan of Toghto's, he engineered his dismissal in 1355. He was later executed.

QANGLI TOGHTO (d. 1327), a Turk of the Qangli tribe, popularly called "Qangli" Toghto in order to distinguish him from many other individuals with the same name. He was a junior aide to Qaishan during the anti-Qaidu campaigns, and was appointed to various high offices during Qaishan's reign as emperor. Later he became a Confucian patron and leader of the opposition group of former Qaishan bureaucrats. Many of his nine sons achieved high positions; the conservative Confucian Temür Tash, for one, was Chancellor of the Left from 1345 until his death in 1347.

QOSHILA (assassinated 1329), Yüan emperor, and "steppe" candidate during the restoration of 1328. He was Qaishan's elder son. He reigned in Mongolia for a few months in 1329. His sons Irinjibal and Toghon Temür later became emperors.

QUBILAI (d. 1294), ruled 1260 to 1294, formally founded the Yüan Dynasty in 1271. All of the succeeding Yüan emperors were descendants of Qubilai through his second son Jingim (d. 1285), whom Qubilai had made heir apparent.

SHIDEBALA (assassinated 1323), Yüan emperor, son and successor of Ayurbarwada, reigned 1320-23. His attempt to shift his support from the Temüder clique to the Confucianists was ultimately responsible for his assassination.

*TANGKISH (killed 1335), son of El Temür's brother Sadun. Bayan defeated and killed him along with the rest of El Temür's family at the time of his rise to power in 1335.

TEMÜR (d. 1307), Yüan emperor, grandson and successor of Qubilai. Temür was Jingim's youngest son; Kammala (father of Yesün Temür) and Darmabala (father of Qaishan and Ayurbarwada) were his older brothers. Temür ruled 1294-1307. His only son predeceased him.

TEMÜR BUQA (executed *ca.* 1335), Uighur Turk, and nominal ruler of the Uighur kingdom of Central Asia. Most of Temür Buqa's career, however, was spent in bureaucratic service in China. He was one of the leaders of the restoration of 1328, and was executed by Bayan.

TING-CHU, a Turk of the Qangli tribe. He served in the Central Chancellery under both Bayan and Toghto, and became Chancellor of the Right after Toghto's dismissal.

TOGHON TEMÜR (d. 1370), last Yüan emperor in China, eldest son of Qoshila. He ruled in China from 1333 to 1368.

TOGHTO (poisoned 1356), a Mongol of the Merkid tribe, son of Majartai, and nephew of Bayan. He led the overthrow of Bayan in 1340, and served as reformist Chancellor of the Right in two incumbencies, 1340-44 and 1349-55. His dismissal in January, 1355, precipitated the collapse of Yüan central authority.

TUGH TEMÜR (d. 1332), Yüan emperor, and figurehead leader of the restoration forces of 1328. He was Qaishan's younger son, and was in part responsible for the assassination of his elder brother Qoshila in 1329. He reigned 1328-32 under the guidance of El Temür.

TUGHTUGHA (d. 1297), a Turk of the Qipchaq tribe, and builder of the Qipchaq inheritance in China. *Chong'ur was his son, and El Temür his grandson.

YEH-ERH-CHI-NI, a Tangut, son of Ch'i-t'ai-p'u-chi. He and his brother Li-jih were commanders to Qaishan during the wars against Qaidu. He was made Censor-in-Chief upon Qaishan's enthronement. Although he did not participate in the restoration of 1328, he was recalled to government in 1329 and made a head of the Chief Military Commission.

YESÜN TEMÜR (d. 1328), Yüan emperor, eldest son of Prince Kammala. He came to the throne after the assassination of

Shidebala in 1323, but repudiated the group which committed that act and backed his enthronement.

*YOCHICHAR, a Mongol of the Hü'üshin tribe. He was a senior aide to Qaishan in the anti-Qaidu wars, and was appointed Chancellor of the Right of the new Mongolian province of Ho-lin (Ling-pei) during Qaishan's reign as emperor. *Yochichar was granted the princely fief of Ch'i-yang, but after Qaishan's death his descendants suffered persecution and the fief was canceled.

Emperors of the Yüan Dynasty in China

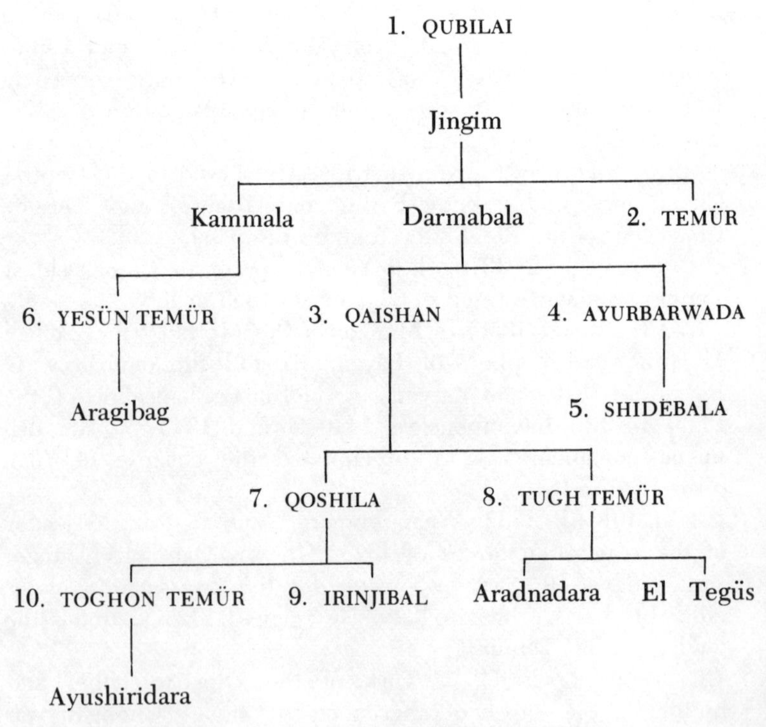

Notes

Chapter I: The Decline of the Steppe in Yüan Politics

1. See my "From Mongol Empire to Yüan Dynasty: Changing Forms of Imperial Rule in Mongolia and Central Asia," forthcoming in *Monumenta Serica*, 1973.

2. Grousset, *L'Empire des Steppes*, pp. 352-53, 359-63; Pelliot, *Notes on Marco Polo*, I, 124-29; Barthold, *Four Studies on the History of Central Asia*, I, 124-27.

3. *YS*, 131.5b-6a; 132.6a; 138.1b, 17a; *MWE*, 10.1a; 74.13a-b; 102.5b. I follow T'u Chi and Grousset (p. 362) in placing the battle in Mongolia; Grousset, however, wrongly states that Qaidu was defeated there. Pelliot places the battle in the western steppes near Lake Balkhash *(Notes*, I, 128). For the name *Chong'ur, cf. Pelliot and Hambis, *Histoire des Campagnes de Gengis Khan*, p. 300. For *Yochichar, cf. Cleaves in *HJAS*, XV (1952), 26.

4. Grousset, pp. 362-63, 442, 459; Barthold, *Zwölf Vorlesungen über die Geschichte der Türken Mittelasiens*, pp. 199-200. News of this development was reported to Philip IV of France and later Edward II of England. For Maragha, cf. Pelliot, *Notes*, I, 128.

5. *MWE*, 10.1b; Pelliot, *Notes*, I, 128; B. Spuler, "Capar," *Encyclopedia of Islam* (new ed., 1965), II, 14.

6. *YS*, 22.1b; *MWE*, 10.1b; Grousset, pp. 410-11.

7. *YS*, 22.2a; 138.17a.

8. *MWE*, 76.5b-7b; O. Franke, *Geschichte des Chinesischen Reiches*, IV, 505-7. For the reading Bulughan, cf. Cleaves in *HJAS*, XXIV (1962-633, 74, n. 75.

9. Rashid ad-Din, *Sbornik Letopisei*, II, 207-10.

10. For the reading Ayurbarwada, cf. Cleaves in *HJAS*, XVII (1954), 17 and 120, n. 309. Pelliot (in Hambis, *Le Chapitre CVII du Yuan Che*, p. 134, n. 4) traces the name to Sanskrit Ayurparibhadra, or a Tibeto-Sanskrit *Ayurparpata.

11. *MWE*, 11, 1a-b. For the doubtful reading *Targi, cf. Hambis, *Le Chapitre CVIII du Yuan Che*, table 2, opp. p. 18. For Harghasun, cf. Cleaves in *HJAS*, XXIV (1962-63), 75, n. 80.

12. *MWE*, 11.1a-b.

13. *YS*, 24.1b.

14. *YS*, 137.8b-9a; *MWE*, 11.1a-b.

15. *YS*, 138.1b-3b; *MWE*, 10.1b-2a.

16. *YS*, 22.2b-3b. The formula later used by Ayurbarwada was more suitable; according to it, Chinggis launched the enterprise through all kinds of difficulty, but it was Qubilai who unified the realm (*YS*, 26.13a).

17. *YS*, 115.10a-12a; *MWE*, 121.1a-4a. Ch'i-t'ai-p'u-chi became Chancellor of the Right in both the *Chung-shu sheng* and later the *Shang-shu sheng* chancelleries, and was given the princely fief of An-chi (not listed by Hambis in *Le Chapitre CVIII*, but cf. *YS*, 23.20a-b for the fact of the enfeoffment). Yeh-erh-chi-ni and Li-jih both achieved the position of Censor-in-Chief.

18. *YS*, 138.1a-5b.

19. *YS*, 136.10a-b. A-sha Buqa died in 1309.

20. *YS*, 23.1b; 128.18b-21b. The girl was Chakir or *Chagir, daughter of the Prince of Ch'u Yaqudu, himself a descendant of Tului through Tului's son Böchög. Cf. Hambis, *Le Chapitre CVIII*, p. 164, n. 5.

21. *Ibid.*

22. *YS*, 138.6b. For the office, cf. Ratchnevsky, *Un Code des Yuan*, pp. 143-46.

23. *YS*, 23.16b; 138.17a. The *Shang-shu sheng* was a chancellery set up by Qaishan to replace the *Chung-shu sheng*. It was abolished immediately after Qaishan's death in 1311. Cf. Ratchnevsky, pp. 118-22.

24. Meng Ssu-ming, *Yüan-tai she-hui chieh-chi chih-tu*, p. 51, n. 290.

25. For the reading Tugh Temür, cf. Ligeti in *TP*, XXVII (1930), 57-61.

26. *YS*, 138.4b. But see *MWE*, 12.1a; 14.1a; and 19.3a, where T'u Chi has it that Ayurbarwada had originally agreed to set up Qaishan's eldest son Qoshila as heir apparent.

27. *YS*, 26.19b.

28. *YS*, 25.11b-13a; 31.1b. An ingot was equivalent to 50 ounces (*liang*) of silver.

29. *MWE*, 121.3b-4a.

30. The commotion in Shensi caused a certain amount of excitement in Mongolia; unfortunately, information on this matter is very vague. Cf. Yü Chi's epitaph for Su Chih-tao in *Yüan wen-lei*, 54.1b.

31. *YS*, 31.1b-2a; *MWE*, 14.1a-b.

32. *MWE*, 14.1b. Cha-ch'i Ssu-ch'in (*Meng-wen Huang-chin-shih i-chu*, p. 121) and Pelliot (*Notes*, I, 254) agree that the "chu-wang Ch'a-a-t'ai" of *YS*, 31.2a, means the princes, or reigning prince, of the Chaghatai Khanate. T'u Chi points out that the reigning prince at this time was Esen Buqa. He also identifies Qoshila's

summer and winter quarters and spring planting grounds as places in the Tarbagatai area, east of Lake Balkhash.

33. *YS*, 27.18a-b; 31.1b.

34. *YS*, 29.8b, 18a; Hambis, *Le Chapitre CVIII*, p. 51.

35. Lu Yu, *Yen-pei tsa-chih*, B.9b. Cf. also H. Franke in *AM*, III (1952), 34-37.

36. For important remarks on the significance of Qubilai's reign from a somewhat different point of view, cf. the following writings by H. F. Schurmann: "Mongolian Tributary Practices of the Thirteenth Century," *HJAS*, XIX (1956), 304-89; "Problems of Political Organization during the Yüan Dynasty," *Trudy XXV Mezhdunarodnogo Kongressa Vostokovedov*, V (Moscow, 1963), 26-30; and *Economic Structure of the Yüan Dynasty*, pp. 1-11. For a brief discussion of the effect of Qubilai's dynastic revolution on the appanage system, cf. Ratchnevsky, "Zum Ausdruck 't'ouhsia' in der Mongolenzeit," pp. 179-80.

37. For the reading Arigh Böke (not Böge), cf. Poppe in *HJAS*, XVII (1954), 306. On Nayan, cf. Pelliot, *Notes*, II, 788-89. E.J.P. Mullie, *De Mongoolse Prins Nayan*, reviewed in *AM*, XII (1966), 130-31 is inaccessible to me.

38. For Qubilai's remission of *ch'ai-fa* (levies and tributes) in 1261, see *MWE*, 74.3a. For his remission of Qaraqorum taxes shortly afterwards, see *MWE*, 74.4a. For what little is known of the taxation of nomads, cf. Munkuev's article in the bibliography, and most recently, John Masson Smith, Jr., "Mongol and Nomadic Taxation," *HJAS*, XXX (1970), 46-85.

39. *MWE*, 74.4b; Grousset, pp. 402-3.

40. *MWE*, 74.5b.

41. For the date of Duwa's accession, cf. *MWE*, 32.6b; 74.7a.

42. Details on these matters may be found in the article cited in note 1, above. Nayan was a descendant of Temüge Odchigin, youngest brother of Chinggis Qan (Hambis, *Le Chapitre CVII*, pp. 39, n. 16, 150-51). Nayan's profession of Nestorian Christianity, in contrast to the official Lama Buddhism of the court, seems to reflect a desire on his part to maintain cultural as well as regional autonomy.

43. For the Ba'arin, cf. *MWE*, 8.28b; *YS*, 15.13b. For the Water Tatars, cf. Pelliot in *TP*, XXVIII (1931), 118; Bretschneider, *Medieval Researches from Eastern Asiatic Sources*, II, 175-76; and Schurmann, *Economic Structure*, p. 163, n. 5. Nayan's revolt was only one episode in a long history of Manchurian dissidence.

44. Nayan's raids seriously damaged Manchurian agriculture; cf. *YS*, 14.18b, 19b; 16.1b.

45. Between 1288 and 1290, Qubilai increased grain tribute shipments from the Yangtze area from 400,000 to 1,500,000 piculs in

order to supply the anti-Qaidu campaign (*YS*, 15.11b; Schurmann, *Economic Structure*, p. 123). Some of the grain was sent directly up the Liao River to supply the anti-Nayan forces (*MWE*, 75.2a). For Qubilai's assembling his own horses in China prior to a campaign in the steppes, see *YS*, 15.21b. There are many references to Qubilai's relief and resettlement policies in the *YS*. Relief in the form of grain allotments, cash grants for the purchase of horses and sheep to restock depleted herds, and gold and silver bullion was commonly given to the loyal steppe princes rather than to the tribes directly.

46. *MWE*, 75.6a. Bayan was able to secure Nayan's post stations through bribery; cf. Cleaves in *HJAS*, XIX (1956), 265-66.

47. Mongolia was made Ho-lin (Qorum) province in 1307, and renamed Ling-pei province in 1312 (*YS*, 24.18b; 58.39a). For Chung-tu, cf. *YS*, 22.4b-28b *passim;* Pelliot, *Notes*, I, 322.

48. Cf. *YS*, 58.39a.

49. The *YS* states that there were 868,000 destitute nomad households in Mongolia at this time. Using the official ratio of four people per nomad household, the total comes to 3,472,000 individuals, surely an improbably high figure. That eastern Mongolia was fully populated, however, may be surmised from a report of 1308 which states that there was not enough room east of the Altai to permit the settlement there of the surrendered people of Duwa and Qaidu (*YS*, 22.24b; 23.20a; 119.25a). Whatever the true figure of the destitute, the government issued them large amounts of aid (*YS*, 23.20a). It may be noted that this aid was given directly, without the mediation of the steppe princes. Other destitute nomads flocked down to the North China border where they were settled on military-agricultural colonies (*YS*, 22.24a).

50. Only a rough indication can be given. Hambis (*Le Chapitre CVIII*) lists 142 such fiefs, of which about 60 percent were held by descendants of the house of Chinggis Qan, 20 percent by members of various consort clans, and 20 percent unknown, unclear, or posthumous. Qubilai awarded around 31 such fiefs; Temür nine, and Qaishan and Ayurbarwada each around 24. Of the first-class fiefs, however, Qubilai awarded around six, Temür none, Qaishan sixteen, and Ayurbarwada eight.

51. The new Chinese-style fiefs were not associated with the appanages (*fen-ti*) earlier given the Mongol nobility; apparently they represented a claim to the imperial bounty rather than to semi-independent sources of revenue. Unenfeoffed "princes of the blood" (*chu-wang*) continued to be used as defenders of the border areas in the steppes.

52. The Imperial Clan Court was not the only agency authorized to adjudicate princely disputes; cf. *YS*, 30.16b.

53. In 1314-15 the Qipchaq *Chong'ur made a raid upon Transoxania (*Ys*, 128.21a-b; *MWE*, 32.8a-b). In 1319 Kebek raided the Tarim area (*MWE*, 32.9a). In 1323, however, Kebek offered peace to the Yüan court (*YS*, 28.15b). For another individual with the same name in Chinese transcription, Cleaves in *HJAS*, XV (1952), 26, gives the reading Kebei. The form "Kebek" is usual among writers on Central Asia who use Persian sources.

54. Qoshila was involved in a campaign against the prince Tuman Temür apparently somewhere along the Kansu border in 1317 (*MWE*, 102.7a). The only notice on this matter comes from the biography of the Qipchaq Ha-tsan-ch'ih (? Qazanchi) in *YS*, 135.17a. See also *YS*, 25.5b-6b. In 1318 Tuman Temür was raised from ordinary prince (*chu-wang*) to Prince of Wu-p'ing; this obviously was a sign of official favor. His genealogy appears to be unknown; cf. Hambis, *Le Chapitre CVIII*, p. 119, n. 3.

55. *YS*, 28.15b.

56. It is doubtful whether the distinction between the tributary terms *hsien* and *kung* was as precisely drawn at this time as H. Franke suggests; cf. H. Franke in *Saeculum*, II (1951), 72. Qoshila's tribute was described as *hsien* in 1325 and *kung* in 1326 (*YS*, 29.29a; 30.16b), whereas the Ilkhan Abu Said's was called *kung* in 1325 and *hsien* in 1326 (*YS*, 29.30b; 30.1b).

57. *YS*, 31.3b-4a; 32.9a; 33.3b. An envoy was sent to Qoshila on December 23, 1328 (*YS*, 32.23b).

58. The itinerary of Qoshila in *YS*, 31.7a-10a, has been explained in full in Pelliot, *Notes*, I, 320-23.

59. Yü Chi, *Tao-yüan hsüeh-ku lu*, 10.10a (colophon on a handwritten edict of Qoshila). Yü Chi wrote this colophon in Qoshila's *ordo* at Ch'ing-ho, probably a stream near the Great Wall north of Peking. Cf. Yanai Wataru, *Yüan-ch'ao ch'ieh-hsieh chi o-erh-to k'ao* [Studies on the *keshig* and *ordo* of the Yüan period] (Taipei, 1963), p. 148, n. 3.

60. *YS*, 31.10a; *KSWS*,1a-b.

61. Barthold, *Four Studies*, I, 51-52.

62. That Eljigitei was a Chaghatai ruler at this time requires some lengthy explanation. The difficulty stems from the problem of the succession to Kebek, who died in 1326 according to Barthold (*Zwölf Vorlesungen*, pp. 203-5), and again according to Barthold and J. A. Boyle in *Encyclopedia of Islam* (new ed., 1965), II, 3-4. Also cf. Arat in *UAJ*, XXXV (1964), 153. The *YS* annals last record an embassy from Kebek in 1326, and a return mission was sent to his subject people in 1327 (*YS*, 30.3b, 18a). According to Grousset (*L'Empire des Steppes*, p. 414), Kebek was succeeded by his brothers Eljigitei and Duwa Temür (read Döre or Töre Temür; H. Franke in *Oriens*, XV [1962], 403, n. 1), both of whom reigned

only a few months. However, again according to the *YS*, Eljigitei succeeded, we are not told to what, at least by the year 1327 when he sent an embassy to announce the fact to the Yüan court, where Yesün Temür was still reigning (*YS*, 30.15b). A little later in the same year, Eljigitei and Qoshila sent a joint tribute mission to the Yüan court (30.16b). Then in February, 1329, September, 1329, and March, 1330, the Yüan court sent embassies to Eljigitei, on the last occasion conjointly with missions to Abu Said of the Ilkhanate and Özbeg of the Golden Horde (*YS*, 33.2a, 17a; 34.7a-b). Consequently it may be presumed that Eljigitei was a ruler of some importance in some part if not all of the Chaghatai Khanate. According to the *YS* biography of Naimantai (*YS*, 139.2a), Naimantai was made Censor-in-Chief of the Shensi Branch Censorate in 1329 and in the same year undertook a mission to "deliver the seal of the imperial elder brother formerly cast by T'ai-tsung (i.e., Ögödei) to his (i.e. the elder brother's) descendant Eljig*edei* [sic]." The reference here must be to the Eljigitei who was in contact with the Yüan court, and who was a descendant of Ögödei's elder brother Chaghatai. After 1330 we hear no more of Eljigitei. We next learn in September, 1331, that Döre Temür, Eljigitei's co-ruler or rival, had been succeeded in his position by Darma, who was *chu-wang* of the Western Regions, the same designation used for Eljigitei in September, 1329. This Darma is to be identified with Darmashiri, or Tarmashirin, a well-known Chaghatai ruler (cf. H. Franke, above). Döre Temür, however, continued to rule somewhere, possibly in the Ili, for as *chu-wang* of the Western Regions he sent an embassy to the Yüan court in January, 1332 (*YS*, 35.27b; *Tō yō rekishi daijiten*, VI, 39). The indications are, therefore, that Eljigitei ruled *ca.* 1327-30 in the eastern portions of the Chaghatai realm.

63. *YS*, 31.4b.

64. The Mongol chronicle called the *Altan Tobchi*, a late compilation, has Qoshila *invading* the south. This version does not square with the contemporary accounts in Chinese. Cf. Cha-ch'i Ssu-ch'in, *Meng-wen Huang-chin-shih i-chu*, pp. 123, 126. In his earlier translation of this work, however, C. R. Bawden stated that the passage in question was corrupt and delivered no sure meaning. See his *The Mongol Chronicle Altan Tobči* (Wiesbaden, 1955), p. 149, n. 4.

65. Two notices of severe drought in Mongolia are reported in *YS*, 31.8a-b.

66. *YS*, 31.5a-b.

67. *YS*, 31.7a.

Chapter II: The Restoration of 1328

1. On the Tung-p'ing school, see Abe Takeo, "*Gendai chishikijin to kakyo,*" pp. 900-6, 917-20; Hsiao Ch'i-ch'ing, *Hsi-yü-jen yü Yüan-ch'u cheng-chih,* pp. 53-61; Sun K'o-k'uan, *Yüan-tai Han wen-hua chih huo-tung,* pp. 109-38. See also the important article by Igor de Rachewiltz, "Personnel and Personalities in North China in the Early Mongol Period," *JESHO,* IX (1966), 88-144.

2. On the early history of Neo-Confucianism in North China under the Mongols, cf. Abe, pp. 906-17; Sun, pp. 155-96.

3. For further discussion of *chiao-hua* and *feng-su,* see Chapter III below.

4. Quoted in Abe, p. 914. A Neo-Confucian view of the proper relationship between ideology and literary training may be seen in the preface to the biographies of eminent Confucians in the *Yuan shih:* "The earlier dynastic histories in their biographical sections always divided the scholars into two. Those specializing in the classics were called 'Confucians' *(ju-lin);* those famous for literary composition were called 'Literati' *(wen-yüan).* But to the scholar who pursues his studies, these two are really the same thing. The Six Classics are where the Way may be found, and literary language is that whereby this Way is expressed. Thus, without literary language, there would be no way for the classics to convey their message; but if literary language is not rooted in the classics, then it hardly deserves the name. From this it is clear that classical study and literary composition cannot be divided and made two separate things" *(YS,* 189.1a).

5. Cf. W. Fuchs in *MS,* XI (1946), 33-64.

6. In this matter alone, apparently, the Tung-p'ing men found themselves in agreement with the ruling finance experts. While opposition to the *t'ou-hsia* was carried on by such Tung-p'ing adherents as Wang Yün (d. 1304), the financiers Aḥmad, Sengge, and later Temüder as a matter of policy squeezed down upon *t'ou-hsia* incomes. Gradually but surely, *t'ou-hsia* incomes fell or were reduced by about 72 percent between the years 1236 and 1319. (Cf. Iwamura Shinobu, *Mongoru shakai keizaishi kenkyū,* pp. 404-69, esp. pp. 457 ff.). Strictly Confucian opposition to the *t'ou-hsia* system seems conspicuously absent. The greatest of the *t'ou-hsia,* the Jalair clan, descendants of Chinggis Qan's general Muqali, patronized Confucianism and won consistent Confucian esteem.

7. Meng Ssu-ming, *Yüan-tai she-hui chieh-chi chih-tu,* pp. 43-69.

8. Qubilai especially appointed such men as the Qangli Buqumu to study under the Confucian Hsü Heng *(YS,* 130.3b-14b); cf. also

Hsiao, pp. 65-68, on the role of the Jalair An-t'ung. See further L. C. Goodrich in *Oriente Poliano,* pp. 3-10; Ch'en Yüan, *Western and Central Asians in China under the Mongols,* pp. 18-79.

9. Abe, pp. 922-24.

10. *YS*, 81.4a-b. At this time the government also canonized the Neo-Confucian fathers Chou Tun-i, the Ch'eng brothers, Chang Tsai, Shao Yung, Ssu-ma Kuang, Chu Hsi, Chang Shih, Lü Tsu-ch'ien, and Hsü Heng, and placed their tablets in the Confucian temple *(YS,* 24.26b). Cf. also O. Franke, *Geschichte der Chinesischen Reiches,* IV, 508-9.

11. Cf. Wang Yün, *Ch'iu-chien chi,* 90.4b-5a for an argument favoring the introduction of *pao-chü.* For the operation of *yin* as the dominant mode of local official recruitment, see Makino Shuji in *Tōhōgaku,* no. 32 (1966), 56-70.

12. *YS*, 83.6b-7a.

13. *YS*, 81.4b-5a.

14. Abe, p. 915; Meng Ssu-ming, pp. 72-73.

15. For *Targi, cf. Chapter I, n. 11.

16. *YS*, 26.3a; 27.6b; 205.26a-27a.

17. The martyrs were Ho Sheng, a Northern Chinese and commandant *(liu-shou)* at Shang-tu; Yang Dorji, a Tangut and Vice Censor-in-Chief; and Hsiao Baiju, a Khitan, and a Chief Administrator. Cf. *YS*, 27.3a; 179.1a-10a; and Yü Chi's two epitaphs for Ho Sheng (a.c. Ho Bayan) in *Tao-yüan hsüeh-ku lu,* 13.1a-5a.

18. *YS*, 28.6b, 8b, 14b, 16a.

19. *YS*, 28.16b-17b; 29.1a-2a; 137.11a-18a; 207.1a-2a. The Prince of Chin's claim to the throne was not a strong one; his father Kammala had voluntarily removed himself from consideration upon Qubilai's death in 1294, and supported the candidacy of Temür. Cf. *YS*, 121.11b.

20. *YS*, 29.13b-14a; 175.4b-6b.

21. *YS*, 32.2a; Cleaves in *HJAS*, XIII (1950), 53, n. 173.

22. *YS*, 32.4b-5a.

23. *YS*, 32.2b; 138.7a.

24. *YS*, 32.2b-3b; 138.7a-8a.

25. *YS*, 32.4a, 5b; 138.17b.

26. *YS*, 32.8a-9b. The edict of enthronement was composed by Yü Chi; cf. *Yüan wen-lei*, 9.15a-16a.

27. *YS*, 30.24b; *MWE*, 13.14b. For the name Aragibag, from the Tibetan Ra-kyi-phag, cf. Hambis, *Le Chapitre CVII*, p. 139, n. 1, and Laufer in *TP*, II (1901), 34.

28. On this paper currency issue, cf. *YS, 32.21b.*

29. *MWE*, 13.15a. For the Yunnan rebellion, see Cleaves in *HJAS*, XXV (1964-65), 31-79, and G. Kara in *AOASH*, XVII (1964), 145-73. The Yunnan and Szechwan troubles did not break out until

after the overthrow of the loyalists at Shang-tu. On the interconnection of the Yunnan and Szechwan rebellions, cf. *YS*, 33.21a.

30. *YS*, 32.10a-15b; 138.8a-12a. The battle accounts in the basic annals (32.10a-15b) and in El Temür's biography (138.8a-12a) derive from two different sources and do not always agree with each other.

31. For the Shensi famine, brought on by a four-year drought, see *YS*, 32.26b; 33.9a, 11b. The population loss was estimated to be from 70 percent to 90 percent; cf. *YS*, 97.13b and T'ung Shu, *Ch'ü-an chi*, 3.9b-10a. The desolation was complete enough to inspire Yü Chi's hopeful suggestion that the property lines might be completely redrawn and the ancient well-field system reestablished there. Cf. *YS*, 181.8b.

32. Two of these dangers were pointed out by the Vice Administrator of the Left Shih Wei-liang; cf. Huang Chin, *Chin-hua Huang hsien-sheng wen-chi*, 26.11b-12a (spirit-way stela for Shih Weiliang).

33. *YS*, 32.3b-13a *passim;* 35.11b; 184.9a. For Lü Ssu-ch'eng's willing cooperation in fulfilling the various new demands, cf. *YS*, 185.1b. Lü was at the time a local magistrate in Hopei.

34. *YS*, 32.3b-15a *passim.*

35. The leading steppe princes who fought on the Shang-tu side were the Prince of Liao Toghto and the Prince of Liang Ongchan. Toghto, a descendant of Chinggis Qan's younger brother Temüge Odchigin, was made Prince of Liao by Ayurbarwada in 1316, and had his power base in northern Manchuria. He had been accused on two occasions of murder by the censors in Ta-tu, but the emperor Yesün Temür protected him. He had therefore a strong interest in supporting the Shang-tu side (cf. *YS*, 29.12a-b; *MWE*, 22.7b-9a; Hambis, *Le Chapitre CVIII*, p. 42). Ongchan and the Prince of Hsiang-ning Balashiri were both nephews of Yesün Temür and were given their fiefs by him (Hambis, *Le Chapitre CVIII*, pp. 6, 91). Other princes on the Shang-tu side included the Prince of Chao Majaqan, an imperial son-in-law and descendant in the fourth generation of the Onggud chief Ala Qush Digid Quri. Majaqan held his fief at least from 1321; the reasons for his loyalty to the Shang-tu side are unclear. He was, in any event, pardoned and given relief after the fighting was over (*YS*, 27.21a; 31.8a; 32.18b; *MWE*, 13.15a; 36.3a; Hambis, *Le Chapitre CVIII*, pp. 23, 25, n. 6; Cleaves in *HJAS*, XII (1949), 527-28). The Prince of Yang-chai T'ai-p'ing, a descendant of Ögödei, was given his fief by Yesün Temür (Hambis, *Le Chapitre CVII*, p. 92, n. 4), as was the Prince of Ju-ning Hula'atai, grandson of Chapar, and great-grandson of Qaidu (Hambis, *Le Chapitre CVII*, p. 80, n. 5; *Le Chapitre CVIII*, p. 96, n. 4). The personal background of six other princes (*chu-wang*) known to have supported Shang-tu appears to be unclear. One

important non-princely commander, the Chief Administrator of Liao-yang province Tümender, had earlier been accused of complicity in the assassination of Shidebala and thus had good reason to support the Shang-tu side (*YS*, 29.12a-b; 143.8a). On the other side, a study of the imperial princes known to have backed the restoration fails to produce any special pattern. Most important was Arad-nashiri, Prince of Hsi-an, and a descendant of Qubilai through his eighth son A-urughchi. Another prominent prince was the Prince of Ch-i Örüg Temür, a descendant of Chinggis Qan's younger brother Jochi Qasar; he was given his fief by Yesün Temür in 1326 (*YS*, 30.6a). After the surrender of Shang-tu on November 14, many more princes began to show support for the restoration and contributed to the remaining operations.

36. Among the elite units thus split were the Asud, or Alan Guards (*YS*, 32.5a; 138.9b); the Tung-lu Meng-ku, or "East-route Mongol" myriarchy, established in Manchuria at the time of Nayan's rebellion (*YS*, 131.16b; 138.12a); and even some *qarachi*, of whom many were of El Temür's own Qipchaq tribe (Yü Chi, 24.3a-b, stela of merit for the princes of Ts'ao-nan). On the *qarachi*, see note 42 below. Other split units included the Lung-chen Guards (*YS*, 32.6a), and the Güyügchi (*YS*, 32.5a-b. On the latter, cf. Pelliot, *Notes*, I, 572-73).

37. *YS*, 32.5a-b.

38. Evidence for a measure of Qunggirad support for both sides may be discerned in a Sino-Mongolian inscription translated by Cleaves in *HJAS*, XIII (1950), 26, 99-100. Many Qunggirad tribesmen were dependent upon relief from Ta-tu, a factor which must have helped prevent total Qunggirad support for Shang-tu (*YS*, 30.2a). The Jalair viceroy (*kuo-wang*) *Dorotai, a Shang-tu partisan, was killed in 1328. His successor was Dorji, a learned Neo-Confucian ideologue, and a Jalair who supported Ta-tu (*YS*, 32.14b; 139.3b). A word about these two clans may be in order here. Aside from the imperial house, Mongol society in China was dominated by a small number of clans whose position and prestige derived from their intimate involvement in the family and personal history of Chinggis Qan. Chief among these were the Qunggirad and Jalair clans. The Qunggirads were descended from Chinggis Qan's father-in-law Dei Sechen. They remained in later times the imperial consort clan par excellence, a privilege expressly affirmed and sanctioned by the *qaghan* Ögödei (Cleaves in *HJAS*, XIII [1950], 13-16; Hambis, *Le Chapitre CVIII*, table 2, opp. p. 18). The clan maintained an official residence of its own, the principality of Lu at Ch'üan-ning (now Wu-tan-ch'eng in north central Jehol; cf. Cleaves, *ibid.*, p. 39, n. 55). It employed its own staff of palace guards and officials. Members of the clan had served in the Mongol armies

from the time of Chinggis. They held at various times thirteen different princely fiefs; their nearest rivals, the Ikires, had three (data from Hambis, *Le Chapitre CVIII*). The clan obtained an enormous annual income from its appanage holdings in various parts of China, which were managed by clan officials (cf. *MWE*, 23.6b-7a, for the holdings). The Qunggirad role in power politics derived not from any commanding position within the Yüan bureaucracy, but rather from its extremely close relationship to the throne, from which it derived its tremendous ability to influence succession questions.

The position of the Jalair clan was significantly different. The Jalair were a clan subservient to the Borjigin clan of Chinggis Qan. The subservient status of the Jalair, like the consort relationship of the Qunggirad, was an ancient one predating Chinggis Qan himself (cf. Vladimirtsov, *Le Régime Social des Mongols*, pp. 58, 80-82). The position of the Jalair clan in China, however, owed much to their ancestor Muqali's having been Chinggis's best general in his North China campaigns. Chinggis gave Muqali the title "viceroy" (*kuo-wang*), and this title was always inherited by one or another of his descendants (cf. Cleaves in *HJAS*, XII [1949], 96, n. 13). The Jalair held no princely fiefs, and did not intermarry with the imperial house. As the first of the hereditary "meritorious subjects" (*hsün-ch'en*), however, the Jalair did possess extensive appanages in China (*YS*, 95.28a). Although Muqali's position as chief commander of the five *t'ou-hsia*, which included the Qunggirad, was lost by his descendants by 1294 when the Yüan military establishment was reorganized and centralized, the Jalair viceroys did continue to control tribal forces (Ratchnevsky, "Zum Ausdruck 'touhsia' in der Mongolenzeit," pp. 173-77; YS, 23.2a). But the real importance of the Jalair clan in later times lay in the fact that its members consistently attained leading positions in the Yüan bureaucracy as Confucians or Confucian sympathizers.

39. *YS*, 32.16a, 17b (Hambis, *Le Chapitre CVIII*, p. 140, misdates and mistranslates this passage), 23b.

40. Cf. Feng Ch'eng-chün in *FJHC*, IV, 2 (June, 1936), p. 6.

41. *YS*, 184.8b; but also cf. *YS*, 32.2a, translated by Cleaves in *HJAS*, XIII (1950), 53, n. 173.

42. *YS*, 128.14a-18b; Yen Fu in *yüan-ch'ao ming-ch'en shih-lüeh*, 3.5b-9a (stela commemorating the ancestral merits of the princes of Chü-jung); Yü Chi, 23.5b-10a (stela on the same subject). The earlier stela, by Yen Fu, does not mention the allotments in lands and households given Tughtugha. For the reading Tughtugha, possibly doubtful in view of Pelliot's remarks in Pelliot and Hambis, *Histoire des Campagnes de Gengis Khan*, pp. 97-98, see Cleaves in *HJAS*, XVIII (1955), 357 n. 2 and 400, n. 254. In *HJAS*, XIII

(1950), 45, n. 120, Cleaves simply transliterated the same as T'u-t'u-ha and offered no reconstruction. On the term *qarachi*, cf. Pelliot and Hambis, *Historie des Campagnes*, p. 280. For the same term, transliterated ha-la-ch'ih, Hambis in *Le Chapitre CVIII*, p. 62, unaccountably offers the tribal name Qalach, which makes no sense. On the specialized functions of the Imperial Guards generally, see Chavannes in *TP*, V (1904), 429-32. For the establishment of the Qipchaq Guards (*wei*), cf. *YS*, 14.4a; 123.19b-20a; Pelliot and Hambis, *Histoire des Campagnes*, p. 109. The most recent general study of the *t'ou-hsia* feudal establishment in China may be found in Iwamura Shinobu, *Mongoru shakai keizaishi kenkyū*, pp. 404-69.

43. Cf. *YS*, 34.25b-26a.

44. *YS*, 138.6b.

45. *YS*, 138.17a. Bayan was made Vice Censor-in-Chief and later Censor-in-Chief of the Southern (Kiangnan) Branch Censorate, and finally Chief Administrator of Kiangche province.

46. *YS*, 28.7a; 138.5b-6a; 207.1b.

47. El Temür was made Chief Minister of the Court of the Imperial Stud (*T'ai-p'u ch'ing*) in 1325, Assistant Vice Commissioner in the Chief Military Commission in 1326, and Assistant Commissioner in early 1328 (*YS*, 138.6b). Bayan was made Chief Administrator of Kiangsi province in 1325, and in 1326 was shifted to the same position in Honan province (138.17b). Bayan was content to ingratiate himself with the new imperial administration; he voluntarily surrendered about half of the office fields assigned him to the emperor and the Imperial Guards.

48. The outstanding senior members of Qaishan's staff included (1) the Hü'üshin Mongol *Yochichar, a descendant of Boroghul, who was one of Chinggis Quan's close companions called the "Four Heroes." Qaishan enfeoffed *Yochichar as Prince of Ch'i-yang and made him Chancellor of the Right of Ho-lin province, i.e., Mongolia. Of *Yochichar's sons, Taraqai attained the Chancellorship of the Right in the central government under Qaishan, but he died in 1308. Another son, Esen Temür, who succeeded to the princedom, participated in the assassination of Shidebala and was executed by Yesün Temür in 1323. The princely fief of Ch'i-yang was apparently then canceled and the family proscribed. None of *Yochichar's sons participated in the restoration (*YS*, 29.3b-4a; *MWE*, 28.12b-13b; Cleaves in *HJAS*, XVIII [1955], 394, n. 220). (2) Nanggiadai, a Naiman, served as a myriarch under Qaishan but left his service sometime before 1307 and joined Prince Ayurbarwada's entourage at Huai-chou. Thenceforth he was clearly Ayurbarwada's man rather than Quaishan's; Ayurbarwada conferred upon him the princely fief of Hsün-tu in reward for his participation in the arrest of Ananda.

The fief was apparently later canceled, and none of Nanggiadai's sons achieved central positions (*YS*, 131.4a-6b). (3) The Alan Yü-wa-shih, commander of the Alan Guards under Qaishan during the steppe wars, died in 1306; his son and grandson who succeeded to his guards post played no known political roles (*YS*, 132.4b-6b). (4) The Ikires Mongol Ash—a descendant of Botu, who was a close supporter of Chinggis Qan—served with distinction in the steppes and was made Prince of Ch'ang by Qaishan. Of Ash's seven sons, we know only about Balashiri, who succeeded as Prince of Ch'ang, but played no known part in the restoration (Chang Shih-kuan in *Yüan wen-lei,* 25.10b-13b [ancestral stela for Ash]; *MWE*, 23.7a-9b; Hambis, *Le Chapitre CVIII*, pp. 29-34; Cleaves in *HJAS*, XVIII [1955], 407). I have discovered only one exception: Qara Batur, whose father San-pao-nu was executed in 1311 as a member of Qaishan's Central Chancellery (*Shang-shu sheng*), aided in the restoration and was given bureaucratic office (*YS*, 24.3a-b; 32.13b; Yü Chi, 10.1a).

49. *YS*, 24.3a-b, 5a-b.

50. One leading personality associated with Qoshila was the Tangut Li-jih, who disappeared after Qoshila's 1316 revolt. His brother Yeh-erh-chi-ni, who held provincial posts in China after Qaishan's death, of his own decision took no part in the coup, but was recalled to court and made head of the Chief Military Commission in 1329. Their father Ch'i-t'ai-p'u-chi died in 1313 (*MWE*, 121.3a-4a). Qabartu, a man long associated with both Qaishan and Qoshila, was impeached by the Censorate in 1330 (*YS*, 34.22a-b).

51. On the location of the Qangli, see Pelliot and Hambis, *Histoire des Campagnes,* pp. 109-10; and Bretschneider, *Medieval Researches from Eastern Asiatic Sources,* I, 301-2. For the origin of the name Qipchaq, cf. Pelliot in *TP*, XXVII (1930), 280-82. On the various transcriptions of the name, cf. Poppe in *CAJ*, I (1955), 39. Also see below, note 53.

52. *YS*, 138.5b-6a; *MWE*, 121.4b.

53. Pelliot in *JA*, ser. XI, vol. XV (1920), 148-49, 165-67; Pelliot and Hambis, *Histoire des Campagnes,* pp. 102-12; Yen Fu in *Yüan wen-lei,* 3.6a. The sources for Qipchaq history are highly confused, as the studies by Marquart in 1914, Pelliot in 1920, and Ts'en Chung-mien in 1936 attest. In view of the recent availability of Yen Fu's inscription for Tughtugha in the photoreprint of the 1335 edition of the *Yüan-ch'ao ming-ch'en shih-lüeh,* the problem is due for reexamination.

54. Among the leading *se-mu* supporters of the restoration were the following men, none of whom was personally connected with Qaishan: (1) The Onggud Ma Tsu-ch'ang, a noted Confucian (*YS*, 143.1a-3a); (2) the Alan Chiao-hua and his son Jaya'an Buqa, both

guards commanders who were rewarded with bureaucratic office for their support of the restoration (*YS*, 123.17b-18a); (3) the Qarluq Taghai, a former *qarachi* follower of Tughtugha's, who also received civil office for his military support of the restoration (*YS*, 122.7a-8a; Cleaves in *HJAS*, XII [1949], 109, n. 73); (4) the Uighur Alin Temür, a literary man of the Han-lin Academy, and a translator of the Chinese classics. he originally gave his support to Qoshila, but later took office under Tugh Temür (*YS*, 124.5b; H. Franke in *JOS*, II [1955], 302; Cleaves in *HJAS*, XII [1949], 115, n. 121); (5) the Prince of Kao-ch'ang Temür Buqa, nominal ruler (*iduq qut*, or "Holy Majesty") of the defunct Uighur kingdom of Qaraqojo, of whom more will be told in the following chapter; (6) the Onggud Chao Shih-yen, a Confucian whom Temüder nearly succeeded in executing in 1320 (*YS*, 27.10b-11a; 180.5a-10a); (7) the brothers Hui-hui and Nao-nao, known as the "twin jewels," of Qangli descent, and avid Confucians. Hui-hui later clashed with El Temür and went into retirement (*YS*, 143.3a-7b; Sung Lien, *Sung Wen-hsien kung ch'üan-chi*, 41.15b-18b [spirit-way stela for Hui-hui]; Cleaves in *HJAS*, X [1947], 1-12); and (8) Arigh Qaya, an Uighur, and strongly pro-Confucian (*YS*, 137, 5b-10b; Yü Chi, 23.1a-2a [stela tor the new Confucian temple school of the Wu Guards]; Cleaves in *HJAS*, XXVII [1967], 96, n. 1 for the name). All of the above men, with the exception of the Alans, were Turkish.

55. Cf. Feng Ch'eng-chün in *FJHC*, IV, no. 2 (June, 1934), p. 7, where he characterizes the restoration as a struggle of Alans and Qipchaqs against the incumbent Mongols and Moslems. The statement is true only in part. It describes the military aspect of the restoration best, but does not take into account the fact that there were Mongols on both sides.

56. *YS*,138.6a-b; Huang Chin, 8.10b-12a (inscription on the ancestral hall of Qangli Toghto's son Temür Tash).

57. *YS*, 140.9a, 11b. Cf. note 54 above.

58. *YS*, 32.19a-b.

59. *YS*, 34.1a-b, 5b; 138.12b. It was Qoshila who reappointed El Temür.

60. *YS*, 138.13b-14a.

61. For the title *Lu chün-kuo chung-shih*, see Otagi and Murakami in *Iminzoku no Shina tōchi kaisetsu*, p. 125. El Temür shared this title with Bayan and the Prince of Kao-ch'ang Temür Buqa. The *Ta-tu-tu-fu* controlled the Left and Right Qipchaq, the Qarluq, the East-route Mongol, the East-route Qipchaq, and the Lung-i Guards (*YS*, 32.25a; 33.1a; 34.13b; 35.10b; 86.24b-27b; 138.12a-b). El Temür commanded the Lung-i Guards personally.

62. As in the summer of 1330 (*YS*, 34.13a-b; 138.14a).

63. The record of censorial activity (*YS*, 33.13a-36.8a *passim*)

during Tugh Temür's reign shows that it was mainly occupied with impeachments. It indicted twenty-seven men, mainly on the grounds of vice, incompetence, corruption, dereliction, and political opportunism.

64. *YS*, 32.9b; 33.5b; 34.3b; 36.3b. For the K'uei-chang-ko Academy, see H. Franke, *Beiträge zur Kulturgeschichte Chinas unter der Mongolenherrschaft*, pp. 74-79; and Cleaves in *HJAS*, XX (1957), 396, n. 20, 456, n. 136. The K'uei-chang-ko appears to have been an ambiguous institution. Although it served as an academy for the arts (cf. Lu Yu, *Yen-pei tsa-chih*, A.32b), it was primarily, according to the description of it in the *Ching-shih ta-tien,* a Confucian institution (cf. the *Yüan wen-lei*, 41.5a). K'o Chiu-ssu, the subject of Cleaves's article above, was a litterateur who was a member of this academy until his impeachment in 1331.

65. There was a strong demand on the part of such Confucian members of the K'uei-chang-ko as Yü Chi to have greater access to and influence over the emperor; cf. *YS*, 181.9a-b.

66. *YS*, 34.7a; 35.11a, 16a; 89.21b-26b. For one of its component activities, textile manufacture at the northern town of Hsün-ma-lin, cf. Pelliot in *JA*, CCXI (1927), 261-79.

67. *YS*, 32.9b; 34.3b; 95.34a. El Temür's annual allotment as Prince of T'ai-p'ing amounted to 10 ingots (*ting*) of gold, 50 of silver, 10,000 in paper cash, plus 500 *ch'ing* (*ca.* 8,000 acres) of land in the T'ai-p'ing area.

68. *YS*, 32.9b; 34.25b-26a; 35.9a, 11a. According to Tughtugha's biography in *YS*, 128.17b, Qubilai gave him 1,000 taxpaying households in the *lu* of Chien-k'ang (Nanking), Lu-chou (Ho-fei, Anhwei), and Jao-chou (P'o-yang, Kiangsi), and designated these as *qarachi* households. To these were added 1,700 captured households; where these were located is not stated. One of Tughtugha's sons was appointed *darughachi* for the purpose of collecting taxes on the *qarachi* households. The *YS*, section on annual allotments (95.32a), states that the year of these grants was 1284, but in contradiction to the above information, says that Tughtugha as *qarachi* was given 4,000 households in Jao-chou *lu*, and that these together yielded an annual income of 160 ingots in cash. In *Chong'ur's time, 1,436 unregistered households provided an annual income of 200 ingots in cash, which sum *Chong'ur did not collect himself (*YS*, 34.25b-26a). These households must be the remnant of the original 1,700 captured households. Now depleted by 15 percent, these households, located in An-feng, An-ch'ing, and Lu-chou (all in present-day Anhwei province), reverted to El Temür's control. It would thus appear that El Temür did not regain control of any *qarachi* households. Since control over the *qarachi* guards troops seems to have passed at an unspecified date into the hands of a Qangli

family (cf. *YS*, 133.16b), control over the *qarachi* households, which provided revenue for the troops' support, may have passed to this same family also. In the Yüan period, a *ch'ing* was roughly 16 acres; cf. Amano in *Jimbun Kenkyū*, XIII (1962), 806.

69. *YS*, 32.19a; 138.12a. There is a large literature on the term *darqan*, lit. "freeman." Cf. Cleaves in *HJAS*, XXIV (1962-3), 75, n. 80. References to some of the literature may be found in de Rachewiltz's article in *JESHO*, IX (1966), 133, n. 1.

70. *YS*, 35.21a.

71. *YS*, 35.12a. For the *sheng-tz'u* ("live sanctuary") cf. C. K. Yang, *Religion in Chinese Society*, p. 174. Also cf. *YS*, 35.16b.

72. *YS*, 32.17b-18a. For *Chong'ur's four wives, cf. Hambis, *Le Chapitre CVIII*, p. 164, n. 5. Here Hambis offers the starred form *Chagir; on p. 120, n. 3, of the same work, he gives the unstarred form Chakir, She was a descendant of Böchög, a brother of Qubilai. She helped plan El Temür's dawn seizure of the palaces; cf. *YS*, 138.7a.

73. Hambis, *Le Chapitre CVIII*, table 15, opp. p. 164.

74. *YS*, 138.15a. Hambis's table fails to show any of these marriages. We know of only one of his wives by name; she was Örüg, and may have been a daughter of Qoshila. Cf. *YS*, 36.1a; Hambis, *Le Chapitre CVIII*, p. 34, n. 9.

75. *YS*, 38.3b. El Temür was, however, opposed to Toghon Temür's enthronement; see Chapter III.

76. *YS*, 32.16a-18b; 34.7b. Hambis, *Le Chapitre CVIII*, p. 119, n. 4, gives no genealogy for Buqa Temür. For the question of Buqa Temür's exact relationship to El Temür, cf. *MWE*, 155.26a-b.

77. *YS*, 34.1b, 24b-25a; 87.15a-23b.

78. *YS*, 33.1a, 21b; 35.4a, where the text, however, seems corrupt. The *Ta-hsi tsung-yin-yüan* is translated as "Court of Ancestral Sacrifice for Grand Blessing" by Cleaves in *HJAS*, XX (1957), 397, n. 33. Cf. also *YS*, 32.14a, 34.20a, and 87.23b-31b. For the Office for Imperial Guisine (*Hsüan-hui-yüan*), cf. Ratchnevsky, *Un Code des Yuan*, pp. 143-46. On p. 145, n. 1, Ratchnevsky quotes Ch'ien Ta-hsin to the effect that only the *Chung-shu-sheng*, the *Shu-mi-yüan*, and the *Hsüan-cheng-yüan* chose their own officials. But on p. 151, n. 3, he states, correctly, that the *Hsüan-hui-yüan* did have this privilege. For the name Sadun, cf. Cleaves in *HJAS*, XX (1957), 436, n. 29. *Tangkish is a tentative reconstruction by Hambis.

79. Qaishan's revival of the *Shang-shu sheng* was a patently Legalist measure undertaken to raise money to pay the exorbitant expenses his enthronement incurred; on this, see H. Franke, *Geld und Wirtschaft in China unter der Mongolen-Herrschaft*, pp. 82-93. Whereas Qaishan never made much mention of Qubilai, Ayurbar-

wada made Qubilai the precedent-setting beacon-light of the dynasty; cf. *YS*, 26.20a.

80. *YS*, 32.5b. A special school (*Kuo-tzu-chien*) for Moslems, set up in 1289 and again in 1314, was already abolished in 1321; cf. O. Franke, *Geschichte*, IV, 509. There is evidence that the Moslems were afraid of too much public prominence; cf. *YS*. 26.4b.

81. *YS*, 32.2b, 8a, 23b.

82. *YS*, 32.6a, 14a; 33.2a; 134.24b.

83. *YS*, 32.8b-9a.

84. *Yüan wen-lei*, 41.37b (preface to a section of the *Ching-shih ta-tien*).

85. *YS*, 175.7a ff. In April, 1329, Buddhist, Taoist, Nestorian, Jewish, and Moslem merchants were all ordered to pay taxes "according to the old regulations" (*YS*, 33.7b), but in April, 1331, commercial tax exemptions were expressly stated to be in effect for Buddhist and Taoist merchants (*YS*, 35.8a-b).

86. *YS*, 32.10b; Tazaka Kōdō, *Chūgoku ni okeru kaikyō no denrai to sono kōtsū*, I, 813-30.

87. *YS*, 32.17b-25b.

88. *YS*, 32.16b; 33.2a; 178.14a-b.

89. *YS*, 35.26a; 138.14a.

90. *YS*, 34.20b-21a.

Chapter III. Bayan and the Anti-Confucian Reaction

1. *Sheng-wu ch'in-cheng lu*, ed. Wang Kuo-wei, pp. 150-51, 183-84. Barthold's reconstruction of these events in *Turkestan down to the Mongol Invasion* (pp. 361-62, 370-72, 415) has been questioned by Pelliot in *TP*, XXVII (1930), 22. Cf. also *Meng-ku pi-shih*, tr. Hsieh Tsai-hsing, pp. 123-25, 151.

2. Wang Yün, *Ch'iu-chien chi*, 50.2a-3a (ancestral stela for the Uriangqa clan); *YS*, 121.2b; 122.10b-11a; Pelliot and Hambis, *Histoire des Campagnes*, pp. 115-16.

3. The inscriptions composed by Yen Fu and Yü Chi for the Qipchaqs (cf. Chapter II, n. 42) make mention of the fugitive Merkids, but there is nothing of the Qipchaqs in Bayan's ancestral record.

4. Bayan's great-grandfather served in the Imperial Guard. Who was ruling at that time is not stated. His grandfather was a minor officer under the *qaghan* Möngke, and is said to have been killed in the course of the wars against the Southern Sung. Bayan's father served as commander of the guard in the palace of the consort of Jingim (d. 1285), Qubilai's son and heir apparent. Cf. *YS*, 138.16a; Hambis in *JA*, CCXLI (1953), 215-16.

5. The Shang-tu partisans had possession of the imperial seal; cf. Chapter II.

6. *YS*, 138.17b-19a.

7. *YS*, 32.21a; 34.5a-b, 17a.

8. *Ys*, 33.16a; 35.1b; 88.7b-8b. The institution for the heir apparent was known as the *Ch'u-cheng-yüan;* for its organization and subordinate agencies cf. YS, 89.1a-4a. There were 400 personal valets (*sügürchi*, lit. "parasol bearer"). For the term, see Cleaves in *HJAS*, XX (1957), 438, n. 41.

9. *YS*, 35.25a, 26b; 89.21b.

10. *YS*, 32.17b; Hambis in *JA*, CCXLI (1953), 248.

11. *YS*, 35.20a, 21a-b, 26b; 35.8a; 36.8a; 143.9a.

12. *YS*, 36.6a. The other place was Cho-chou (Cho-hsien, Hopei). Why a stela should have been placed there is unclear to me.

13. *YS*, 37.1b. El Tegüs was originally named Gunadara; cf. *YS*, 36.4b; Hambis, *Le Chapitre CVII*, p. 141, n. 2. Tugh Temür had a third son, T'ai-p'ing-nu, of whom practically nothing is known. El Tegüs remained a possible imperial candidate until his murder in 1340 (*YS*, 40,8a; *KRS*, I, 558).

14. *YS*, 37.1b-2a; 38.1b; 138.14b. Irinjibal's edict of accession was composed by Yü Chi; see *Yüan wen-lei*, 9.18a-19a. For the name Irinjibal, cf. Cleaves in *HJAS*, XIII (1950), 35, n. 35.

15. *YS*, 37.5a.

16. *YS*, 143.2b; 181.11b; 183.15b; Huang Chin, *Chin-hua Huang hsien-sheng wen-chi*, 26.14a-b (epitaph for Shih Wei-liang).

17. *YS*, 33.20b. The *Chiang-Huai ts'ai-fu tu-tsung-kuan-fu*, established as the empress's personal patrimony in 1329, managed eleven revenue-producing agencies in the lower Yangtze region (*YS*, 89.20a-21a; Ratchnevsky, *Un Code des Yuan*, p. 293, n. 5). The number of its subordinate agencies, however, varied; at the time of its abolition in 1335 the bureau controlled three such agencies (*YS*, 38.14a-b).

18. *KSWS*, 3a; *YS*, 143.14b. The evidence from the *KRS*, I, 555, does not seem clear enough to determine a definite date. The YS biography of El Temür consists of two parts; the first part, down to 1331, is based upon official documents and laudatory inscriptions; the second, beginning with 1333, is based solely upon anecdotal materials.

19. *YS*, 38.9b.

20. *YS*, 38.15a-b; *KSWS*, 3b.

21. *YS*, 38.14a.

22. *YS*, 38.14b-15b; *KSWS*, 1b-3b.

23. *YS*, 38.14b-15b; 39.7b; *KSWS*, 4a. Toghon Temür's next empress was a member of the Qunggirad clan.

24. Cf. Toghon Temür's edict in *YS*, 38.14b-15a.

25. *YS*, 39.2b, 3b. Bayan received the 1,500 households in Central China, originally given Tughtugha by Qubilai; the house-

holds in Chü-jung which Qaishan had given *Chong'ur as part of his fief; and half of El Temür's brother Sadun's valuables. The other half of Sadun's property went to Ting-chu, a Qangli adherent of Bayan's. For Ting-chu's biography, cf. *HYS*, 210.6a-7a; also *MWE*, 155.24a.

26. *YS*, 39.7a-b. Another adherent of Bayan's, the Tangut Narin, arranged for this. His biography is in *YS*, 142.13a-15b; those of his ancestors are in *YS*, 125.11a-13b. For the name Narin, cf. Pelliot in *JA*, CCXVII (1930), 258.

27. *YS*, 38.4b, 12b; 39.3a.

28. *YS*, 40.1b. Cf. Hambis in *JA*, CCXLI (1953), 245, n. 1, for a discussion of one of these stelae, done in 'Phags-pa script, now cemented into the Great Wall and inaccessible. Bayan's *sheng-tz'u* in Pien-liang and Cho-chou were also refurbished (*YS*, 37.14a).

29. *YS*, 40.2b-3a.

30. *YS*, 38.5a. Bayan's former fief of Shun-ning was of the third grade. For the fief rankings, cf. Hambis, *Le Chapitre CVIII*, pp. v-x.

31. According to an unofficial account (*KSWS*, 4b), Bayan hastened to explain that "Ch'in" referred not to Shensi, as one would expect, but to the city of Kao-yu on the Grand Canal, known also as Ch'in-yu, where he had a fief in property *(shih-i)*. It might be pointed out that Bayan was not the first outsider to obtain a first-class fief; he was preceded in this by El Temür's brother Sadun, appointed Prince of Jung in December, 1333 (*YS*, 38.4b; Hambis, *Le Chapitre CVIII*, pp. 56-59). Jung, however, was a newly created fief, and Sadun was the first holder of it.

32. The note-maker was Yang Yü, cf. H. Franke, *Beiträge zur Kulturgeschichte Chinas unter der Mongolenherrschaft*, pp. 67-68, 71-73, 107-9. For a study of Yang Yü, cf. H. Franke in *JOS*, II (1955), 302-8.

33. Before the destruction of the Qipchaqs, both Sadun and Bayan were allowed three concurrent positions (*YS*, 38.3b). After that, Bayan was sole holder of the privilege.

34. Toghon Temür's probable mother, Mai-lai-ti, a Qarluq, died soon after Toghon Temür's birth. The fate of Irinjibal's mother, Naimanjin, appears uncertain.

35. *YS*, 38.15b; 143.14b; 182.10a. Budashiri's YS biography has been translated by Cleaves in *HJAS*, XIII (1950), 35, n. 35.

36. *YS*, 38.2a.

37. Much has been written on the subject of Toghon Temür's paternity. Ch'uan Heng (*KSWS*, 9b-10b), probably repeating the version current in official circles, has it that Toghon Temür was actually the son of the Chinese scion of the defunct Sung imperial house and a Moslem girl, and had been adopted by Qoshila. See also *YS*, 181.11b, where it is stated that Tugh Temür himself

ordered it written down that Toghon Temür was not a son of Qoshila. In an edict of 1340, issued after the dismissal of Bayan, Toghon Temür for the first time denounced vigorously the aspersions cast on his ancestry; cf. *YS*, 40.6b.

38. During Tugh Temür's reign, there was a certain amount of submerged friction between Bayan and El Temür. As Censor-in-Chief, Bayan appears to have used the censorial voice to pressure the emperor and El Temür for larger rewards. This led first to the appointment of another man as concurrent Censor-in-Chief and later to the removal of Bayan from the Censorate altogether (*YS*, 32.5b, 24a-b, 25b). Following this, in September, 1329, Bayan was appointed Chancellor of the Left, second in command to El Temür within the Central Chancellery. A month later, however, Bayan gave notice of "illness" and departed the capital in order to convalesce, but he was soon called back. In January, 1330, both El Temür and Bayan resigned outright their Chancellery positions, but were "consoled" and reinstated. These charades ended in March, when Bayan left the Chancellery altogether. From that point, as an edict made clear, El Temür was in charge in the Chancellery and Bayan in the Chief Military Commission (*YS*, 33.13a, 18b; 34.1a-b, 5a-b). The Korean sources state that Bayan and El Temür clashed strongly over the question of the Korean royal succession, and that Bayan "hated El Temür's monopoly of power" (*KRS*, I, 555).

39. For the first plot, in July, 1330, cf. *YS*, 34.15b; 40.6b-7a; *KRS*, I, 552. Toghon Temür was exiled in the same month; in 1332, he was moved from Korea to Kwangsi (*YS*, 38.1b; *KRS*, I, 555; H. Franke in *Oriens*, III [1950], 122). For the second plot, cf. *YS*, 34.13a-b; 38.2b, 138.14a.

40. *YS*, 34.26b. Aradnadara died in February 1332 (*YS*, 35.2b).

41. Hsü Yu-jen, 44.1a-6a (inscription for a Confucian temple at Shang-tu).

42. *YS*, 38.17a.

43. *YS*, 38.17b-18a, 183.9a.

44. *YS*, 39.8b.

45. There is a good deal of evidence that many Chinese advanced into office through competence in the Mongol language; several of the epitaphs in Huang Chin's written works, for example, show this. Bayan's order forbidding language study was soon rescinded; cf. *YS*, 182.10b.

46. *YS*, 138.20a.

47. *YS*, 38.17a; 142.12b. This "community chest" system for the support of Confucian students has been described by Ho Ping-ti in *The Ladder of Success in Imperial China*, pp. 203-5.

48. *YS*, 182.10a-b.

49. *KSWS*, 4a-b; cf. Schulte-Uffelage, *Das Keng-shen wai-shih*, pp. 31-32.

50. *YS*, 81.12b; Otagi and Murakami in *Iminzoku no Shina tōchi kaisetsu*, p. 132.

51. *YS*, 142.11b-12a, translated into Japanese by Miyazaki Ichisada in *Tōyōshi kenkyū*, XXIII (1965), 448. For the biographies of Chang Meng-ch'en (Chang Ch'i-yen), Ma Po-yung (Ma Tsu-ch'ang), and Ou-yang Hsüan, cf. *YS*, 182. 1a-4a; 143. 1a-3a; 182. 4a-7a. The three men together with Hsü were all *chin-shih* of 1315.

52. Cf. Yü Chi, *Tao-yüan hsüeh-ku lu*, 6.2a-b (preface to poems written in honor of the *chin-shih* Chou Tung-yang, about to take up his post as assistant magistrate in Ling-ling county); Hsü Yu-jen, *Chih-cheng chi*, 32.3b-4a (a departing message for the inspector [*chao-mo*] Feng). For the bitterness and frustration that existed among the large numbers of underpaid clerks hoping for appointment to the regular bureaucracy, cf. Hu Chih-yü, *Tzu-shan ta-ch'üan-chi*, 23.17b. The clerkships themselves were generally filled on a hereditary basis by the sons of low-ranking officials; cf. Makino Shūji in *Tōhōgaku*, no. 32 (1966), p. 62.

53. *YS*, 183.12b-13a.

54. Cf. *YS*, 185.10a-b.

55. *YS*, 81.7a-b. The triennial *chü-jen* quota was 300, divided equally among the four ethnic classes. The 11 percent figure may be a little too high if the quotas were not filled each time.

56. For example, the Confucian Huang Chin began his career as a local clerk; for committing some misdemeanor he was flogged, and so quit his job and studied. He passed the 1315 examination for the *chin-shih* degree. His biography in *YS*, 181-18b-21a, neglects to mention his clerkly experience; this we learn from Ch'ang-ku Chen-i, *Nung-t'ien yü-hua*, A.20b-21a. Yüan Ming-shan (d. 1322), who was very closely associated with the Confucian movement, came up through the clerkly ranks; cf. *YS*, 181.1a-4a.

57. This is evident from the large number of epitaphs and biographies written by Confucians for relatives or acquaintances who, in order to support their families, are said to have had no recourse but to accept clerkships. Ayurbarwada's Chinese mentor once remarked to him: "There are, after all, worthy men among the clerks; it is simply a matter of encouraging and transforming them." Ayurbarwada supposedly replied: "You are a Confucian, one would think that you would be unsympathetic towards them, yet you make this concession to them. Truly you speak as a superior man." (*YS*, 175.19a-b).

58. Chieh Hsi-ssu, *Chieh Wen-an kung ch'üan-chi*, 9.5b.

59. Chieh Hsi-ssu, 9.5b-7a (a departing message for Yesüderchi). Part of this piece has been translated by Ch'ien and Goodrich in

their English translation of Ch'en Yüan, *Western and Central Asians in China under the Mongols*, p. 38. I have paraphrased rather than translated this long and rather rambling souvenir.

60. These metaphors and illustrations are borrowed from Yüan writings of the 1340s and 1350s; cf. Hu Han, *Hu Chung-tzu chi*, 3.8a-b (a second discussion on medicine); and Liu Chi, *Ch'eng-i-po wen-chi*, p. 109 (a departing message to the magistrate Chang of the subprefecture of Hai-ning, leaving office upon the fulfillment of his term), and p. 188 (miscellaneous explanations).

61. *YS*, 39.6a, 8a-b.

62. *YS*, 39.6b-7a; Lu Shen, *P'ing-hu lu*, p. 1; *KSWS*, 5a. In a rare slip, Cleaves mistranslated *Pang Hu* ("Stick" Hu) as "cudgel barbarians." Cf. *HJAS*, XV (1952), 50.

63. *YS*, 39.8a. His self-given title "Chao king of the Southern Court" makes it clear that he had the Sung Dynasty (960-1279) in mind.

64. *YS*, 39.13b, 14a; 188.9a-b.

65. *YS*, 39.8a; 40.1b.

66. Yeh Tzu-ch'i, *Ts'ao-mu-tzu*, 3.6b.

67. *YS*, 39.8b-9a; 182.10b.

68. *YS*, 182.10b.

69. *YS*, 143.10b-11a.

70. *KSWS*, 10b-11a.

71. Ch'ang-ku Chen-i, *Nung-t'ien yü-hua*, A.9a-b.

72. *YS*, 39.9a; Ch'ang-ku Chen-i, A.9b; and *KSWS*, 5a, all report the same rumor.

73. *YS*, 39.12a.

74. *KSWS*, 5a.

75. Otagi in *Iminzoku no Shina tōchi kaisetu*, p. 121; Otagi and Murakami in *ibid.*, p. 132; *YS*, 81.5b. Northern Chinese made up 15 percent of the registered households, and Southern Chinese 82 percent, based on figures of the late thirteenth century. The non-Chinese were encouraged to take the more difficult examinations, with the reward of appointment at a higher grade if they passed. Examples of examination questions put to non-Chinese candidates may be found in Huang Chin, 20.1a ff.

76. *YS*, 81.12b. Miyazaki Ichisada makes the assumption I use here in *Tōyōshi Kenkyū*, XXIII (1965), 447-48.

77. Otagi and Murakami in *Iminzoku*, p. 132.

78. A possible exception is Ma Tsu-ch'ang, *chin-shih* of 1315, who was for a time a Vice Commissioner in the Chief Military Commission. Cf. *YS*, 143.2b; Ch'en Yüan, *Western and Central Asians*, p. 78.

79. On the basis of the *chin-shih* list of 1333, Ho Ping-ti notes that "practically all the Mongol candidates who gave their family statuses were from families of Mongol garrisons." Cf. *The Ladder*

of Success in Imperial China, p. 55. The case of Chieh Hsi-ssu's friend, the Qarluq Yesüderchi, was thus not an isolated one. On the provincial level, relations between the sons of Mongol or *se-mu* commanders and the Chinese scholar gentry were sometimes close, and led, as in Yesüderchi's case, to intermarriage. The Suldus (Mongol) Örüg Buqa, whose father was a chiliarch in Kiangche, studied under the famous Confucian teacher Han Hsing and attained the *chin-shih* degree in 1333 (*YS*, 145.4b-5a; 190.12b-13b). Although he obtained no degree, the Salji'ud (Mongol) Tegüder, a commander in Kiangche, was able to discuss the classics with the local scholar gentry (Cheng Yü, *Shih-shan hsien-sheng wen-chi*, 144(7).2b stela of appreciation). The Baya'ud (Mongol) Tai Buqa, born in the South China coast city of T'ai-chou, studied under the Confucian master Chou Jen-jung, and at the age of seventeen attained the *chin-shih* degree. He was also a calligrapher, author, and compiler. His father was a local civil official (*YS*, 143.14a-17b; 190.16a-b; Pelliot and Hambis, *Histoire des Campagnes*, p. 106). Hsü Yu-jen devotes an inscription to a Khotanese Moslem who had a Chinese mother and passed the *chin-shih* examination of 1315 (*Chih-cheng chi*, 51.4b-8a). The examination system was important to these provincials, who had little opportunity to enter the Imperial Guards at Ta-tu, the main recruiting base for Mongol and *se-mu* officials.

80. The most famous examples of such Confucian patrons were the Jalair clansmen, descendants of Muqali. Many other examples could be selected from among the Qanglis, the Uighurs, etc.

81. *YS*, 139.3a.

82. *YS*, 139.1a-5b.

83. Yü Chi, *Tao-yüan hsüeh-ku lu*, 23.1a-2a; also cf. Chapter II, note 54. We last hear of Arigh Qaya in September, 1334, when he was dismissed as Chief Administrator (*YS*, 38.10b). In April, 1336, his personal library was confiscated (*YS*, 39.1b). Arigh Qaya's is one of the YS biographies which was never completed; cf. *YS*, 137.5b-10b, of which the source was probably an officially ordered stela of merit (*YS*, 35.17a).

84. *YS*, 145.1b.

85. *YS*, 38.16b; 138.15b-16a; Huang Chin, *Chin-hua Huang hsien-sheng wen-chi*, 25.6b (spirit-way stela for the Kereid Pa-shih). For the term Qonqor, cf. Pelliot in *TP*, XXXVII (1944), 77, n. 1.

86. H. Franke, *Beiträge zur Kulturgeschichte Chinas*, p. 101.

87. Temür Buqa's *YS* biography (*YS*, 122.4a-5a) stops with the cession of his titles to his younger brother in 1329. Ch'en Ssu-ch'ien owed his career to Temür Buqa's recommendation; cf. *YS*, 184.9b. Franke's doubt (*Beiträge*, p. 101, n. 4) whether this Temür Buqa was indeed the ex-*iduq qut* appears to be unnecessary; cf. Liu Chi,

Ch'eng-i po wen-chi, p. 154 (inscription commemorating the official accomplishments of the Kiang-Huai salt transport commissioner Sung).

88. *YS*, 39.7b; 138.16a; *KSWS*, 4b.

89. *YS*, 183.3a. Cf. also *YS*, 41.17a; 186.2a; 187.8a; 139.5a.

90. *YS*, 117.6b-8a, 9a; 144.8b. For the correct order of Qubilai's sons, cf. Pelliot, *Notes*, I, 569.

91. *KSWS*, 6b-8a; also cf. *YS*, 40.3a; 186.6a-b. Other references, mostly brief, to the Fan Meng incident may be found in *YS*, 185.3a; 139.4a; Huang Chin, 24.7b (spirit-way stela for Tung Shou-chien); Liu Chi, pp. 153-54; Su T'ien-chüeh, *Tzu-ch'i wen-kao* (Tientsin, 1931), 27.15a-17b.

92. *YS*, 139.4a; 185.3a; Liu Chi, pp. 153-54.

93. *YS*, 139.4a.

94. *YS*, 138.25b.

95. I know of only one man who was personally distressed over the murder of Qoshila: the Qangli Hui-hui (cf. Chapter II, note 54).

96. On the overthrow of Bayan, cf. *YS*, 40.3b-4a; 138.21a-22a, 24b-26a; *KSWS*, 8b-9b; Ch'ang-ku Chen-i, B.16b-17a; Sung Lien, *Sung Wen-hsien kung ch'üan-chi*, 41.7a (account of conduct for Wu Chih-fang); and Yang Yü in H. Franke, *Beiträge zur Kulturgeschichte Chinas*, pp. 33-34, 61-62. Yang Yü had the foresight to have the emperor provide extra rice supplies ahead of time for the people of the captial in order to prevent rising prices caused by the locking of the gates.

Chapter IV. The Triumph of Confucian Politics

1. *YS*, 40.6a-7a (dated July 9, 1340; the same text is given in *KRS*, I, 558, there dated May 25); 40.8a-10a; 36.10a; *KSWS*, 9b.

2. The use of the term *keng-hua* in this context may be found in Huang Chin, 26.15a (spirit-way stela for Shih Wei-liang); and in Wang I, *Wang Chung-wen kung chi*, 168(3).6a-7a, where he speaks of the Chih-cheng period as being one of *keng-hua*.

3. *YS*, 142.12b; 182.10b. Hsü Yu-jen's *YS* biography has been translated by Cleaves in *HJAS*, XV (1952), 46, n. 54.

4. These were Shih Wei-liang (Huang Chin, 26.15a); Keng Huan; and Chang Yu-liang (*YS*, 40.5a).

5. *YS*, 40.8b; *MWE*, 16.11a-b. The *KSWS* (11b ff.) insists that a certain *iduq qut* was Chancellor of the Right during this time, an assertion for which I have found no corroborating evidence whatever. It may be that the KSWS author somehow confused the present Temür Buqa with the ex-*iduq qut* Temür Buqa, who was executed by Bayan (cf. Chapter III, note 87). The KSWS is often inaccurate, especially for the period before 1351.

6. *YS*, 140.1a-3b, 9a; *MWE*, 157.34b; Hsü Yu-jen, 49.1a-5a.

7. *YS*, 138.25b.

8. *YS*, 113.3b-4a.

9. *YS*, 181.20a; 182.2b-3a, 5b-6a; Sung Lien, 41.11b (account of conduct for Huang Chin).

10. For the translation "Classics Mat," cf. Cleaves in *HJAS* XIV (1951), 35, n. 13. The establishment of the Classics Mat had long been a Confucian demand in the Yüan period; cf. *YS*, 178.12b, and Wang Chieh, *Wang Wen-chung chi*, 4.3b-4a, where it was put first in the famous eight points on government which Wang Chieh submitted to the emperor Temür. It was finally set up under Yesün Temür. For its interruption under Bayan, cf. *YS*, 187.1b. Before the reopening of the Classics Mat, the young emperor Toghon Temür had already learned the rudiments of Confucian political and moral ideology from his tutors, the Uighurs Alin Temür and his son Sharabal. Cf. *YS*, 124.5b, and H. Franke, *Beiträge zur Kulturgeschichte Chinas*, pp. 63, 66.

11. For example, it was probably Huang Chin who recommended Cheng T'ao of the famous Cheng clan of P'u-chiang (in present-day Chekiang province) to the Classics Mat, where he compiled the discussions held there into a book, now apparently lost. Cf. Wang I, 163(3).6a-7a, and 172(7).3a. The importance of the appointment in the eyes of the region may be discerned in Wang I's disquisition on the true nature of the Confucian, presented to Cheng on his departure; cf. *ibid.*, 166(1).21b-23b.

12. These included Yang Yü of Hang-chou and Wu Chih-fang of P'u-chiang, plus Fan Hui from Kiangsi and a few others whom I am unable to identify.

13. The basic source for the life of Wu Chih-fang is Sung Lien's detailed account of conduct in *Sung Wen-hsien kung ch'üan-chi*, 41.5a-8b. The Confucian slogan Wu used to justify the ouster was *ta-i mieh-ch'in*, translated by Legge as "great righteousness is supreme over the affections" (cf. *The Chinese Classics* [London and Hong Kong, 1872] Vol. V, part I, p. 17), but perhaps translatable in the circumstances of 1340 as "for the sake of great righteousness, one may destroy relatives." The phrase is from the *Tso chuan*. Wu Chih-fang died in 1356. His son Wu Lai was a noted Confucian philosopher; cf. *YS*, 181.21a-b; Sung Lien, 41.1a-2b; and E. H. Schafer in *Oriente Poliano* (Rome, 1957), pp. 67-69.

14. He patronized Wu Chih-fang, and also one Lou Shih-pao from the same area; cf. Sung Lien, 49.11b-13a.

15. *YS*, 40.5b.

16. *YS*, 40.8a. On this matter, see Ch'en Yüan, *Western and Central Asians*, pp. 226-75 and esp. pp. 249-52. The Qipchaq Sadun, for example, had married his maternal aunt; cf. Huang Chin, 26.13b. In November, 1340, a non-Chinese censor further proposed

that Moslem and Jewish women be forbidden to marry their uncles (*YS*, 40.9a).

17. *YS*, 40.8b; 138,23a, 26b.

18. *KSWS*, 11b-12a, 16b.

19. Thus the philosopher Cheng Yü of She county in Kiangche discussed approvingly several precedents from T'ang history, which he must certainly have written with recent Yüan events in mind. On the justifiability of T'ang T'ai-tsung's removal of his father from the throne (for which read the justifiability of Toghto's removal of Bayan and/or Majartai), cf. Cheng Yü, 140(3).1b-3a; for his strictures against the T'ang empress Wu (for which read his approval of the elimination of the grand empress dowager Budashiri), cf. *ibid.*, 140(3).3a-4a and 4a-6a. In a preface to Cheng Yü's writings the Confucian Wang I expressed his earlier strong diagreement with these views; cf. Wang I, 178(13).32b-33b.

20. *YS*, 40.4b.

21. *YS*, 39.15a; 92.15b-16a; 138.26b, 27b; 190.22b-23a.

22. *YS*, 138.26b, 28a.

23. *YS*, 40.8a. The Tangut Irinjinbal, who suffered exile under Bayan, was appointed to this post on August 1, 1340; Esen Temür was appointed to the same post on August 24. Probably they served concurrently for a time. This close alliance between the Chancellor of the Right and the Censor-in-Chief seems to have prompted the demand on the part of the lower censors that they be allowed to memorialize the throne directly, without going through the Censor-in-Chief (*YS*, 187.4b).

24. For example, Yü Chi's proposal during the reign of Yesün Temür, suggesting that the need for the annual rice shipments from the Yangtze delta could be obviated if the North China coast were dyked and reclaimed, was turned down on the grounds that it would only open opportunities for official corruption (*YS*, 181.7b-8a; Yü Chi, 6.9b-10a [a departing message to two envoys sent to offer sacrifice to the goddess of the sea]). Similarly, his plan to take advantage of the Shensi famine of 1328 to carry out a basic redistribution of land on the ancient well-field model was not given serious consideration (*YS*, 181.8b; cf. Chapter II, note 31).

25. *YS*, 41.1b; *KSWS*, 14a-b.

26. *YS*, 181.17b; 182.6a. Another project undertaken at this time was the compilation of the *Chih-cheng t'iao-ko;* cf. Ratchnevsky, *Un Code des Yuan*, pp. xix, xxi ff. For the *Chin-shih* compilation, see Chan Hok-lam in *JOS*, VI (1967), 125-63.

27. *YS*, 182.11a; *KSWS*, 12a-b.

28. *YS*, 138.26b-27a.

29. *YS*, 66.17b-18a.

30. *YS*, 66.18a-b. The *YS* historiographers add: "We append this incident here as a warning to those who may in future recklessly discuss hydraulics."

31. *YS*, 40.11a-15b, *passim;* 41.2b.

32. *YS*, 41.1a-2a.

33. *YS*, 40.13a, 15a; 41.2a-b.

34. *YS*, 138.27b-28a; *KSWS*, 16a-b.

35. Cleaves in *HJAS*, XIX (1956), 394, n. 220; Hambis, *Le Chapitre CVIII*, pp. 145-48. For the reading Arughtu, cf. Hambis, p. 96.

36. *YS*, 139.12b-13a.

37. *YS*, 139.13b-14a. According to Arughtu's biography (*YS*, 139.13b-14a), he resigned at once after being attacked by the censor. "Arughtu's in-laws were all dissatisfied over this. They pleaded: 'What you the Chancellor did was entirely good. The censor spoke nonsense. Why don't you see the emperor and state your case? The emperor will certainly understand.' Arughtu replied: 'I am the heir of Boghorchu. Do you think I want to be Chancellor? But when the emperor so appointed me, I dared not refuse. Now a censor has denounced me and I must go at once. The Censorate was set up by Shih-tsu (Qubilai). If I oppose the censor, then I also oppose Shih-tsu. Speak of it no more.' "

38. *YS*, 41.11a-b.

39. *YS*, 140.1b, 2b, 10a-b. In 1342 as Chancellor of the Left of Kiangche province, Berke Buqa was credited with highly popular and effective measures for the relief of the Hang-chou fire. Both he and his first-ranking Chief Administrator, the Qangli Temür Tash, handled the distribution of famine relief in 1345.

40. *YS*, 41.6a-b.

41. *YS*, 41.6a. For the reading *a'urugh*, cf. Cleaves in *HJAS*, XII (1949), 112, n. 102; and in *HJAS*, XXVII (1967), 92, n. 71. On the *a'urugh*, cf. Pelliot in *JA*, CCXVII (1930), 259; and Iwamura Shinobu in *Tōhō gakuhō*, no. 24 (1954), 19, n. 5.

42. *YS*, 41.9a.

43. *YS*, 41.10b-11a.

44. *YS*, 41.8b.

45. *YS*, 185.12b.

46. *YS*, 183.19b.

47. Ch'ang-ku Chen-i, B.2b-3a.

48. *YS*, 41.9b-42.3b *passim*. This was a rising of Yao tribesmen under one Wu T'ien-pao.

49. Thus Chieh Hsi-ssu viewed the various frontier disturbances with alarm, fearing that similar trouble could easily flare up in China proper. Cf. Chieh Hsi-ssu, 9.10b-11b (a departing message to Hsieh

Yüan-p'u). Also cf. Sung Lien, 10.19b-21b (epitaph for Chou Ting). The Kiangsi Confucian teacher Chou Ting was profoundly worried about the possibility of general rebellion in China.

50. *YS*, 41.11b.

51. *YS*, 41.12a.

52. *YS*, 140.10b-11a. *KSWS*, 17a-b, purports to reproduce some of Toghon Temür's personal exhortations.

53. *YS*, 41.12a, 13b; 140.4b. During 1347 the emperor asked for candid advice on how his rule might be improved, provoking at least one "ten-thousand word memorial" and undoubtedly many more. Cf. Wang I, 167(2).25a-26a. It is surprising that the *YS* does not mention this move of the emperor's, which was very praiseworthy from a Confucian standpoint.

54. Cf. Hsiao Ch'i-ch'ing, pp. 59-61.

55. Two old officials at the end of their careers, Ching Yen and Wang I, served as Chief Administrators in 1328 and 1329 respectively. For their biographies, cf. *HYS*, 201.7a-10a, 14a.

56. *YS*, 27.6b; 169.1a-3b, 179.1a-3a.

57. *YS*, 41.6a; 140.3b, Ch'ien Ta-hsin, *Nien-erh-shih k'ao-i*, p. 1507. Ho Wei-i's son Ho Chün was similarly renamed Esen Qudu (*YS*, 140.8a).

58. *YS*, 139.4b, 5b. Dorji acted very much in the Confucian tradition of the Jalair house. Very similar roles were played by his distant relatives An-t'ung, whom Qubilai used as a figurehead Chancellor of the Right mainly in order to exploit his popularity with the Confucianists; and Baiju, a Confucianizing Chancellor under the emperor Shidebala (cf. Hsiao Ch'i-ch'ing, pp. 63-65; *YS*, 137.11a-18a). An-t'ung and his grandson Baiju were descendants of the oldest son of Muqali's son Bo'ol; Dorji's branch of the Jalair descended from the second son of Bo'ol. Cf. Hambis, *Le Chapitre CVIII*, table 5, opp. p. 40). "As prime minister, Dorji was committed to preserving the transcendant order *(ta-t'i)*, while T'ai-p'ing (i.e., Ho Wei-i) took an equal share in managing the administration. At the time, the powers of state were mainly exercised by T'ai-p'ing, and many men attached themselves to him. Dorji was impassive in the face of this, and did not try to compete with him. But T'ai-p'ing could also be deferential and exhaust decorum; people inside and out hailed him as a worthy prime minister" (*YS*, 139.5b). For Muqali and Bo'ol (Bōl), cf. de Rachewiltz in *JESHO*, IX (1966), 127-28.

59. *Ys*, 41.14a.

60. *YS*, 41.15a, 16b. Cheng Yü's inscription of 1348, which describes the honors accorded the Kereid Mongol Qara Buqa, *darughachi* in Hui-chou *lu*, Kiangche province, notes that on April 28 a panel of six men recommended Qara Buqa's name to the

emperor. The six men included two Imperial Guardsmen, a *sügürchi* (parasol-bearer) and an *üdüchi* (sword-bearer); the Palace Censor Bolod Temür, the Supervising Secretary Maiju; the Assistant Administrator Fu-shou; and the Bureau Director Teri Temür. On June 8 an envoy from the capital arrived in Hui-chou with the honors, and the crowds thronged the streets in order to see him. The inscription ends with a short account of the emperor's recent and praiseworthy attempts to improve local government. Cf. Cheng Yü, 144(7).1a-2a.

61. *YS*, 41.16a. The *she*, or community system, was set up under Qubilai to inculcate better farming methods among the peasants and keep order in the villages. The system operated on a sub-official level; the community chiefs *(she-chang)* were unpaid local men, and probably few of them performed, or were capable of performing, as the government intended. Cf. Schurmann, *Economic Structure*, pp. 43-48.

62. *YS*, 41.16a; 42.1b; 185.17a.

63. *YS*, 41.4a; 66.1a.

64. *YS*, 41.4a-b; 66.1a-b; K'ung Ch'i, *Ching-chai chih-cheng chih-chi*, 3.25a.

65. *YS*, 41.4b-42.2a *passim*. The Baya'ud Tai Buqa, a *chin-shih* and President of the Board of Rites, was dispatched by the emperor to sacrifice to the god of the Yellow River. Tai Buqa proposed getting laborers to stir up the silt and sand deposits where the prospective new bed of the Yellow River would enter the sea, so that the tides could take away the loose sediment. The project was begun but ended half completed, because the laborers were needed to open military-agricultural colonies (*YS*, 143.15a).

66. The Yellow River flooded in August, 1345; December, 1347; and February, 1348 (*YS*, 41.5b, 13b, 14b).

67 Nakayama Hachirō in *Wada hakushi koki kinen tōyōshi ronsō* (Tokyo, 1960), p. 653.

68. *YS*, 97.9b-11a; 187.5b; *KSWS*, 20a. In May, 1349, it was necessary to cut salt production at Ho-chien by 30,000 *yin* owing to flooding (*YS*, 42.1b).

69. The government was hard pressed for cash to meet expenses. In 1347 the Board of Revenue complained that, because of the high cost of suppressing rebellions in Yunnan and Hukuang, it could no longer meet expenditures. It urged that cuts be made in the ranks of the Imperial Guards in order to release funds for current need. The emperor, overwhelmed by protesting guardsmen, had to put a three-year moratorium on the question of reducing guards expenditures (*YS*, 41.13a).

70. *YS*, 97.1b-2a. Around 1342 it was reported that only ten of an original forty patrol boats were still in existence, and that

these actually never left port (*YS*, 183.4a-b). A Yüan picul was roughly 2.8 bushels. Cf. Amano in *Jimbun Kenkyū*, XIII (1962), 806.

71. E.g., see the cases of piracy in 1344 listed by Wang I, 173(8).19a-21b (record of law cases in Shao-hsing).

72. *YS*, 143.15b; *MS*, III, 1570; Yeh Tzu-ch'i, 3.6b-7a; *Lu-ch'iao chih-lüeh*, 6.7a-8a (Chang Chu's spirit-way stela for Fang Kuo-chang). According to Chang Chu's flattering account of Fang Kuo-chen's elder brother, Fang Kuo-chen voluntarily took the captured chiliarch to the Kiangche Administrative Vice Commissioner, who rewarded the Fangs out of gratitude. This version does not square with the other accounts. According to *YS*, 143.15b, Fang Kuo-chen refused the title offered him. According to *MS*, III, 1570, Fang accepted the title *Ting-hai wei*, or "Commandant who Pacifies the Seas."

73. *YS*, 186.8a-b. The Fang Kuo-chen affair was used as ammunition in the censorial attack upon Berke Buqa; cf. *YS*, 186.1b-2a.

74. *YS*, 194.7a.

75. Even with the development of an efficient maritime route for shipping Yangtze delta grain to the capital, the inland canal transport routes continued to be used for a certain amount of such shipping. On the development of the Yüan maritime and canal routes, see Lo Jung-pang in *FEQ*, XIII (1953-54), 263-85; and Schurmann, *Economic Structure*, pp. 108-16.

76. *YS*, 120.6a; 205.29b.

77. Berke Buqa's father was Aqutai, executed by Ayurbarwada for having backed Ananda for the throne in 1307. Cf. Chapter I.

78. *YS*, 41.13b, 14a. On the Branch Censorates of the Yüan period, cf. Hucker, *The Censorial System of Ming China*, pp. 26-27.

79. *YS*, 41.13b, 16a; 140.5a.

80. *YS*, 186.1b-2a.

81. *YS*, 39.13a, 15b. This move of Bayan's was strictly illegal in that Qubilai had set no precedent for it. It was a point the opposition seized upon when marshaling support for Bayan's overthrow.

82. *YS*, 138.25a-b; *MWE*, 125.2a.

83. *YS*, 41.3b; *MWE*, 127.2a.

84. *YS*, 139.8b-9a. Dorjibal was also descended from the second son of Bo'ol. As a participant in the Classics Mat in 1341, he compiled a book of Neo-Confucian maxims which the emperor entitled "Complete Instructions on the Fundamentals of Rule." Cf. *YS*, 139.8a, 12a. Huang Chin wrote an inscription for his study; cf. Huang Chin 14.7b-9a (inscription for the Pao-chung t'ang).

85. *YS*, 140.3a; 145.2a; 185.12a-b. Li Chi was a *chin-shih* of 1327. Ko Yong-bok's biography is in *KRS*.

86. *YS*, 182.3a.

87. *YS*, 41.14b; 142.14a; 185.3b-4a.

88. *YS*, 42.2a; 205.29b-30a.

89. *YS*, 39.7b; *MWE*, 19.18b-19b. For the reading of Qudu, cf. Pelliot and Hambis, *Histoire des Campagnes*, pp. 104, 284-85.

90. *YS*, 181.17a-b; Yamamoto Takayoshi in *Tōhōgaku*, no. 11 (1955), pp. 81-99.

Chapter V. In Pursuit of "Merit and Profit"

1. *YS*, 42.2a-b; 140.3a-b, 5b; 205.29b-30a.

2. These lower-level men were Wu-ku-sun Liang-chen, Kung Po-sui, Ju Chung-po, and Beg Temür (*YS*, 138.28a-b). Wu-ku-sun was a Jürched, classified as Northern Chinese during the Yüan period. He obtained office through the *yin*, or hereditary route (*YS*, 187.1a-4a). Kung Po-sui was from the Huai region; he was a former protégé of the Onggut Confucian Ma Tsu-ch'ang (*YS*, 181.11a). The other two men I cannot identify.

3. *YS*, 141.1a; *HYS*, 210.6a. T'u Chi (*MWE*, 155.24a) thinks that Ting-chu was probably a descendant of Ya-ya, and hence related to the Qangli Toghto and his sons Temür Tash, Dash Temür, etc. Toghto refused to allow Ting-chu to retire when he asked to do so in October, 1349 (*YS*, 42.3a). The names Temür Tash and Dash Temür are peculiar as a pair, for one means "iron rock" and the other "rock iron." For the d/t alternation in Turkish, cf. Barthold, *Four Studies*, III, 124; and Cleaves in *HJAS*, XII (1949), 527-28. However, Huang Chin (8.10b) gives the first name as Temür Dash.

4. *YS*, 42.2b; 125.17b; *MWE*, 155.16b; 157.37b. For the name Chösgem, cf. Cleaves in *HJAS*, XV (1952), 30.

5. For the name Üch Qurtuqa, cf. Pelliot and Hambis, *Histoire des Campagnes*, p. 240; and L. Rásonyi in *AOASH*, XII (1961), 52. The name in Turkish means literally "three old women" and has a magical significance. Üch Qurtuqa was a son of the Qangli Toghto.

6. *YS*, 184.14a; 185.11b.

7. *KSWS*, 19a-b; cf. Schulte-Uffelage, *Das Keng-shen wai-shih*, p. 56.

8. *YS*, 42.3a; 92.5b; 183.10a-b. Li Hao-wen, a Northern Chinese and a *chin-shih* of 1321, assiduously complied a number of texts consisting mainly of extracts from Confucian works for Ayushiridara's education. Cf. *YS*, 183.10a-11b. Ayushiridara began learning Uighur letters in May, 1348, and Chinese characters in July, 1349 (*YS*, 41.15a; 42.2a).

9. *YS*, 42.3a.

10. *HYS*, 213.4a-b.

11. *YS*, 186.8a.

12. *YS*, 42.5a; *HYS*, 213.4b; *MWE*, 45.5b. For Hsieh Che-tu's family, established in Kiangsi province, cf. Ou-yang Hsüan, *Kuei-*

chai chi, 11.3a-13a. In 1343 the Confucian Chieh Hsi-ssu, also from Kiangsi, had proposed the issuance of copper cash, but he was turned down by Toghto at that time (*YS*, 181.17b).

13. *YS*, 42.5b, 8b; 97.5a. On the currency reform of 1350, see H. Franke, *Geld und Wirtschaft in China unter der Mongolen-Herrschaft*,pp. 93-100; Ch'üan Han-sheng in *CYYY*, XV (1948), 41-43; and Maeda Naonori in *Rekishigaku Kenkyū*, no. 126 (1947), p. 47. If I understand correctly Iwamura Shinobu's argument that the reform was intended to stop inflation, I disagree with it entirely. Cf. Iwamura in *Tōhō gakuhō*, no. 34 (1964), pp. 122 ff. Gordon Tullock's article in *Economic History Review*, 2d ser., IX (1956-57), 393-407, is disappointingly inadequate.

14. *YS*, 43.1a. Of this amount, 1,900,000 ingots was in the new currency, and 100,000 in the old. The ingot (*ting*) was a unit equivalent to 50 taels in silver; cf. L.S. Yang, *Money and Credit in China*, pp. 45-46. On Yüan currency units, see Maeda Naonori in *Shakaikeizai shigaku*, XIV (July, 1944), 1-22.

15. On the Yüan paper money system in general, besides H. Franke's monograph mentioned above, see also Schurmann, *Economic Structure*, pp. 131-45. Since the withdrawal of the precious metal reserves by the financier Ahmad after 1276, it appears that the paper money was no longer fully backed. Cf. Ch'üan Han-sheng, *CYYY*, XV, 18-20; and Maeda in *Rekishigaku kenkyū*, no. 126 (1947), p. 44. Paper money was instituted in China by Qubilai largely in order to prevent the drain of Chinese silver to Central Asia and the Middle East; cf. Blake in *HJAS*, II (1937), 325-28.

16. The Yellow River project, completed in December, 1351, cost a total of 1,845,636 ingots in new (Chung-t'ung) paper currency; cf. *YS*, 66.10b. During 1351 the government printed a total of 1,900,000 ingots in new currency; cf. note 14 above. The implication seems clear that the government financed the project by using this unbacked, or inadequately backed, paper money to pay for materials and labor.

17. Cf. Chapter II, note 14.

18. Cf. H. Franke in *Oriens*, II (1949), 226. For the years 1292-93, Schurmann calculates that salt revenues covered somewhat over 50 percent of government expenditures. Franke's figures derive from explicit data for the year 1329, however. Cf. Schurmann, *Economic Structure*, pp. 169-70.

19. For salt prices, which rose from about 1/5 ingot per *yin* in 1276 to 3 ingots in 1315, cf. Schurmann, p. 172. In 1342 the price was still 3 ingots; cf. Maeda in *Rekishigaku kenkyū*, no. 126 (1947), p. 33. For salt production quotas down to 1329, cf. Schurmann, p. 190. For the downward revision of salt quotas after that date, cf. *YS*, 97.9b-25b.

20. *YS*, 184.17a.

21. *K'un-shan hsien-chih*, 9.8b-9a.

22. *YS*, 42.5b; Wang I, 185(20).3b-4a (epitaph for Chao Kuan-kuang); Hsü I-k'uei, *Shih-feng kao*, 3.11b-12a (epitaph for Tsou Shih-wen); *Che-chiang t'ung-chih*, 33.30a.

23. Cf. Wang I, 185(20).4a; 168(3).12b (a departing message for T'ang Tzu-ch'eng).

24. *YS*, 140.12a-b; Hsü I-k'uei, 14.1b-2a (epitaph for Yeh Ying-huai). Dash Temür was a son of the Qangli Toghto's.

25. *YS*, 140.12a-b; 143.15a.

26. According to the Confucian Yeh Tzu-ch'i, Chia Lu was all along a staunch Toghto partisan and had had a hand in the Chin-k'ou canal project—the chief purpose of which, according to Yeh, was to provide irrigation. Yeh Tzu-ch'i was, however, a hostile witness. Cf. Nakayama in *Wada hakushi koki kinen tōyōshi ronsō* (Tokyo, 1960), p. 651. But this might explain why it was the emperor, rather than the Berke Buqa leadership, that appointed Chia Lu at that time.

27. *YS*, 138.28b; 186.18a-b.

28. Actually, public opinion did not seem to be so definite on this point. Earlier, *ca.* 1344, the Tangut Confucian Yü Ch'üeh was of the opinion that the natural bed of the Yellow River lay north of the Shantung peninsula, and that it should be tamed by diverting its lower course into multiple channels; cf. Yü Ch'üeh, *Ch'ing-yang chi*, 129(1).2a-4a (a departing message for the clerk-registrar [*ching-li*] Yüeh Yen-ming [Örüg Buqa], about to take up position in the Branch Directorate of Water Control); and *YS*, 145.4b-5a. Also at this time, however, the Confucian Sung Lien took what was essentially the position of Chia Lu and Toghto, that the best route lay south of the Shantung peninsula, and away from the Huai River system. Sung asserted that many other people shared this view. See Sung Lien, 43.1b-2a (a discussion of Yellow River control). A certain Wang Hsi, whom I cannot identify, proposed dividing the Yellow River in two sections along its lower course, half flowing north of the Shantung peninsula, and the other half south, the latter along much the same route suggested by Sung Lien. Cf. Wang Hsi, *Chih-ho t'u-lüeh*, with maps. For the name Tughlugh, cf. Cleaves in *HJAS*, XII (1949), 55, n. 152. For the reading of Örüg, cf. Cleaves in *HJAS*, XV (1952), 30.

29. *YS*, 186.18a-b.

30. Yü Ch'üeh, 133(5).5b (colophon to Ho-lu I-chih's "Song of the Old Man of Ying-chou").

31. *YS*, 41.7b-8a; *KSWS*, 20a; Liu Chi, p. 154.

32. Chieh Hsi-ssu, 9.11a-b.

33. *YS*, 41.13a, 14a.

34. *YS*, 41.9b, 14a, 17a.

35. *YS*, 42.5a; 92.13a.

36. *YS*, 42.6a, 7a; 92.17b.

37. *TTSL*, I, 276. The Uighur Lien Qaishan Qaya, *chin-shih* of 1321 and Vice Administrator of the Right of Honan province, protested the whole project on the grounds that the labor recruitment was causing disturbances everywhere (*YS*, 145.4a).

38. *YS*, 42.6b.

39. *YS*, 66.2a.

40. *YS*, 66.10b. Ou-yang Hsüan's commemorative inscription on the rerouting of the Yellow River has been copied verbatim into the *YS* (66.2a-10b).

41. Cf. L. S. Yang's remarks on this in *Les Aspects Économiques des Travaux Publics dans la Chine Imperiale*, pp. 44-46.

42. *YS*, 42.7a; *MS*, III, 1560; *KSWS*, 20a ff.; Yeh Tzu-ch'i, 3.7b-8a; Yen Han-sheng in *Li-shih chiao-hsüeh* (August, 1955), p. 8.

43. For an interpretive account of these rebellions, cf. my article in *JAS*, XXIX(1970), 540-49, and the literature cited therein.

44. Thus a popular rhyme reported by T'ao Tsung-i goes:

Majestic the Great Yüan
Where the evil and specious monopolize power.
When they opened the Yellow River and changed the currency
That was the beginning of the trouble.
They incited thousands and myriads of Red Turbans.
The administrative laws are a mess;
The punishments are heavy.
The common people are angry
And people eat each other.
With paper money one buys paper money;
Never has such a thing been seen before.
Bandits become officials
And officials become bandits.
Fools and wise men are mistaken for each other;
Alas, how pitiful it is.

Cf. T'ao Tsung-i, *Cho-keng lu*, p. 338. T'ao said that everyone from the capital to South China could recite the poem. For a study of T'ao, cf. F. W. Mote in *Silver Jubilee Volume of the Zinbun Kagaku Kenkyusyo* (Kyoto, 1954), pp. 279-93.

45. *YS*, 139.9b; *KSWS*, 22b. According to the latter, the original document reporting the rebellion was simply entitled "The Rebellion," which Toghto reworded to read "The Rebellion of the Honan Chinese."

46. *YS*, 144.11b.

47. *YS*, 42.7b.

48. *KSWS*, 23a-b. For the usage of *hui-hui* in the sense of Christian here, cf. Pelliot, *Notes*, I, 22-23. Ch'üan Heng says that over half of Tughchi's forces died of disease. Tughchi was, however,

rewarded for later success in the Honan campaign (*YS*, 42.19b-20a). He later accompanied Toghto against Hsü-chou (*YS*, 138.30a). That many of the Alans were Roman Catholics is, of course, a fact well known.

49. *KSWS*, 24b. For the name *Gongbubal, cf. Hambis, *Le Chapitre CVIII*, p. 142.

50. *YS*, 42.8a-b; 138.29a. There were a total of only some 350,000 Mongol and *se-mu* troops stationed around the capital and in the provinces; cf. *Iminzoku no Shina tōchi kaisetsu*, pp. 139-40. Ch'üan Heng (*KSWS*, 24b) says that Esen Temür had 300,000 troops, surely an exaggeration. For Köncheg, or *Könchege, a presumed descendant of Möngke, cf. Hambis, *Le Chapitre CVIII*, p. 35, n. 5, where 1341 is an error for 1351; and Hambis, *Le Chapitre CVII*, pp. 157-58.

51. *YS*, 42.9a.

52. *YS*, 42.10a.

53. *YS*, 42.16a; 138.29a; *KSWS*, 24b-25a. We have no more precise date for Esen Temür's rout than April-May, 1352, possibly because an immediate report was not made on it. Cf. also Yeh Tzu-ch'i, 3.8b-9a.

54. *YS*, 141.1a-b.

55. Cf. note 48 above. Another case was the commander Lao-chang, one of the heads of the Chief Military Commission, who proved dilatory under Esen Temür's command (*YS*, 42.8b; 141.1a-b). In February, 1353, however, he improved sufficiently to be rewarded for recapturing a town in the western part of Honan (*YS*, 43.2a). Later on he accompanied Toghto in the Kao-yu campaign. I cannot identify the nationalities of either Tughchi or Lao-chang; chances are they were not Chinese.

56. *YS*, 42.17a; 138.29b; 139.10b; 187.11b.

57. *YS*, 145.2a-b; *KSWS*, 24b-25a.

58. *YS*, 139.10a-b. On the "Hairy Gourds," cf. also D. M. Farquhar in *MS*, XXV (1966), 380.

59. *YS*, 140.12b.

60. *YS*, 188.1b-2a. Chiao-hua was not a Chinese.

61. *YS*, 42.14a-b, 15a, 17a-b, 21b; 142.1a-2a. For the Salji'ud tribe of the Mongols, cf. Pelliot and Hambis, *Histoire des Campagnes*, pp. 398-99. For the name Badulugh, cf. Cleaves in *HJAS*, XIX (1956), 395, 398, n. 46. For the term *tamachi*, cf. below, note 68.

62. *YS*, 144.13a-b; 145.2b.

63. *YS*, 42.21b; 188.2a-3b; Ku Ying, *Yü-shan p'u-kao, chia-wu*, 8b-11b (a song of victory in ten stanzas and a short departing message for the Assistant Administrator Tung T'uan-hsiao).

64. *YS*, 42.11a-b; 138.29b; 187.7b-8a; *KSWS*, 24a; *TTSL*, I, 276. Ch'üan Heng gives a total of 30,000 men.

65. *YS*, 42.12a-21a *passim*..

66. *YS*, 43.7a-b; 144.6b-8a.

67. *YS*, 42.12a, 21b; 43.5a; 117.7a; 185.5a-b. The "Darqan Army" that campaigned in Hukuang was made up of Chinese villagers; cf. *YS*, 139.11a-b.

68. *YS*, 142.1b-2a. Dash Badulugh also had contingents of Yunnan tribal forces under his command. The meaning of the term *tamachi* seems to have changed through the centuries. It seems originally to have meant "escort officials" and later "vanguard" (cf. the reviewer's remarks in *Shigaku zasshi*, LXXVI [1967], 217; and Cleaves in *HJAS*, XII [1949], 440-41), but later it apparently came to refer to the tribal or national affiliation of the troops, rather than to their function. Cn this, see Schurmann, *Economic Structure*, p. 63, n. 46; and most recently Ratchnevsky in *Collectanea Mongolica* (Wiesbaden, 1966), p. 184, n. 1, where it is pointed out that the *tamachi* troops were other than true Mongols. The Naiman Chaghan Temür was a *tamachi*, as was the Chinese Liu Qara Buqa. Cf. *MWE*, 154.5b; *KSWS*, 25a; *YS*, 188.7a.

69. *YS*, 42.9a, 12a-b; 92.2a; 184.14a. In Honan, supply was the responsibility of the provincial administration (*YS*, 187.11b-12a).

70. *YS*, 42.10a-b.

71. *YS*, 186.19a.

72. *YS*, 183.6b.

73. *YS*, 185.13a. A similar decision on this matter was made in the 1330s or 1340s; cf. *YS*, 187.4b.

74. *YS*, 139.10b-11b.

75. *YS*, 186.19a-b.

76. *YS*, 144.14a. Both the central government and Huainan province were ordered to supply Toghto's Hsü-chou campaign with everything it needed. Hsü-chou was itself in Honan province (*YS*, 42.19a).

77. *YS*, 42.17a, 21b-22a.

78. *YS*, 42.21a.

79. *YS*, 42.21b; 43.1a-3a; 138.30a; 187.3a; Ch'en Chi, *I-po-chai kao*, 17.5b (a departing message for Li Te-chung); 15.4b (preface to poems for Ch'iang Yen-li, departing for the capital); Cheng Yüan-yu, *Ch'iao-wu chi*, 8.9b (a departing message for Hsü Yüan-tu); *KSWS*, 25b. There were various supporting activities connected with this agricultural project: pasture offices for the rearing of plow oxen were established in Hsü-chou, Ju-ning, Nan-yang, and Teng-chou—all in Honan in former rebel-occupied territory. State agricultural offices were established at Pien-liang, in Liaoyang, and in the Yangtze delta (*YS*, 42.22a; 43.2b-3a, 8a; 187.10a). Wang I puts the agricultural project together with the Yellow River project as Toghto's largest and most expensive programs; cf. Wang I,

168(3).17a-18a (a departing message for Örüg Buqa, Vice Director of the Board of Civil Office).

80. *YS*, 42.11b. For the Pacification Commissions, cf. Hucker, *The Censorial System of Ming China*, pp. 26-27.

81. *Ibid.* The prince is here listed as Prince of Ning, not Hsi-ning; Hambis, *Le Chapitre CVIII*, p. 103, does not note this discrepancy. On Yaghan-shah, see further H. Franke in *AM*, XI(1965), 120-27.

82. *YS*, 43.10a-b; 142.2a.

83. *YS*, 142.14a-15a.

84. *YS*, 43.7a; 144.6b-8a, 9-10b; Sung Lien, 34.1a-4a (epitaph for Shinggi). Both Buyan Temür and Shinggi were Tanguts. The Esen Temür mentioned here was not the younger brother of Toghto.

85. *YS*, 42.14b-15a; 92.7b.

86. A Taoist who was Administrator (*chang-shih*) in the princely establishment of the Prince of Chen-nan led a cavalry expedition in Honan; cf. Wang Feng, *Wu-ch'i chi*, 5.28b. For the prince's pacification office, cf. *YS*, 194.16b-18a. The prince was an admirer of Chinese literature; cf. Ch'ang-ku Chen-i A.20b.

87. *YS*, 194.16b-18a.

88. *YS*, 42.15a.

89. It is true that one can find numerous references to a decline in the quality of the regular Yüan armies. Hu Chih-yü, *Tzu-shan ta-ch'üan-chi*, 22.29b-39a, devoted a discussion to the matter, as did Hsü Yu-jen in *Chih-cheng chi* (printed ed., K'ai-feng, 1911), 77.28a-b. Detailed reports of abuses in the military system may be found in the *Yüan tien-chang:* cf. 34.15b-17a (for the year 1299); 34.17a-19b (for the year 1311); and *hsin-chi, ping-pu* 1a-10a (for 1320). Both Yeh Tzu-ch'i and Ch'ang-ku Chen-i give stories purporting to show how the Red Turban rebels in 1351 and 1352 completely overwhelmed the lazy and swinish Yüan military officers. Cf. Yeh Tzu-ch'i, 3.6a-b; Ch'ang-ku Chen-i, A. 3a. The picture these sources give, however, is too one-sided. Despite the abuses of 1299, 1311, and 1320, the dynasty was able successfully to conclude the steppe wars, and El Temür had no difficulty fielding an army to fight the civil war of 1328. In the Red Turban rebels, the Yüan armies were opposed not by regular and trained armies, but by mobs of frenzied religious rioters, which seem to have unnerved them.

90. *YS*, 187.6a-b.

91. *YS*, 42.9a-b; cf. note 40, above.

92. *YS*, 42.10a. How many households Toghto was allotted is not stated. On the function of the hunter and falconer households, cf. Ebisawa Tetsuo in *Shichō*, no. 95 (1966), p. 34.

93. *YS*, 42.19b.

94. *YS*, 42.20b.

95. *YS*, 42.21a.

96. *Ibid.* Cf. also Hambis, *Le Chapitre CVIII*, p. 65, n. 3. Toghto had been made Prince of Cheng at the time of his retirement in 1344, but his biography states that he declined the honor (*YS*, 138.27b).

97. *YS*, 43.2b.

Chapter VI. The Growth of Yüan Regionalism

1. *YS*, 43.4a; 194.17b; Wu K'uan, 2a-3a; T'ao Tsung-i, p. 439.

2. *YS*, 194.14b-15b. Shih P'u was killed while directing the Kao-yu attack, and the historians of the Yüan *shih* have entered his biography among the "loyal and righteous" *(chung-i)* who died in the cause of the dynasty. The exact date of Shih P'u's attack is not given.

3. *YS*, 43.11a; 138.30a-b; 142.5a; *KRS*, I, 583; Yeh Tzu'ch'i, 3.9a. Chang had made several attempts upon Yang-chou, but the impending Yüan attack forced him to withdraw; cf. *YS*, 43.10b; T'ao Tsung-i, pp. 439-40.

4. Ch'ang-ku Chen-i, B.5a.

5. The rivalry among the various military units to take the city was perhaps intense enough to cause Toghto to change his tactics from assault to siege. The *Koryŏ sa* reports this about the Korean contingent: "Our nationals at Yen-ching (i.e., Ta-tu) plus the expeditionary force under Yu T'ak and others numbered 23,000 men and was used as a vanguard. When the City [of Kao-yu] was about to go under, the Tatar Lao-chang, a head of the Chief Military Commission, who was jealous of our nationals' having monopolized success, sent out an order which said: 'Today it is late, we will take it tomorrow.' . . . That night the rebels strengthened the walls and set up defenses. The next day when they were attacked, they could not be subdued" (*KRS* I, 584).

6. *YS*, 43.12a-b; 138.30b-31a; 205.29a-32a.

7. The quotation is from *YS*, 138.31b. Cf. also *YS*, 43.12a-b; Ch'ang-ku Chen-i, B.5a-b; *KSWS*, 27a-28b; T'ao Tsung-i, p. 440.

8. *YS*, 43.12b-13a; 138.31b-33a; 139.5a-b; 187.3b; 205.32a; *KRS*, I, 584-85; Ch'ang-ku Chen-i, B.5b; T'ao Tsung-i, p. 440; Wu K'uan, 4a.

9. Three such newly appointed Southern Chinese censors are known: Wu Tang, Chou Po-ch'i, and Kung Shih-t'ai. Chou Po-ch'i, a former Imperial University student, took a prominent and vocal part in support of the main Censorate's counterattack against the Shensi Branch Censorate. Cf. *YS*, 42.13a; 187.8b-13a.

10. *YS*, 183.6b-7a. Wang Ssu-ch'eng was a *chin-shih* of 1321 and a Northern Chinese.

11. *YS*, 139.5a-b.

12. *YS*, 140.6b.

13. *YS*, 182.11b-12a.

14. The memorial of impeachment against the two brothers read: "As to Toghto's campaign, for three months he has not had an inch of success, and he has wasted the state's resources for his own purposes. Also, his younger brother Esen Temür is of low talent and meager capacity. He has sullied the purity of the Censorate, so that governmental controls are in disuse, and a psychology of greed and corruption becomes more pronounced daily" (*YS*, 43.12a-b).

15. The conservative Hsü Yu-jen's complaint was that "rewards are too heavy and punishments too light, and thus the generals and troops plunder and steal and have no will to fight" (*YS*, 182.12a). It is, perhaps, curious that both the conservative and reform wings of Neo-Confucianism were borrowing different aspects of traditional Legalist ideology. In the late Yüan, the conservative concern with rewards and punishments was matched by the reform emphasis on purposive institutional centralism, both of Legalist and not Confucian derivation.

16. *YS*, 114.9b-10b; 138.31a. According to her biography, Bayan Qudu gave birth to a boy named Jingim, who died at the age of one. The date of his death is not known. Ayushiridara had another younger brother named Toghus Temür; who his mother was or when he was born appear to be unknown. Cf. M. Honda in *UAJ*, XXX (1958), 235-36.

17. Toghto's close adherent Wu-ku-sun Liang-chen was keenly in favor of Ayushiridara; there is no indication that he and Toghto were divided on the succession question. Cf. *YS*, 187.3a.

18. It may be significant that the preliminary installation of Ayushiridara as heir apparent in July, 1353, was carried out not in Ta-tu, but in the summer capital of Shang-tu. It is possible that Toghto, who was busy with the North China agricultural project about this time, was not present for the ceremony, even though his presence was ceremonially required (*YS*, 43.4a; 67.14b-19b). It may also be significant that on November 24, 1354, the emperor ordered the Central Chancellery, the Chief Military Commission, and the Censorate henceforth to forward all memorials to the heir apparent for review *(ch'i)* before submitting them to the throne. At the time the emperor issued this order, Toghto was not in the capital but was approaching Kao-yu with his army. The timing of the order seems to indicate that it was issued without Toghto's knowledge, perhaps against his wishes (*YS*, 43.12a). The full investiture of Ayushiridara was carried out in April, 1355 (*YS*, 44.3a-b).

19. *YS*, 205.31b. Toghon Temür was the last ruler of the dynasty, and traditional historiography, as is well known, lays much of the

blame for the fall of dynasties on bad last emperors. Consequently the *YS* describes Toghon Temür's foibles at great length. This does not, however, necessarily mean that such description is totally false.

20. Pelliot and Hambis, *Histoire des Campagnes*, p. 271; *Sheng-wu ch'in-cheng lu*, ed. Wang Kuo-wei, pp. 150-51; Rashid ad-Din, *Sbornik Letopisei*, I, i, 151-52. On the name Toghto, meaning "fixed" or "determined," cf. Cleaves in *HJAS*, XV (1952), 51.

21. After his fall, many of Toghto's men are said to have been executed. Cf. *YS*, 185.11b.

22. *YS*, 44.4a-5a.

23. *YS*, 44.12a-14a *passim;* Wu K'uan, 4a-6b; T'ao Tsung-i, pp. 127 ff., 440 ff., 466 ff., Ch'ang-ku- Chen-i, A.4a-b; Yao T'ung-shou, *Le-chiao ssu-yü*, 3b-4a; YS, 187.10a-b.

24. Wu K'uan, 4a-5a; T'ao Tsung-i, p. 441.

25. *YS*, 45.5a-b; 97.1b-3a; 140.12b-13b; 187.12a; Wu K'uan, 7b-8a; T'ao Tsung-i, p. 442; Liu Jen-pen, *Yü-t'ing chi*, 135(2).7a-8b; Otagi Matsuo in *Bunka*, XVII (1953), 611.

26. *YS*, 42.21a-b; 43.1b-9b *passim.*

27. *T'ai-chou fu-chih*, 133.6a-7a; *Lu-ch'iao chih-lüeh*, 6.13a-b.

28. *YS*, 44.13a-b.

29. *YS*, 45.5a.

30. On Fang's administration, cf. *T'ai-chou fu-chih*, 133.8a-9a.

31. I have attempted a fuller analysis of this matter in *JAS*, XXIX (1970), 549-53.

32. This point is forcefully put by a contemporary observer, quoted by Ch'ien Ch'ien-i in *Kuo-ch'u ch'ün-hsiung shih-lüeh*, 1.26a-b.

33. *YS*, 42.21a; 144.10b; Sung Lien, 34.1a-4a.

34. *YS*, 144.7b-8a.

35. *YS*, 139.10b-11b. Dorjibal functioned well enough, even though he was a conservative and was under suspicion from Toghto for having impeached Esen Temür earlier.

36. *YS*, 144.5b-6a. On the *Buringkil Dörben tribe, to which Örüg Temür belonged, cf. Pelliot and Hambis, *Histoire des Campagnes*, p. 400. When he was appointed Chief Administrator of Kiangche province in 1352, he attempted to convince Toghto that he could save the area from the rebels if he were authorized to "act at convenience." Toghto openly and flatly refused this authorization (*YS*, 144.5b). Toghto permitted such plenipotentiary power to one leading provincial official in Szechwan, Hukuang, Kiangsi, Kiangche, and Huainan, and to Narin, Censor-in-Chief of the Kiangnan Branch Censorate (*YS*, 42.15b-16a; 43,4a, 5a).

37. *YS*, 145.2b.

38. Ch'en Yu-liang gave posthumous honors to the Tangut Yü Ch'üeh for his heroic defense of the city of An-ch'ing; so too did

Chu Yüan-chang and the Yüan authorities (*YS*, 143.20b-21a). There are many other such examples.

39. That Chaghan Temür was a Naiman is proved by T'u Chi, who quotes from a stela of merit composed for him by Kuei Ch'ang (*MWE*, 154.5b). The Naiman were classified as *se-mu* in the Yüan period and appear to have been a partially Mongolized Turkish tribe. Cf. S. Maruyama in *CAJ*, IV (1958-59), 188-98; Pelliot in *TP*, XXXVII (1944), 35-71; and William Hung in *HJAS*, XIX (1956), 31, n. 6.

40. *YS*, 141.4a-b; *KSWS*, 27a; *MWE*, 129.8b; *MS*, III, 1579.

41. *Wen-hsien chih*, 6.3b (epitaph for Kuan-kuan, written by Chang Chu).

42. Sung Lien, who composed his otherwise laudatory epitaph, had an opportunity to mention such a matter, but instead he passes over Li's early life in complete silence (Sung Lien, 15.3b-4a). Li was a warlord in northwest China at the time of his surrender to the Ming in 1369. Cf. also his biography in *TTSL*, IV, 1619-20. There is a good discussion of the functions of the *tien-shih* in Cheng Yü, 141(4).3b-4a (a departing message for the *tien-shih* Chao). Some other early associates of Chaghan's were Pao-pao, or Lao-pao, with the surname Li, from Yang-wu (in present-day Honan); and Wei Sain Buqa, from Hsi-chou in Honan. Their ethnic origins are unknown (*HYS*, 220.14a-b; *TTSL*, II, 419).

43. *YS*, 141.4a-b. His biography goes on to add: "He was constantly frustrated, for he had a will to change the world."

44. *Wen-hsien chih*, 6.3b-4a. Kuan-kuan is there said to have recruited "over ten thousand" men, an improbably high number.

45. *YS*, 42.22a; 141.4b. According to *KSWS*, 27a, the emperor himself saw to it that Chaghan and Li received the above posts in an effort to show that "the court does not slight the Northern Chinese."

46. *Wen-hsien chih*, 6.4a, describes some of these actions, but the chronology is confused. The rebel Sung did not establish its capital in Pien-liang in 1354, as the epitaph would have it.

47. *YS*, 44.10b; 141.4b-5a; 142.2b; *KSWS*, 29a. These Miao, or Yao, under their leader Wu T'ien-pao, had earlier been in rebellion in the 1340s in what is now Hunan province; cf. *YS*, 41.9b ff.

48. *YS*, 44.4b-8a; 141.1b-2a; 142.2b.

49. *YS*, 141.5a; 142.2b-3a. Liu Qara Buqa, a Chinese from Kiangsi who was a *tamachi* and a protege of Tai Buqa's, was also successful against the rebel forces at this time (*YS*, 188.7a-b).

50. *YS*, 44.10a; 142.3a-b. The chronology in Dash Badulugh's *YS* biography is confused; I follow T'u Chi's reconstruction in *MWE*, 129.2a-b. After the second unsuccessful encounter, the court ordered Dash Badulugh to place his camp at Ch'en-liu, directly

between Po-chou and Pien-liang. The Sung regime fled to An-feng in the Huai region.

51. *YS*, 142.3b.

52. *YS*, 44.14b-15a; 45.1b; 141.5a-b; 142.3b; *Wen-hsien chih*, 6.4a (where the year is wrongly given as 1357). Tai Buqa was made Chancellor of the Left of Hukuang on December 16, 1355 (*YS*, 44.9a-b), and at the same time was given back his imperial patent as Chancellor of the Left of Honan. Apparently he occupied both positions at once. Dash Badulugh, however, remained as Chancellor of the Left of Honan, too.

53. Dash Badulugh was a Salji'ud, a Mongol clan closely related in the male line to Chinggis Qan's Borjigins (cf. Pelliot and Hambis, *Histoire des Campagnes*, pp. 397-400; Rashid ad-Din, *Sbornik Letopisei* I, i, 178-80). He traced his ancestry in the fifth generation to a certain Boroldai, who served in Chinggis's *keshig*, or guard, and later participated in the invasion of Honan under Ögödei (for the name Boroldai, cf. Cleaves in *HJAS*, XIX [1956], 404, n. 100). His great-great-grandfather T'ai-ta-erh (? Taidar, d. 1255) took part in Möngke's campaigns first against the Qipchaqs and Alans, and later against the Southern Sung in Szechwan. His great-grandfather Ne'üril continued this work and played a prominent part in the conquest of Szechwan. His grandfather Yesüder campaigned there and also in Yunnan, becoming Chancellor of the Left of Yunnan province by the time of Qaishan's reign (*YS*, 129.3b-7a). Dash Badulugh's family, whose fortunes were so closely connected to the conquest of west China, first achieved prominence under Ne'üril. But it suffered a sharp reverse when Dash Badulugh's father Nanggiatai, Chief Administrator of Szechwan, declared his independence in that province in December, 1328, only to be executed in the market place by El Temür after his surrender to the restoration in May, 1329 (*YS*, 32.24a; 33.8a, 13b). Dash Badulugh inherited the position of myriarch in the Lo-lo Pacification Office in Yunnan; he might have spent the rest of his life managing tribesmen had not the Red Turban rebellion afforded him a chance to operate in China proper. Thanks to the rebels, he was able to recoup his family fortunes. With no stake at court in the first place, it was entirely possible for him to link his personal interests to a growth in regional power.

54. *YS*, 44.5a-b; 45.2b. The Qunggirad Tai Buqa, as his biography makes clear, was not at all interested in establishing himself provincially. As a member of a tribe with a high and secure position in the Yüan capital, he was interested mainly in power at the central level, and considered his service in Honan as something close to exile. He had acted quickly enough to put down the Red Turbans in western Honan in 1352. After Toghto's dismissal, he was promoted from Chief Administrator to Chancellor of the Left of Honan,

with authority over the various armies of Shantung and Hopei; he succeeded to the command of a third of the army that Toghto had led against Kao-yu. Apparently, there was poor morale in his army. His biography tells us that he was despondent, and refused to obey orders from the capital. Insufficiently supplied, he let his troops plunder the villages, and was not at all eager to engage his forces in battle. These were the grounds for his impeachment in 1355 (*YS*, 141.1a-2a). In June, 1358, he was again impeached, and murdered en route to his place of exile (*YS*, 45.10b; 141.2b-4a).

55. *YS*, 142.3a. Dash Badulugh organized a military-agricultural colony at Chung-mou.

56. Cf. note 50, above.

57. For further detail on these renewed rebel activities, cf. my article in *JAS*, XXIX (1970), 549 ff.

58. *YS*, 44.14a-b; 45.1b.

59. *YS*, 139.10a.

60. Aradnashiri was a descendant in the fourth generation of Qubilai, through his seventh son A'urughchi. During the restoration of 1328 he was an important backer of El Temür. Cf. Hambis, *Le Chapitre CVII*, pp. 62, 123; and *Le Chapitre CVIII*, pp. 51-52, 101-2. For the reading A'urughchi, cf. Schurmann, *Economic Structure*, p. 129, n. 19. Hambis reads it Oghruqchi.

61. *YS*, 44.2a, 13b.

62. *YS*, 183.7a-b. This is the same Wang Ssu-ch'eng who earlier memorialized the emperor about increasing the powers of the provincial governments.

63. *YS*, 141.5a-b.

64. *YS*, 45.1b; 141.5a-b; 183.7b.

65. *YS*, 45.6a-b; 141.6a-b.

66. *YS*, 45.8a.

67. *YS*, 45.12b.

68. *YS*, 45.8a-10a *passim*.

69. *YS*, 45.12b.

70. *YS*, 45.16b.

71. This we learn from an epitaph written by Sung Lien for K'ung K'o-chien, a lineal descendant of Confucius who served in the Shensi Branch Censorate. Cf. Sung Lien, 31.17b. The *YS* does not seem to report this event. In 1360 Teri Temür succeeded in irrigating and opening to agriculture 45,000 *ch'ing* of land along the Ching River north of Feng-yüan (Sian), as a supply base for the regular government (*YS*, 66.16b). Using Amano's figure of 773.5 sq. yds. per Yüan *mou*, 45,000 *ch'ing* would equal about 720,000 acres. Cf. Amano in *Jimbun Kenkyū*, XIII (1962), 806. I am unfortunately unable to find any biographical information about Teri Temür.

72. *YS*, 45.3b-6b; *Lu-ch'eng hsien-chih*, 3B.55b-56a (a stela of

merit); *Wen-hsien chih*, 6.4a-b. The stela places the event in 1358. I follow the *Shansi t'ung-chih*, 86.15a-b, which places it in 1357.

73. This contingent proceeded through Shang-tu, which it destroyed, and then into Manchuria and Korea.

74. *YS*, 141.6b; *Hsieh-chou chih*, 13.22b.

75. *YS*, 141.6b-7a. While Chaghan proceeded to build his own regional army, appoint his own local officials, and arrange for his own supplies, he was content to let his merits and those of his men be recognized and rewarded by the court. It is, however, difficult to determine precisely what the official positions Chaghan and his men obtained really meant. When Kuan-pao and Kuan-kuan were appointed to posts in the Pacification Office in Shansi, there was a clear connection between their military commands and their official positions. On the other hand, when Li Ssu-ch'i in Shensi province was given an official post in Szechwan, or when Chou Ch'üan in Honan was given one in Hukuang, it is unlikely that the positions were anything other than honorary, or perhaps anticipatory. But in Chaghan Temür's own case, he held offices in three provinces at once, and although he had forces in each of them, he himself obviously could not sit in all three offices at once. We simply do not know to what extent his positions in the Shensi provincial bureaucracy, the Shensi censorate, or the Honan Branch Military Commission allowed him to influence or control those bodies. It may perhaps be presumed that these offices were mainly tokens legitimizing his possession of a power which was really extrabureaucratic and in normal circumstances illegal.

76. *YS*, 45.11a.

77. *YS*, 45.7b; 186.3a.

78. *YS*, 45.8a-16b *passim;* 140.6a; 141.8b; 142.7a; 188.6b-9b.

79. *YS*, 45.15b.

80. This is also evident from Wu T'ing-hsieh's tables of the leading Yüan provincial bureaucrats; cf. *Yüan hsing-sheng ch'eng-hsiang p'ing-chang cheng-shih nien-piao*, 9b-10a.

81. *YS*, 45.15b; 141.7a-b.

82. *YS*, 45.16b; 141.7b-8a; *MS*, III, 1560-61.

83. *YS*, 45.6a, 7a. Dash Badulugh died on February 8, 1358, after an unsuccessful encounter with the rebels in November and December, 1357. His biography says he died of dismay. The rebels knew Dash Badulugh was under official suspicion for failing to press his campaign, and in an effort to discredit him completely, they forged a letter in which he offered to make peace with them. They left this document on the road where the envoys from the court would be sure to find it. It was found, and evidently Dash Badulugh was unable to clear himself. It is impossible to say whether this incident is authentic or not. Cf. *YS*, 142.3b-4a; *MWE*, 129.3a.

84. *YS*, 45.4b-14a *passim;* 207.2b-3a. Bolod Temür's former post

in Hopei was given to a government commander by the name of Uriangqatai, whose army consisted of a mixture of Chinese and Mongol (Ta-ta) units, some of them formerly under the command of the Qunggirad Tai Buqa, and others recently detached from the armies of Bolod and Chaghan.

85. *YS*, 45.19a-b; 207.3a.

86. *YS*, 45.20a-b.

87. *YS*, 207.3b.

88. *YS*, 45.19b-20a. The growing tension between Chaghan and Bolod seems to have precipitated the disintegration of Uriangqatai's army in late 1359 or early 1360. As a head of the Chief Military Commission, Uriangqatai was the central government's major representative in the field. Yet his power and prestige were insufficient to prevent the defection of four of his generals together with their men to the side of either Chaghan or Bolod, their former masters (cf. *YS*, 45.19b-20a). After this happened, Uriangqatai drew together the "Tatar" troops that remained and marched back to the capital. If it were Uriangqatai's purpose to provide a military counterweight to the regionalist forces of Chaghan and Bolod, his mission was a complete failure. The generals who deserted him were the first to press for an open battle between Bolod and Chaghan (cf. *YS*, 45.17a-b, 19a).

89. *YS*, 45.10a, 13b-14a.

90. *YS*, 45.17b.

91. As the Sung movement gathered strength in 1357-58, a number of loyalist commanders of militia *(i-ping)* armies in the east, sensing the weakness of the Yüan court, defected to the rebel side with all of their men (cf. *YS*, 45.8b-11b *passim; KSWS*, 30b-31b). Defection was an option perhaps not entirely closed to Chaghan Temür. If in his own case such an eventuality was unlikely, owing to his Naiman nationality, there were Chinese among his subordinate commanders and adherents to whom the idea of a Sung restoration and the possibility of achieving a degree of personal independence by joining it might not have been unattractive in the right circumstances.

92. Li Shih-chan, *Ching-chi wen-chi*, 1.10a-12a (letter to the Chief Administrator Chaghan). Cf. *HYS*, 216.3b-5a, where the letter has been abridged and partly reworded. From Chaghan's *YS* biography, one learns little of these matters. His *YS* biography hurries through the year 1360 with only a brief reference to his war with Bolod, and a statement saying that it was all Bolod's fault. For this, there are political reasons. At the time when the *YS* was being compiled, the Ming emperor Chu Yüan-chang still hoped to win Chaghan's foster son Kökö Temür to his cause. The *YS* editors put the biography of Bolod Temür, who left no powerful heirs, into the "rebellious minister" *(ni-ch'en)* section of the work.

93. Li Shih-chan, 6.13a (biography of Liu Tse-li).

94. *YS*, 45.20b; 46.1a-b; 207.3b-4a.

95. *YS*, 46.2a-3a.

96. *YS*, 46.2b-3a; 141.8b-9b; *Wen-hsien chih*, 6.4b. The local militarists, formerly loyalists, were T'ien Feng at Tung-p'ing, Yü Pao at Ti-chou, and Liu Kuei at Tsi-nan.

97. Cf. the stela rubbing no. 04699 (Academia Sinica, Taiwan), taken from an inscription celebrating this occasion. Chaghan's forces are styled "the emperor's army" *(wang-shih)*.

98. *YS*, 46.3b-4a; 141.9b.

99. Liu Ch'en, *Kuo-ch'u shih-chi*, 10a; *T'ai-chou fu-chih*, 133.10a; *YS*, 46.2b-5a.

100. *KSWS*, 38a-39a. Ch'üan Heng's words are these: "For several months T'ien Feng often went to Chaghan Temür's camp to discuss affairs. When he saw how superciliously Chaghan treated the court envoys, and how calculating and lacking in loyalty and righteousness his actions were, he said angrily: 'I surrendered all of Shantung to you and pacified the coastal cities for you. I cooperated with you, believing you were the man who was leading the restoration of the Yüan Dynasty. But you are not; you are merely a Ts'ao Ts'ao. If you can be a Ts'ao Ts'ao, so can I'" (*KSWS*, 38b). The speech is of course literary embroidery, but it gives a more credible motive for the assassination than Chaghan's *YS* biography, which has it that T'ien and Wang were in covert league with the rebels at I-tu.

101. *YS*, 46.6a-b; 140.10a-b. Chaghan's father Arghun, still alive and residing at Shen-ch'iu, was given 200 *ch'ing* (*ca.* 3,200 acres) of fields. Honan and Shantung were ordered to build temples where seasonal sacrifices could be carried out in Chaghan's memory.

Epilogue: The Last Days of The Yüan Court in China

1. *YS*, 44.3a-b.

2. *YS*, 44.4a, 9b; 205.32a-33a; *HYS*, 210.6b-7a.

3. *YS*, 45.13a; 140.6b; 205.34b-35a.

4. *YS*, 140.6b-7a; 205.35a-b.

5. *YS*, 140.7b-8a; 186.11a-12b; 204.4b-6a. In 1360 Ho Wei-i retired in the face of pressure from Ayushiridara and Chösgem. With the death of the Vice Administrator of the Left Ne'üdigei in 1360, Ho was deprived of a powerful adherent; Ne'üdigei was a descendant of Boghorchu, one of Chinggis Qan's "Four Heroes." The emperor meanwhile appointed Pai-sa-li, one of the nine sons of the Qangli Toghto, as Chancellor of the Right, and Pai-sa-li attempted to get Ho to return as Chancellor of the Left. This move was blocked by Ayushiridara and Chösgem. Pai-sa-li was overthrown, and Ho accused of treason for attempting to return to the

capital. Chösgem further had the Censorate impeach the Vice Administrator of the Left Ch'eng Tsun, a *chin-shih* of 1333, together with four other supporters of Ho Wei-i, on the grounds of corruption. They were flogged to death. Cf. *YS*, 139.14b-15a; 140.7a; 186.20b; *HYS*, 200.7a, 11a.

6. *YS*, 46.6b-12a *passim.*
7. *YS*, 46.13b-15b; 114.12a; 141.11b; 145.8b-10a; 204.6a-b; 205.35b-36a; 207.4a-6b; *Ning-wu fu-chih,* 12.7a-b. An official of Fang Kuo-chen's (Fang was an ally of Kökö's) noted of the northern situation in 1364: "The heir apparent is with his army in Shansi. He wants to wipe out the great evil, but the officials at court and in the provinces are confused as to which side to follow, and are quick to take advantage of the weakness of one side." Cf. Li Chi-pen, *I-shan wen-chi* (Hu-pei hsien-cheng i-shu ed.), 4.23a-b.
8. *YS*, 46.16a-17a; 141.11b-12a; 142.9a; 207.6b-7b; *MWE*, 17.22a; *KSWS*, 42b-46b.
9. *YS*, 45.18b; 46.9b; 47.1b.
10. *YS*, 140.7a; Cheng Yü, 138(1).1a-2b.
11. *YS*, 45.2a-4b *passim.*
12. *YS*, 45.21a; 46.3a-b; 140.7b; 206.7a-8a; *KSWS*, 36b-37a.
13. *YS*, 114.12a; *KRS*, I, 610; III, 669-71.
14. *YS*, 44.8b-11b; 45.14b-15b.
15. *YS*, 46.17b-18b; 47.4b; 141.12a-b.
16. *MS*, III, 1579; *KSWS*, 47b.
17. *YS*, 47.1a-5a; 141.12b-13a. Ch'üan Heng attributes these words to Li Ssu-ch'i, when Kökö tried to get him to join him against Chang Liang-pi: "You stinking milksop *(ju-ch'ou-erh)*! You still have not lost your baby fuzz, yet you order me around? Your father (i.e., Chaghan) and I came from the same village. When your father shared wine with me, he always bowed three times before drinking. You have no standing-place before me, and yet now you openly call yourself the commander and order me around" (*KSWS*, 48b).
18. *YS*, 47.2b-3a; *MS*, III, 1579; *TTSL*, I, 317-19, 344. At the time, however, Chu interpreted these thrusts as enticements to get him to enter recklessly into Northern territory, where he would be beaten.
19. *YS*, 47.3a-b; Ch'en Kao, *Pu-hsi chou-yüchi* (Ching-hsiang-lou ts'ung-shu ed.), appendix la; Wu Ssu-tao, *Ch'un-ts'ao-chai chi* (MS ed.), 10.11a-12a.
20. *YS*, 47.5a-6a.
21. *YS*, 47.6a-8b; 92.2b; 141.13a-14a, *KSWS*, 49b-52a.
22. *YS*, 47.8a-10a.
23. *YS*, 47.10b-14a; 141.14a-15b; 145.10b-11a; *KSWS*, 52a-55a.

Summary and Conclusion

1. *YS*, 81.4a.

2. Bayan eventually hanged himself on the political legacy of Qubilai; as Toghto's mentor Wu Chih-fang pointed out, Qubilai had never issued an order barring Chinese from the leading positions in the Provincial Surveillance Offices *(Lien-fang-ssu)*, as Bayan in the wake of the Fan Meng case was attempting to do. Cf. *YS*, 138.25a.

3. *YS*, 143.5a. The Confucian movement should not be understood as a movement for ethnic assimilation. For one matter, the idea of ethnic privilege by right of conquest was not clearly in violation of any recognized Confucian principle. There was a possible contradiction involved between Mencius's dictum that worthy men should be employed regardless of their origins and Qubilai's rule that ethnic affiliation was also a primary qualification for office holding. In his argument with Bayan, however, Hsü Yu-jen used Mencius's saying to justify the claim of examination graduates to office, not as an argument against ethnic preference. In addition, there was also the classical principle of the eight categories of legally privileged persons, of which the first two were the relatives of the sovereign *(ch'in)* and the old friends of the sovereign *(ku)*, and the fifth and sixth the meritorious *(kung)* and the noble *(kuei)*. This principle was once invoked by the Central Chancellery official Wang K'o-ching in defense of El Temür. Cf. *YS*, 184.6a-b; T'ung-tsu Ch'ü, *Law and Society in Traditional China* (Paris, 1961), pp. 177-79.

4. Sung Lien, 41.7a.

5. These terms are used by Wang I, 180(15).24b-25a (Words with my wife).

6. Yü Ch'üeh, 133(5).1a-2a (Colophon to the Assistant Magistrate Ku's letter discussing cliques).

Bibliography

ABBREVIATIONS

HYS, K'o Shao-min. *Hsin Yüan shih*
KRS, *Koryŏ sa*
KSWS, Ch'üan Heng, *Keng-shen wai-shih*
MS, *Ming shih*
MWE, T'u Chi, *Meng-wu-erh shih-chi*
TTSL, *Ming T'ai-tsu shih-lu*
TS, *Yüan shih*

I. Sources and Works in Traditional Style

A. WORKS PRIMARILY HISTORICAL

Ch'ien Ch'ien-i 錢謙益 *Kuo-ch'u ch'ün-hsiung shih-lüeh* 國初群雄史略 [Historical extracts concerning the warlords of the early Ming]. Shih-yüan ts'ung-shu ed.

Ch'ien Ta-hsin 錢大昕 *Nien-erh-shih k'ao-i* 廿二史考異 [Study of discrepancies in the twenty-two dynastic histories]. Ts'ung-shu chi-ch'eng ed.

Ch'üan Heng 權衡 *Keng-shen wai-shih* 庚申外史 [Unofficial history of the last Yüan emperor]. Hsüeh-chin t'ao-yüan ed.

For a translation of this work, see Schulte-Uffelage under "Modern Studies" below.

K'o Shao-min 柯劭忞 *Hsin Yüan shih* 新元史 [New Yüan history]. Jen-shou-pen erh-shih-wu-shih ed.

Koryŏ sa 高麗史 [Koryŏ dynastic history]. 3 vols. Tokyo, 1908-9.

Liu Ch'en 劉辰 *Kuo-ch'u shih-chi* 國初事蹟 [Notes on the events of the early Ming]. Chieh-yüeh shan-fang hui-ch'ao ed.

Lu Shen 陸深 *P'ing hu lu* 平胡錄 [Account of the pacification of the Yüan barbarians]. Ts'ung-shu chi-ch'eng ed.

Ming shih 明史 [Ming dynastic history]. 6 vols. Taipei: Kuo-fang yen-chiu-yüan, 1962.

Ming T'ai-tsu shih-lu 明太祖實錄 [Veritable records of the first Ming emperor]. 8 vols. Academia Sinica ed.

Sheng-wu ch'in-cheng lu 聖武親征錄 [Record of the campaigns of Chinggis Qan]. *Meng-ku shih-liao ssu-chung* 蒙古史料四種 [Four sources on Mongol history]. Edited by Wang Kuo-wei 王國維 Taipei: Chung-cheng shu-chü 1962.

This work has been partially translated by Pelliot and Hambis: see "Modern Studies" below.

T'u Chi 屠寄 *Meng-wu-erh shih-chi* 蒙兀兒史記 [History of the Mongols]. 8 vols. Taipei: Shih-chieh shu-chü, 1962.

Wang Hsi 王喜 *Chih-ho t'u-lüeh* 治河圖略 [Yellow River plans]. Mo-hai chin-hu ed.

Wu K'uan 吳寬 *P'ing Wu lu* 平吳錄 [Record of the pacification of Chang Shih-ch'eng]. Chieh-yüeh shan-fang hui-ch'ao ed.

Wu T'ing-hsieh 吳廷燮 *Yüan hsing-sheng ch'eng-hsiang p'ing-chang-cheng-shih nien-piao* 元行省丞相平章政事年表 [Chart of the provincial chancellors and chief administrators of the Yüan]. Ching-she t'ang ed.

Yüan-ch'ao ming-ch'en shih-lüeh 元朝名臣事略 [Extracts from the biographies of outstanding Yüan ministers]. Edited by Su T'ien-chüeh 蘇天爵 Peking: Chung-hua shu-chü, 1962.

Yüan shih 元史 [Yüan dynastic history]. Po-na-pen ed.

Yüan tien-chang 元典章 [Casebook of Yüan administrative law]. Sung-fen-shih ts'ung-k'an ed.

Yüan wen-lei 元文類 [Classified literary pieces of the Yüan]. Edited by Su T'ien-chüeh. Taipei: Shih-chieh shu-chü, 1962.

B. INDIVIDUAL LITERARY WORKS

Ch'ang-ku Chen-i, pseud. 長谷真逸 *Nung-t'ien yü-hua* 農田餘話 Pai-pu ts'ung-shu chi-ch'eng ed.

Ch'en Chi 陳基 *I-pai-chai kao* 夷白齋稿 Ssu-pu ts'ung k'an ed.

Cheng Yü 鄭玉 *Shih-shan hsien-sheng wen-chi* 師山先生文集 Ch'ien-k'un cheng-ch'i-chi ed.

Cheng Yüan-yu 鄭元祐 *Ch'iao-wu chi* 僑吳集 MS ed.

Chieh Hsi-ssu 揭傒斯 *Chieh Wen-an kung ch'üan-chi* 揭文安公全集 Ssu-pu ts'ung-k'an ed.

Hsü I-k'uei 徐一夔 *Shih-feng kao* 始豐稿 Wu-lin wang-che i-chu ed.

Hsü Yu-jen 許有壬 *Chih-cheng chi* 至正集 MS ed.

Hu Chih-yü 胡祇遹 *Tzu-shan ta-ch'üan-chi* 紫山大全集 San-i-t'ang ts'ung-shu ed.

Hu Han 胡翰 *Hu Chung-tzu chi* 胡仲子集 Chin-hua ts'ung-shu ed.

Huang Chin 黃溍 *Chin-hua Huang hsien-sheng wen-chi* 金華黃先生文集 Ssu-pu ts'ung-k'an ed.

Ku Ying 顧瑛 *Yü-shan p'u-kao* 玉山樸稿 Tu-hua-chai ts'ung-shu ed.

K'ung Ch'i 孔齊 *Ching-chai chih-cheng chih-chi* 靜齋至正直記 Yüeh-ya-t'ang ts'ung-shu ed.

Li Shih-chan 李士瞻 *Ching-chi wen-chi* 經濟文集 Hu-pei hsien-cheng i-shu ed.

Liu Chi 劉基 *Ch'eng-i-po wen-chi* 誠意伯文集 Kuo-hsüeh chi-pen ts'ung-shu ed.

Liu Jen-pen 劉仁本 *Yü-t'ing chi* 羽庭集 Ch'ien-k'un cheng-ch'i chi ed.

Lu Yu 陸友 *Yen-pei tsa-chih* 研北雜志 Pao-yen-t'ang pi-chi ed.

Ou-yang Hsüan 歐陽玄 *Kuei-chai wen-chi* 圭齋文集 Ssu-pu ts'ung-k'an ed.

Sung Lien 宋濂 *Sung Wen-hsien kung ch'üan-chi* 宋文憲公全集 Ssu-pu pei-yao ed.

T'ao Tsung-i 陶宗儀 *Cho-keng lu* 輟耕錄 Ts'ung-shu chi-ch'eng ed.

T'ung Shu 同恕 *Ch'ü-an chi* 榘菴集 Ssu-k'u ch'üan-shu chen-pen ch'u-chi ed.

Wang Chieh 王結 *Wang Wen-chung chi* 王文忠集 Ssu-k'u ch'üan-shu chen-pen ch'u-chi ed.

Wang Feng 王逢 *Wu-ch'i chi* 梧溪集 Chih-pu-tsu-chai ts'ung-shu ed.

Wang I 王禕 *Wang Chung-wen kung chi* 王忠文公集 Ch'ien-k'un cheng-ch'i-chi ed.

Wang Yün 王惲 *Ch'iu-chien hsien-sheng wen-chi* 秋澗先生文集 Ssu-pu ts'ung-k'an ed.

Yao T'ung-shou 姚桐壽 *Le-chiao ssu-yü* 樂郊私語 Yen-i chih-lin ed.

Yü Chi 虞集 *Tao-yüan hsüeh-ku lu* 道園學古錄 Ssu-pu pei-yao ed.

Yü Ch'üeh 余闕 *Ch'ing-yang chi* 青陽集 Ch'ien-k'un cheng-ch'i-chi ed.

C. PROVINCIAL AND LOCAL GAZETTEERS

Che-chiang t'ung-chih 浙江通志 (Chekiang). 1561.

Hsieh-chou chih 解州志 (Shansi). 1881.

K'un-shan hsien-chih 昆山縣志 (Kiangsu). 1538.

Lu-ch'eng hsien-chih 潞城縣志 (Shansi). 1885.

Lu-ch'iao chih-lüeh 路橋志略 (Chekiang). 1935.

Ning-wu fu-chih 寧武府志 (Shansi). 1857.

Shan-hsi t'ung-chih 山西通志 (Shansi), ed. Tseng Kuo-ch'üan 曾國荃, n.d.

Wen-hsien chih 温縣志 (Honan). 1759.

II. Modern Studies

ABBREVIATIONS

AM, Asia Major
AOASH, Acta Orientalia Academiae Scientarum Hungaricae
CAJ, Central Asiatic Journal
CYYY, Chung-yang yen-chiu-yüan li-shih yü-yen yen-chiu-so chi-k'an
FEQ, Far Eastern Quarterly
FJHC, Fu-jen hsüeh-chih
HJAS, Harvard Journal of Asiatic Studies
JA, Journal Asiatique
JAS, Journal of Asian Studies
JESHO, Journal of the Economic and Social History of the Orient
JOS, Journal of Oriental Studies
MS, Monumenta Serica
UAJ, Ural-Altaische Jahrbücher

Abe Takeo. "Where was the Capital of the West Uighurs?" *Silver*

Jubilee Volume of the Zinbun Kagaku Kenkyusyo, Kyoto University (Kyoto, 1954), 435-50.

——— 安部健夫 "Gendai chishikijin to kakyo." 元代知識人と科擧 [Yüan intellectuals and the examination system]. *Shirin* XLII (1959), 885-924.

Amano Motonosuke 天野元之助 "Gendai no nōgyō to sono shakai kōzō." 元代の農業とその社會構造 [Yüan agriculture and its social structure], *Jimbun kenkyū*, XIII (1964), 801-18.

Arat, R. Rahmeti. "Der Herrschertitel Iduq-qut," *UAJ*, XXXV (1964), 150-57.

Barthold, W. *Turkestan down to the Mongol Invasion.* Translated by H. A. R. Gibb. 2d ed. London: Luzac, 1958.

——— *Zwölf Vorlesungen über die Geschichte der Türken Mittelasiens.* Hildesheim: George Olms, 1962.

Barthold, V. V. *Four Studies on the History of Central Asia.* Translated by V. and T. Minorsky. 3 vols. Leiden: Brill, 1956-62.

Blake, Robert P. "The Circulation of Silver in the Moslem East down to the Mongol Epoch," *HJAS*, II (1937), 291-328.

Bretschneider, E. *Medieval Researches from Eastern Asiatic Sources.* 2 vols. London: Kegan, Paul, Trench, Trübner, n.d.

Cha-ch'i Ssu-ch'in 札奇斯欽 [S. Jagchid]. "Meng-wen Huang-chin-shih i-chu." 蒙文黃金史譯註 [A Chinese translation of the Altan Tobchi, with annotations]. *Chung-yang tung-ya hsüeh-shu yen-chiu chi-hua wei-yüan-hui nien-pao,* no. 2 (1962), pp. 1-248.

Chavannes, Édouard. "Inscriptions et pièces de chancellerie chinoises de l'époque mongole," *TP*, V (1904), 357-447; *TP*, VI (1905), 1-42.

Ch'en Yüan. *Western and Central Asians in China under the Mongols.* Translated by Ch'ien Hsing-hai and L. Carrington Goodrich. (*Monumenta Serica* monograph XV). Los Angeles: University of California Press, 1966.

Ch'üan Han-sheng 全漢昇 "Yüan-tai ti chih-pi." 元代的紙幣 [The paper currency of the Yüan period]. *CYYY*, XV (1948), 1-48.

Cleaves, F. W. "K'uei-k'uei or Nao-nao?" *HJAS*, X (1947), 1-12.

——— "The Sino-Mongolian Inscription of 1362 in Memory of Prince Hindu," *HJAS*, XII (1949), 1-133.

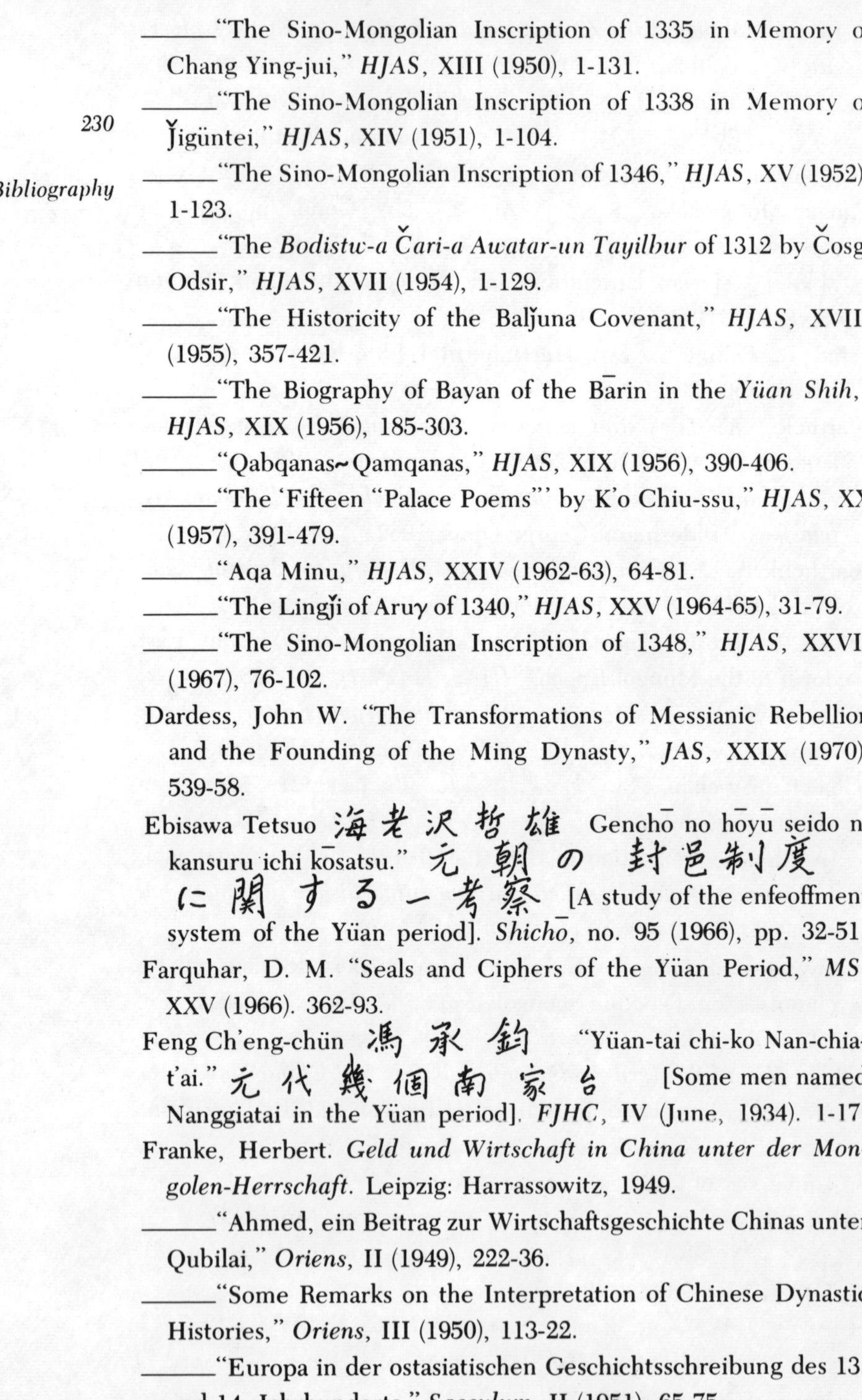

_____"The Sino-Mongolian Inscription of 1335 in Memory of Chang Ying-jui," *HJAS*, XIII (1950), 1-131.

_____"The Sino-Mongolian Inscription of 1338 in Memory of J̌igüntei," *HJAS*, XIV (1951), 1-104.

_____"The Sino-Mongolian Inscription of 1346," *HJAS*, XV (1952), 1-123.

_____"The *Bodistw-a Čari-a Awatar-un Tayilbur* of 1312 by Čosgi Odsir," *HJAS*, XVII (1954), 1-129.

_____"The Historicity of the Balǰuna Covenant," *HJAS*, XVIII (1955), 357-421.

_____"The Biography of Bayan of the Bārin in the *Yüan Shih*," *HJAS*, XIX (1956), 185-303.

_____"Qabqanas~Qamqanas," *HJAS*, XIX (1956), 390-406.

_____"The 'Fifteen "Palace Poems"' by K'o Chiu-ssu," *HJAS*, XX (1957), 391-479.

_____"Aqa Minu," *HJAS*, XXIV (1962-63), 64-81.

_____"The Lingǰi of Aruγ of 1340," *HJAS*, XXV (1964-65), 31-79.

_____"The Sino-Mongolian Inscription of 1348," *HJAS*, XXVII (1967), 76-102.

Dardess, John W. "The Transformations of Messianic Rebellion and the Founding of the Ming Dynasty," *JAS*, XXIX (1970), 539-58.

Ebisawa Tetsuo 海老沢哲雄 Genchō no hōyū seido ni kansuru ichi kōsatsu." 元朝の封邑制度に関する一考察 [A study of the enfeoffment system of the Yüan period]. *Shichō*, no. 95 (1966), pp. 32-51.

Farquhar, D. M. "Seals and Ciphers of the Yüan Period," *MS*, XXV (1966). 362-93.

Feng Ch'eng-chün 馮承鈞 "Yüan-tai chi-ko Nan-chia-t'ai." 元代幾個南家台 [Some men named Nanggiatai in the Yüan period]. *FJHC*, IV (June, 1934). 1-17.

Franke, Herbert. *Geld und Wirtschaft in China unter der Mongolen-Herrschaft*. Leipzig: Harrassowitz, 1949.

_____"Ahmed, ein Beitrag zur Wirtschaftsgeschichte Chinas unter Qubilai," *Oriens*, II (1949), 222-36.

_____"Some Remarks on the Interpretation of Chinese Dynastic Histories," *Oriens*, III (1950), 113-22.

_____"Europa in der ostasiatischen Geschichtsschreibung des 13. und 14. Jahrhunderts," *Saeculum*, II (1951), 65-75.

———"Could the Mongol Emperors Read and Write Chinese?" *AM*, III (1952), 28-41.

———"Some Remarks on Yang Yü and his *Shan-chü hsin-hua.*" *JOS* II (1955), 302-8.

———*Beiträge zur Kulturgeschichte Chinas unter der Mongolenherrschaft. Das Shan-kü sin-hua des Yang Yü. (Abhandlungen für die Kunde des Morgenlandes* XXXII, no. 2). Wiesbaden: Franz Steiner, 1956.

———"Zur Datierung der mongolischen Schreiben aus Turfan," *Oriens*, XV (1962), 399-410.

———"A 14th Century Mongolian Letter Fragment," *AM*, XI (1965), 120-27.

Franke, Otto. *Geschichte des Chinesischen Reiches.* 5 vols. Berlin: Walter de Gruyter, 1930-52.

Fuchs, W. "Analecta zur mongolischen Übersetzungsliteratur der Yüan-Zeit," *MS*, XI (1946), 33-64.

Grousset, René. *L'Empire des Steppes.* Paris: Payot, 1948.

Goodrich, L. Carrington. "Westerners and Central Asians in Yüan China," *Oriente Poliano*, (Rome: Istituto Italiano per il Medio ed Estremo Oriente, 1957), pp. 1-21.

Hambis, Louis. *Le Chapitre CVII du Yuan Che. Les généalogies impériales mongoles dans l'histoire chinoise officielle de la dynastie mongole; avec des notes supplémentaires par Paul Pelliot.* (Supplement to *T'oung Pao,* XXXVIII). Leiden: Brill, 1945.

———*Le Chapitre CVIII du Yuan Che. Les fiefs attribués aux membres de la famille impériale et aux ministres de la cour mongole d'après l'histoire officielle de la dynastie mongole. (T'oung Pao* monographs, III). Leiden: Brill, 1954.

———"Notes préliminaires à une biographie de Bayan le Märkit." *JA*, CCXLI (1953), 215-48.

Ho Ping-ti. *The Ladder of Success in Imperial China. Aspects of Social Mobility 1368-1911.* New York: Columbia University Press, 1962.

Honda, M. "On the Genealogy of the Early Northern Yüan," *UAJ*, XXX (1958), 232-48.

Hsiao Ch'i-ch'ing 蕭啟慶 *Hsi-yü-jen yü Yüan-ch'u cheng-chih.* 西域人與元初政治 [Central Asians and the politics of the early Yüan dynasty]. Taipei: Taiwan University, 1966.

Hucker, Charles O. *The Censorial System of Ming China.* Stanford: University Press, 1966.

Hung, William. "Three of Ch'ien Ta-hsin's Poems on Yüan History." *HJAS*, XIX (1956), 1-32.

Iminzoku no Shina tōchi kaisetsu 異民族の支那統治概説 [Outline of foreign rule in China]. Tokyo: Tōa Kenkyūjo, 1943.

Iwamura Shinobu 岩村忍 "*Gentenshō* keibu no kenkyū—keibatsu tetsuzuki." 元典章刑部の研究—刑罰手續 [A study of the punishments section of the *Yüan tien-chang*—the punishments process]. *Tōhō gakuhō*, no. 24 (1954), pp. 1-114.

______"Gen jidai ni okeru shihei infurēshon." 元時代に於ける紙幣インフレーション [Paper money inflation in the Yüan period]. *Tōhō gakuhō*, no. 34 (1964), pp. 61-133.

______*Mongoru shakai keizaishi kenkyū.* モンゴル社會經濟史研究 [Studies on the social and economic history of the Mongols]. Kyoto: Kyōto daigaku jimbun kagaku kenkyūjo, 1968.

Kara, G. "L'inscription mongole d'Aruγ, prince de Yun-nan (1340)," *AOASH*, XVII (1964), 145-73.

Laufer, Berthold. "Über ein tibetisches Geschichtswerk der Bonpo," *TP*, II (1901), 24-44.

Ligeti. Louis. "Les noms mongols de Wen-tsong des Yuan," *TP*, XXVII (1930), 57-61.

Lo Jung-pang. "The Controversy over Grain Conveyance during the Reign of Qubilai Qaqan, 1260-94," *FEQ*, XIII (1953-54), 263-85.

Maeda Naonori 前田直典 "Gendai no kahei tan'i." 元代の貨幣單位 [Currency units of the Yüan period]. *Shakai keizai shigaku*, XIV (July, 1944), 1-22.

______"Genchō jidai ni okeru shihei no kachi hendō." 元朝時代に於ける紙幣の價値變動 [Fluctuations in the value of paper currency during the Yüan period]. *Rekishigaku kenkyū*, no. 126 (1947), pp. 26-48.

Makino Shūji 牧野修二 "Gendai shōkan kitei ni tsuite no ichi kōsatsu: toku ni kannanjin rofushūkenkan no baai." 元代昇官規定についての一考察；特に漢南

人路府州縣官の場合 [A study of the rules for official advancement during the Yüan period, with special reference to Northern and Southern Chinese in local offices]. *Tōhōgaku* no. 32 (1966), pp. 56-70.

Marquart, J. "Über das Volkstum der Komanen." *Abhandlungen der Königlichen Gesellschaft der Wissenschaften zu Göttingen. Philologisch-Historische Klasse.* N. F. XIII (1912-14), 25-238.

Maruyama, S. "Sind die Naiman Türken oder Mongolen?" *CAJ*, IV (1958-59), 188-98.

Meng Ssu-ming 蒙思明 *Yüan-tai she-hui chieh-chi chih-tu.* 元代社會階級制度 [The social class system of the Yüan dynasty]. (*Yen-ching hsüeh-pao* monograph no. 16). Peiping, 1938.

Meng-ku pi-shih. 蒙古祕史 [Secret history of the Mongols]. Translated into modern Chinese by Hsieh Tsai-shan. 謝再善 Peking: K'ai-ming shu-tien, 1951.

Miyazaki Ichisada 宮崎市定 "Genchō chika no mōkoteki kanshoku o meguru mōkan kankei." 元朝治下の蒙古的官職をめぐる蒙漢關係 [Sino-Mongol relations and the question of Mongol offices under Yüan rule]. *Tōyōshi kenkyū*, XXIII (1965), 428-51.

Mote, F. W. "Notes on the Life of T'ao Tsung-i." *Silver Jubilee Volume of the Zinbun Kagaku Kenkyusyo, Kyoto University* (Kyoto, 1954), pp. 279-93.

Munkuev, N. Ts. "O formakh ekspluatatsii mongol'skikh aratov v XIII-XIV vekakh." [On the modes of exploitation of the Mongol commoners in the 13th and 14th centuries]. *Materialy po istorii i filologii tsentral'noi Azii*, II (Ulan-Ude, 1965), 68-86.

Nakayama Hachirō 中山八郎 Shisei jūichinen ni okeru kōkin no kiji to Ka Ro no kakō." 至正十一年に於ける紅巾の起事と賈魯の河工 [The Red Turban rising of 1351 and Chia Lu's Yellow River engineering]. *Wada hakushi koki kinen tōyōshi ronsō* (Tokyo, 1960), pp. 649-63.

Otagi Matsuo 愛宕松男 "Shu Gokoku to Chō Gokoku: shoki Min ōchō no seikaku ni kansuru ichi kōsatsu." 朱吳国と張吳國:初期明王朝の

性格に関する一考察 [The Wu states of Chu Yüan-chang and Chang Shih-ch'eng: a study on the nature of the early Ming government]. *Bunka*, XVII (1953), 597-621.

Pelliot, Paul. "À propos des Comans." *JA*, ser. xi, vol. XV (1920), 125-85.

_____"Une ville musulmane dans la Chine du nord sous les Mongols," *JA*, CCXI (1927), 261-79.

_____"Les mots mongols dans le Korye să," *JA*, CCXVII (1930), 253-66.

_____"Notes sur le 'Turkestan' de M. W. Barthold," *TP*, XXVII (1930), 12-56.

_____Sur la légende d'Uγuz-khan en écriture ouigoure," *TP*, XXVII (1930), 247-358.

_____"Une tribu méconnue des Naiman: les Bätäkin," *TP*, XXXVII (1944), 35-71.

_____"Les forms avec et sans q- (k-) initial en turc et en mongol," *TP*, XXXVII (1944), 73-101.

_____*Notes on Marco Polo.* 2 vols. Paris: Imprimerie Nationale, 1959-63.

Pelliot, Paul, and Louis Hambis. *Histoire des Campagnes de Gengis Khan. Cheng-wou ts'in-tcheng lou.* Leiden: Brill, 1951.

Poppe, N. "The Turkic loanwords in Middle Mongolian," *CAJ*, I (1955), 36-42.

Rachewiltz, Igor de. "Personnel and Personalities in North China in the Early Mongol Period," *JESHO*, IX (1966), 88-144.

Rashid ad-Din. *Sbornik Letopisei.* [Collection of chronicles]. Translated by L. A. Khetagurov *et al.* 3 vols. in four parts. Moscow-Leningrad: Izdatel'stvo Akademii Nauk SSSR, 1946-60.

Rásonyi, L. "Les noms de nombre dans l'anthroponymie turque," *AOASH*, XII (1961). 45-71.

Ratchnevsky, Paul. *Un Code des Yuan. (Bibliothèque de l'Institut des Hautes Études Chinoises*, vol. IV). Paris, 1937.

An index to this work by Françoise Aubin may be found in *Mélanges Publiés par l'Institut des Hautes Études Chinoises* II (1960), 423-515.

_____"Zum Ausdruck 't'ouhsia' in der Mongolenzeit." *Collectanea Mongolica* (Wiesbaden, 1966), pp. 173-91.

Schafer, Edward H. "A Fourteenth Century Gazetteer of Canton." *Oriente Poliano* (Rome: Istituto Italiano per il Medio ed Estremo Oriente, 1957), pp. 67-93.

Schulte-Uffelage, H. *Das Keng-shen wai-shih. Eine Quelle zur Späten Mongolenzeit (Ostasiatische Forschungen sonderreihe Monographien*, vol. II). Berlin, 1963.

Schurmann, H. F. *Economic Structure of the Yüan Dynasty. Translation of Chapters 93 and 94 of the Yüan shih. (Harvard-Yenching Institute Studies*, vol. XVI). Cambridge: Harvard University Press, 1956.

______"Mongolian Tributary Practices of the Thirteenth Century." *HJAS*, XIX (1956), 304-89.

For a dissenting view, see now John Masson Smith, Jr., "Mongol and Nomadic Taxation," *HJAS*, XXX (1970), 46-85.

______"Problems of Political Organization during the Yüan Dynasty." *Trudy XXV Mezhdunarodnogo Kongressa Vostokovedov*, Vol. V (Moscow, 1963), 26-30.

Sun K'o-k'uan 孫克寬 *Yüan-tai Han wen-hua chih huo-tung.* 元代漢文化之活動 [Chinese cultural activity in the Yüan period]. Taipei: Chung-hua shu-chü, 1968.

Tazaka Kōdō 田坂興道 *Chūgoku ni okeru kaikyō no denrai to sono kōtsū.* 中国における回教の傳來とその弘通 [Islam in China, its introduction and development]. (*Tōyō bunko ronsō*, no. 43). 2 vols. Tokyo, 1964.

Ts'en Chung-mien 岑仲勉 "Tsai-shuo Ch'in-ch'a." 再說欽察 [Another discussion on the Qipchaqs]. *FJHC*, V (December, 1936), 1-32.

Umehara Kaoru 梅原郁 "Gendai saekihō shōron." 元代差役法小論 [Short discussion of the Yüan labor service system]. *Tōyōshi kenkyū*, XXIII (1965), 399-427.

Vladimirtsov, B. *Le Régime Social des Mongols.* Translated by Michel Carsow. Paris: Librairie d'Amérique et d'Orient, 1948.

Yamamoto Takayoshi 山本隆義 "Gendai ni okeru kanrin in ni tsuite." 元代に於ける翰林院について [On the Hanlin Academy of the Yüan period]. *Tōhōgaku*, no. 11 (1955), pp. 81-99.

Yang Lien-sheng. *Money and Credit in China.* Cambridge: Harvard University Press, 1952.

——— *Les Aspects Économiques des Travaux Publics dans lá Chine Impériale.* Paris: College de France, 1964.

Yen Han-sheng 閻瀚生 "Liu Fu-t'ung fen-mu tiao-ch'a hsiao-chi." 劉福通墳墓調查小記 [Short note on the investigation of Liu Fu-t'ung's tomb]. *Li-shih chiao-hsüeh* (August, 1955), p. 8.

Index

'Abd ar-Raḥmān, 110
Abu Said, *see* Ilkhans
Afghanistan, 27
Agricultural development: North China, 93, 112-13, 122, 212*n*79; Shensi, 219*n*71
Aḥmad, 37, 183*n*6
Alan Guards, 17, 54, 186*n*36, 189*n*48
Alans, 105, 110, 211*n*48, 218*n*53
Alin Temür, 190*n*54, 201*n*10
Alqui, 110
Altai Mountains, 11-12, 19, 23, 25
Altan Tobchi, 182*n*64
Alughu, 22
An-chi, princely fief, 172, 178*n*17
An-t'ung, 184*n*8, 204*n*58
Ananda, Prince of An-hsi, 13, 15, 188*n*48
Aqutai, 13, 206*n*77
Aradnadara, 55, 59, 171, 196*n*40
Aradnashiri, Prince of Hsi-an, later Prince of Yü, 138, 139, 171, 186*n*35, 219*n*60
Aragibag, 40, 42
Aral Sea, 45
Arghun, 132, 222*n*101
Arigh Böke, 22
Arigh Qaya, 70, 190*n*54, 199*n*83
Arugh, 76
Arughtu, 81, 89, 171, 203*n*37
Ash, Prince of Ch'ang, 189*n*48
A-sha Buqa, 16-17, 178*n*19
Asud, *see* Alan Guards; Alans
A'urugh, military camps, 83
Ayurbarwada, 9, 17-18, 43, 99, 171, 180*n*50, 185*n*35, 188*n*48; and China-centered imperial candidacy, 13-15; revival of examinations under, 35-36; and factions, 37; and clerks, 63, 197*n*57; and canonization of Neo-Confucian fathers, 184*n*10
Ayushiridara, 97, 125-26, 147-55, 171, 207*n*8, 215*n*18, 222*n*5
Ba'arin, Mongol tribe, 23
Ba'atur, a title, 12
Baiju, 204*n*58
Balashiri, Prince of Ch'ang, 189*n*48
Balashiri, Prince of Hsiang-ning, 185*n*35
Balkhash, Lake, 10-11, 23, 45
Bayan, 10, 12, 17-18, 32, 76, 78, 90-93, 104, 158, 171; ancestry, 53, 193*n*4; early career, 43-44, 188*nn*45, 47; and 1328 coup, 39, 53-54; position in Tugh Temür's court, 46, 54-55, 59; and El Temür, 52, 56, 59, 196*n*38; and succession to Tugh Temür, 55-59, 159; private wealth, 55, 57-58, 194*n*25; and the *Ching-yen*, 201*n*10; initial policies as Chancellor, 60-61, 97, 99; and rebel outbreaks, 66-67; later policies and political persecutions, 67-72, 224*n*2; *see also under* Censorate; Central Chancellery; Confucianism; Ethnic class system
Bayan, Kashmiri, 96
Bayan Buqa, 114
Bayan Qudu, 92, 125, 215*n*16
Beg Temür 207*n*16
Berke, *see* Golden Horde
Berke Buqa, 76, 171; early career, 82, 203*n*39; policies as Chancellor and Grand Guardian, 81, 83-89, 97, 102, 163, 166; and Bayan's partisans, 82, 91, 93; and Toghto, 81, 89-91; and monarchy, 126; dismissal and exile, 126; *see also under* Censorate; Central Chancellery; Confucianism
Black Sea, 45
Böchög, 178*n*20, 192*n*72
Boghorchu, 81, 222*n*5
Bolod Buqa, Prince of Chen-nan, 115, 121, 213*n*86
Bolod Temür, 135, 142-45, 148-50, 171
Bo'ol, 204*n*58, 206*n*84
Budashiri, 55-58, 75, 159, 172
Bulughan, 13, 15

Buqa Temür, 49, 192*n*76
Buqumu, 183*n*8
Buyan Temür, 114, 131

Caspian Sea, 10, 45
Censorate: and financial cliques, 37; and El Temür, 47, 52, 158, 190*n*63; and Bayan, 54, 58; and Toghto, 77, 90-92, 96, 122-23, 202*n*23; and Berke Buqa, 86, 92, 206*n*73; institutional role of, 91, 161, 166-67; and North China regionalism, 136-37; and factionalism, 147 ff., 223*n*5
Central Chancellery: and Qoshila, 28; under El Temür, 52; and Budashiri, 58; under Toghto's first administration, 75-76; under Berke Buqa, 84-86; under Toghto's second administration, 96-97; and ethnic class system, 85; and Han-lin Academy, 94; and Red Turban rebellions, 111; and Confucianism, 161
Chaghan Temür, 130, 162, 172; ancestry and early career, 132-37, 217*n*39; in Shensi, 137-39; in Shansi 139-40; bureaucratic positions, 220*n*75; victory over rebel Sung regime, 140-41; defends autonomy in Shensi and Shansi, 141-45, 221*n*88; final campaign and assassination, 145-46; nature of biographical sources for, 221*n*92, 222*n*100
Chaghatai, 10, 182*n*62
Chaghatai Khanate, 1, 10, 21, 23, 25, 27-29, 181*n*62; *see also* Alughu; Duwa; Eljigitei; Esen Buqa; Kebek
*Chagir, 49, 178*n*20, 192*n*72
Chang Ch'i-yen, 62, 76, 197*n*51
Chang Liang-pi, 151-52, 155
Chang Meng-ch'en, *see* Chang Ch'i-yen
Chang Shih-ch'eng, 104, 109, 112, 118-20, 127-30, 152-54, 172
Chang Yu-liang, 200*n*4
Ch'ang-shih fu, princely staff, 18
Chao Shih-yen, 190*n*54
Chao-kung wan-hu-fu, palace office, 78
Chao-kung wan-hu tu-tsung-shih-ssu, palace office, 55
Chapar, 11, 12, 174
Chechegtü, Prince of T'an, 70
Ch'en Ssu-ch'ien, 199*n*87
Ch'en Tsu-jen, 148
Ch'en Yu-liang, 130-32, 216*n*38
Cheng, princely fief, 214*n*96
Cheng Yü, 202*n*19, 204*n*60
Ch'eng Tsun, 101-2, 112, 223*n*5
Ch'eng-tsung, *see* Temür
Cherig Temür, 61
Chi-hsien Academy, 123
Ch'i-t'ai-p'u-chi, 16, 172, 178*n*17, 189*n*50
Ch'i-yang, princely fief, 176, 188*n*48
Chia Lu, 101, 116-17, 209*n*26
Chiang-Huai ts'ai-fu tu-tsung-kuan-fu, palace agency, 194*n*17
Chiao-hua, moral suasion, 34, 65-66, 82-83, 165
Chiao-hua, non-Chinese official, 107
Chiao-hua, Alan Guards commander, 189*n*54
Chief Military Commission, 16, 39, 47, 54, 77, 105, 189*n*50
Chieh Hsi-ssu, 64-66, 76, 93-94, 203*n*49, 208*n*12
Chih-cheng, reign title, 75
Chih-cheng t'iao-ko, compilation of, 202*n*26
Chih-ku River, project, 99
Chih-yüan, reign title, 61
Chin Dynasty (1115-1234), 79
Chin-k'ou canal, project, 79-80, 96, 209*n*26
Chin-shih, see Examination system
Ch'in, princely fief, 57, 195*n*31
Ching Yen, 204*n*55
Ching-shih ta-tien, compilation of, 47, 73, 78
Ching-yen, imperial seminar, 76, 86, 161, 201*n*10
Ch'ing, unit of land measurement, 192*n*68
Chinggis Qan, 4, 16, 81, 155, 218*n*53; and Merkids, 53, 126
*Chong'ur, 11, 17, 43, 172, 181*n*53, 191*n*68, 192*n*72
Chösgem, 96, 147-49, 172, 222*n*5
Chou, princely fief, 18, 26
Chou Jen-jung, 199*n*79
Chou Po-ch'i, 214*n*9
Chou Ting, 204*n*49
Chu River, 53
Chu Yüan-chang, 1, 3, 130-32, 147, 151-55, 168-69, 172, 217*n*38
Ch'u-cheng yüan, palace office, 194*n*8
Chü-jung, princely fief, 17, 43, 48-49, 57, 195*n*25

Ch'üan Heng, quoted, 96-97, 105, 222*n*100, 223*n*17
Chung-shu, metropolitan province (incorporating modern Shantung, Shansi, Hopei): and 1328 coup, 40; banditry in; 80-81, 102-3; Yellow River flood in, 87; military supply in, 111-13; rebel invasion of Shansi sector, 130; Chaghan Temür and Bolod Temür struggle in Shansi sector, 140-45; rebel Sung retreat to Shantung sector, 145; defense of Shantung against Chu Yüan-chang, 152-54; Kökö Temür position in Shansi, 154-55
Chung-shu sheng, see Central Chancellery
Chung-shu fen-sheng, "detached" office, 111
Chung-tu, 24
"Classics Mat", *see Ching-yen*
Clerks, 83, 217*n*42; advancement prospects, 63-64, 197*n*52; Confucian attitude toward, 66, 197*n*57
Commercial Tax Bureau, 48
Commercial tax exemptions, 193*n*85
Confucianism, Confucianists: Legalism in 215*n*15; as unitary factional movement, 32-33, 37-38, 52, 60, 159, 161; "reformist" variety, 2, 79-80, 93-94, 116-17, 163-64; "conservative" variety, 2, 82, 89, 94, 104, 122, 124-25, 148, 163-67; and Central Chancellery under El Temür, 51-52; and Bayan, 60, 64-66, 72-73, 159-60; and Toghto, 74-78, 93, 162; and Berke Buqa, 82; and rebellion of Fang Kuo-chen, 100; and Censorate, 124; and growth of regionalism, 123, 138; and Mongols and *se-mu,* 160, 198*n*79, 224*n*3; and appanaged Mongol nobility, 183*n*6; and Chinese literary tradition, 183*n*4; *see also* Examination system
Confucianization, 3; of government, 31; at ministerial level, 82, 93-94
Currency: reform and expansion under Toghto, 97-99, 122, 208*nn*12-16; special issues 40, 139

*Darindari, 49
Darma, *see* Tarmashirin
Darmabala, 13, 175
Darmashiri, *see* Tarmashirin
Darqan, a title, 48-49, 77, 117, 192*n*69
Darqan Army, 212*n*67
Darughachi, 17, 83, 85-86, 191*n*68, 204*n*60
Dash Badulugh, 107, 110, 113, 134-37, 142, 162, 172, 218*n*53, 220*n*83
Dash Temür, 100
Daula-shah, 42, 51, 95, 172
Döre Temür, 181*n*62
Dorji, 69-70, 72, 84, 86, 95, 124, 163-64, 172-73, 204*n*58
Dorjibal, 91, 107, 112, 131, 173, 206*n*84
Duwa, 11-12, 23, 174
Duwa Temür, *see* Döre Temür
Dynastic histories (Liao, Chin, Sung), compilation of, 78-79, 81

El Tegüs, 55, 58, 73, 75, 159, 173, 194*n*13
El Temür, 10, 17, 26-27, 32, 55, 75, 78, 93, 159, 168, 173, 190*n*54; ancestry, 42-43, 45; early career, 43-44, 188*n*47; and 1328 coup, 39-42, 53; domination of Tugh Temür's court, 46-48, 50, 190*nn*67, 68; private wealth, 48-49, 57, 191*n*67, kin ties, 49-50; and purge of opposition, 51, 59; and Confucianism, 52, 158; and succession to Tugh Temür, 55; biographical sources for, 194*n*17
Eljigedei, *see* Eljigitei
Eljigitei, 28-29, 181*n*62
Esen Buqa, 19, 178*n*32
Esen Qudu, *see* Ho Chün
Esen Temür, younger brother of Toghto, 76, 78, 106-7, 110, 117, 121-22, 173, 202*n*23
Esen Temür, son of *Yochichar, 188*n*48
Esen Temür, Ḥukuang Chief Administrator, 114
Ethnic class system, 35, 45, 85, 160; and examination system, 36; and Central Chancellery, 85; reinforced by Bayan, 61, 196*n*45, 224*n*2; revised by Toghto, 123; and Confucianism, 224*n*3
Examination system, 35-37, 79, 150, 198*n*75; cancellation by Bayan, 60-66, 160; graduates in bureaucracy, 62, 64-65; and Mongols and *se-mu*,

Examination system (*Continued*), 68-69, 132, 161-62, 198*n*79; revived in Honan by Chaghan Temür; 140-41

Fan Hui, 201*n*12
Fan Meng, incident, 71-72, 90, 224*n*2
Fang Kuo-chen, 88-89, 99-101, 109, 112, 128-29, 173, 206*n*72, 223*n*7
Feng-su, 34, 65-66
Financial cliques, 32, 37, 38, 157, 183*n*6; *see also* Ahmad; Temüder
Fukien province, rebellion in, 67

Genghis Khan, *see* Chinggis Qan
Golden Horde, 1, 22, 26, 182*n*62
*Gongbubal, 105, 110
Grand Canal, 89, 99, 101, 104, 109, 112, 206*n*75
Great Chin, rebel dynasty, 66
Great Chou, rebel dynasty, 128
Guaranteed recommendations, *see* *Pao-chü*
Gunadara, *see* El Tegüs
Güyügchi Guards, 186*n*36

Hainan, Tugh Temür in, 20
Hairy Gourd militia, 107, 120
Han Fa-shih, 66
Han Hsing, 199*n*79
Han Yüan-shan, 96
Han Yung, 96
Han-chia-nu, 90, 92, 95
Han-jen, *see* Ethnic class system
Han-lin Academy, 33, 94
Harghasun, 14
Ho Bayan, *see* Ho Sheng
Ho Chün, 95
Ho Sheng, 184*n*17
Ho Wei-i, 84-87, 90, 95, 124, 148, 150, 163-64, 173, 222*n*5
Honan province: Ayurbarwada in, 13-14; and 1328 coup, 40, 53-54; and enthronement of Toghon Temür, 56; Fan Meng putsch in, 71-72; Yellow River flood in, 87; banditry in, 102; Red Turban rebellion in, 103-9; military supply in, 111-12; rebel Sung dynasty established in, 130-38; rise of Chagan Temür in, 132-37; *see also* Huainan province
Hopei, *see* Chung-shu
Hsi-li-mu, 135

Hsiao Baiju, 184*n*17
Hsieh Che-tu, 98, 207*n*12
Hsien-tsung, *see* Möngke
Hsü Heng, 34, 183*n*8
Hsü Shih-pen, 150
Hsü Yu-jen, 62-63, 75-76, 79, 83, 124, 215*n*15, 224*n*3
Hsüan-hui yüan, *see* Office of Imperial Cuisine
Hsüan-k'o t'i-chü-ssu, *see* Commercial Tax Bureau
Hsün-tu, princely fief, 188*n*48
Huai, princely fief, 20
Huai-ch'ing, princely fief, 13
Huai-ning, princely fief, 11
Huainan province, 109, 114-15, 119
Huang Chin, 76, 197*n*56, 201*n*11
Hui-hui, 190*n*54, 200*n*95
Hukuang province: and 1328 coup, 40; rebellions in, 80, 84; Red Turbans in, 109; military supply in, 110, 112
Hula'atai, Prince of Ju-ning, 174, 185*n*35
Hülegü, *see* Ilkhans

Iduq qut, Uighur royal title, 70, 113, 190*n*54, 200*n*5
Ikires, Mongol clan, 187*n*38
Ili region, 28, 182*n*62
Ilkhans, 1, 11, 22, 26, 181*n*56, 182*n*62
Imperial Guards, 17, 42, 52, 54, 61-62, 85, 105, 132, 199*n*79, 205*nn*60, 69
Imperial University, 33, 123
India, 27
Ingot, unit of currency, 178*n*28
Irinjibal, 55, 173
Irinjinbal, 70, 89, 92, 107, 124, 131, 173, 202*n*23
Irtysh River, 12, 23, 53

Jalair, Mongol clan, 41, 183*n*6; role in conquest establishment, 187*n*38, 204*n*58
Jasagh, 10
Jaya'an Buqa, 189*n*54
Jen-tsung, *see* Ayurbarwada
Jingim, second son of Qubilai, 13, 175
Jingim, son of Toghon Temür, 215*n*16
Ju Chung-po, 120, 207*n*2
Jung, princely fief, 195*n*31
Jürcheds, 23, 35

Kalka, battle of the, 53

Kammala, Prince of Chin, 16, 175, 184*n*19
Kansu province: raids upon, 181*n*54; and 1328 coup, 40; Majartai's exile in. 90; Toghto's sons exiled to, 122
Kebek, 26, 28, 181*nn*53, 62
Keng Huan, 200*n*4
Keng-hua, 75-76, 78-79, 93, 200*n*2
Keshig, see Imperial Guards
Khubilai, *see* Qubilai
Khitans, 35
Kiangche province: and 1328 coup, 40; piracy in, 88; Red Turbans in, 107-8; as supply base for Kao-yu campaign, 119; *see also* Chang Shih-ch'eng; Fang Kuo-chen
Kiangnan (Branch) Censorate, 18, 114-15, 216*n*36
Kiangsi province: and 1328 coup, 40; rebellion in, 67; Confucian ideology in, 93; Red Turbans in, 107, 109
Ko Yong-bok, 92
K'o Chiu-ssu, 191*n*64
Kökö Temür, 133, 146, 148-56, 173
Kökötei, 132
Köncheg Buqa, Prince of Wei-shun, 71, 114
Korea, Koreans, 23, 35, 40, 59, 67, 92, 120, 125-26, 128, 150, 214*n*5
Kuan-kuan, 133-34, 136
Kublai, *see* Qubilai
Kuei Ch'ang, 71, 97
K'uei-chang-ko Academy, 48, 72-73, 191*n*64
Kung Po-sui, 207*n*2
Kung Shih-t'ai, 214*n*9
Kung-hsiang tu-tsung-kuan-fu, palace office, 48, 191*n*66
Kung-li, 79, 94, 105, 118, 124
K'ung Hsing, 151, 154
Kuo-tzu chien, see Imperial University
Kwangsi province: Toghon Temür's exile in, 56; rebellion in, 80
Kwangtung province, rebellion in, 66

Lao-chang, 211*n*55, 214*n*5
Lao-pao, *see* Pao-pao
Lao-ti-sha, 148
Left Guards, 43
Li Ch'a-han, *see* Chaghan Temür
Li Chi, 91-92
Li Hao-wen, 207*n*8
Li Shih-chan, 144-45
Li Ssu-ch'i, 133-34, 136, 138-39, 145, 152, 154-55, 173-74
Li T'an, 33
Li-chin, see Clerks
Li-jih, 16, 19, 174, 178*n*17, 189*n*50
Liang, unit of weight, 178*n*28
Liao valley, 24
Liaoyang province, 24, 112; and 1328 coup, 40
Lien Qaishan Qaya, 210*n*37
Lingpei province, 180*n*47; and 1328 coup, 40; *see also* Mongolia
Liu Qara Buqa, 212*n*68; 217*n*49
Lou Shih-pao, 201*n*14
Lu chün-kuo chung-shih, military policy position, 47, 54, 190*n*61
Lu Lu-tseng, 108
Lü Ssu-ch'eng, 185*n*33
Lung-chen Guards, 110, 186*n*36
Lung-i Guards, 190*n*61

Ma Po-yung, *see* Ma Tsu-ch'ang
Ma Tsu-ch'ang, 62, 189*n*54, 197*n*51, 198*n*78, 207*n*2
Mai-lai-ti, 195*n*34
Majaqan, Prince of Chao, 185*n*35
Majartai, 73, 77, 82, 90, 174
Manchuria: Nayan's revolt in, 22-24; other revolts in, 80; *see also* Liaoyang province
Manggala, 13
Manzi Qaya, 114
Maragha, Ilkhan seat, 11
Maritime grain transport, 79, 87-89, 99, 112, 179*n*45
Merkids, Mongol tribe, 53, 126
Miao army, 110, 115, 134, 217*n*47
Ming Dynasty, 1, 3, 127, 132, 154, 168-69
Ming T'ai-tsu, *see* Chu Yüan-chang
Ming-tsung, *see* Qoshila
Mo Kao, 152-55
Möngke, 10, 70, 218*n*53
Mongol Empire, 1, 7-9, 22, 28, 30, 157, 168
Mongol language: translations into, 34; competence in, 196*n*45
Mongolia, 8, 12, 21-26, 29-31, 176, 180*n*47; and Shensi revolt of 1316, 178*n*30; *see also* Lingpei province
Moslems, 13, 21, 27, 51, 80, 193*n*80, 199*n*79
Muqali, 183*n*6, 187*n*38, 204*n*58

Naiman, Turkish tribe, 132, 217*n*39
Naimanjin, 195*n*34
Naimantai, Jalair viceroy, 70, 182*n*62
Naimantai, grandfather of Chaghan Temür, 132
Nan-jen, *see* Ethnic class system
Nanggiadai, 189*n*48
Nanggiatai, 218*n*53
Nao-nao, 161, 190*n*54
Narin, 92, 114, 174, 195*n*26, 216*n*36
Nasr ad-Dīn, 115
National History *(kuo-shih)*. 47
Nayan, 22-24, 179*n*42
Neo-Confucianism, *see* Confucianism
Ne'üdigei, 222*n*5
Ne'üril, 218*n*53
Ning-tsung, *see* Irinjibal
Nököd, 158, 161

Office of Imperial Cuisine, 17, 49, 192*n*78
Ögödei, 10, 132, 182*n*62; patrimony of, 11-12, 23, 174
Öljei Qudu, née Ki, 92, 125, 149
Öljeitü, *see* Ilkhans
Ongchan, Prince of Liang, 42, 185*n*35
Orqon River, 11
Örüg, 192*n*74
Örüg Buqa, 199*n*79
Örüg Temür, Kiangche Chief Administrator, 131, 216*n*36
Örüg Temür, Prince of Ch'i, 186*n*35
Ou-yang Hsüan, 62, 76, 93, 197*n*51, 210*n*40

Pai-sa-li, 222*n*5
Pao-chü, 36
Pao-pao, 217*n*42
Peking, *see* Ta-tu
P'eng Ying-yü, 67
Persia, 27
Picul *(shih)*, unit of measure, 206*n*70
Pien-i hsing-shih, authorization to "act at convenience", 111, 119, 135, 139, 216*n*36

Qabartu, 189*n*50
Qadī, office of, in Ta-tu, 51
Qaghan, qaghanate, 4, 7, 9-10, 22, 27-28, 30, 45, 132, 157, 168
Qaidu, 10-11, 22-23, 27, 158, 174
Qaishan, 9, 18, 43, 99, 174; and anti-Qaidu resistance, 10-12; and clique of adherents, 12, 16-19, 44, 188*n*48; assumes throne, 13-18; administration in Mongolia, 24, 180*n*49; enfeoffs princes, 25, 180*n*50; as factional symbol, 42, 44, 46, 50, 61, 158; *see also Shang-shu sheng*
Qama, 120-21, 123, 125-26, 147, 174
Qan, 4, 158, 161, 168
Qangli, Turkish tribe, 43, 45
Qangli Guards, 17
Qangli Toghto, 11, 16, 76, 174, 207*nn*3, 5, 222*n*5; as factional leader, 43-44; ancestry, 45; and Confucianism, 45-46
Qara Batur, 189*n*48
Qara Buqa, 204*n*60
Qarachi, 42, 186n36, 190*n*54, 191*n*68
Qarajang, 155
Qaraqojo, Uighur kingdom of, 23, 53, 70, 132, 190*n*54; *see also Iduq qut*
Qaraqorum, 7, 10, 12, 23-25, 29, 38, 179n38
Qarimtu, 114
Qarluq Guards, 190*n*61
Qipchaq, Turkish tribe, 10, 42, 45, 49, 53, 70, 73, 110, 159, 186*n*36, 189*n*53, 218*n*53; *see also* El Temür
Qipchaq Guards, 17, 43, 47, 190*n*61
Qonqor Buqa, 115
Qonqor Temür, Prince of Chia, 70
Qoshila, 9, 18, 52, 72, 157, 174; and revolt in Shensi, 19-20, 44; retreat to steppes, 26, 28, 181*n*54, 182*n*62; assumption of throne, 26-29; line restored, 75, 159
Qubilai, 1, 4, 7-8, 13, 15-16, 25, 85, 157, 164, 174-75; policies in Inner Asia, 21-24, 179*nn*38, 45, 46; and factions, 35, 183*n*8; as political symbol, 50, 61, 159-60, 192*n*79, 224*n*2
Qunggirad, Mongol consort clan, 41, 49, 57, 159, 186*n*38
Quriltai, 7

Rebellions: in Bayan's administration, 66-67; in Toghto's first administration, 80-81; in Berke Buqa's administration, 84, 88; in Toghto's second administration, 102-9; shift in general strategy after 1355, 130-32; *see also* Fang Kuo-chen; Chang Shi-ch'eng; Red Turbans; Sung

Red Turbans, 104-10, 113, 115, 129, 131, 133, 135
Regionalism: development of under Chang Shi-ch'eng, 128; under Fang Kuo-chen, 128-29; under Chaghan Temür, 130, 132 ff.

Sadun, 49, 195*nn*25, 31, 33, 201*n*16
Salt monopoly, 208*n*18; at Ho-chien, 87; prices, 98-99, 208*n*19
San-pao-nu, 189*n*48
Se-mu (Central Asians), 2-3, 29, 33, 35, 45-46, 61, 67-69, 72, 77, 86, 96, 110, 115-16, 132, 160-62, 189*n*54, 211*n*50, 217*n*39; *see also* Confucianism; Ethnic class system; Examination system
Sengge, 183*n*6
Shang Yang, 79-80
Shang-shu sheng, chancellery, 17, 44, 178*n*23, 189*n*48, 192*n*79
Shang-tu, 15, 27-28, 105; as center of Yesün Temür's supporters, 26, 38-42, 54
Shansi, *see* Chung-shu
Shantung, *see* Chung-shu
Sharabal, 201*n*10
She, local control system, 86, 205*n*61
Sheng-tz'u, temple, 49, 55
Shensi Branch Censorate, 19, 90, 106-7, 123-24, 138-39
Shensi province: defense against Qaidu, 13; Qoshila's revolt in, 19, 44; and 1328 coup, 40; famine in, 40, 185*n*31; military pacification in, 111; rebel invasion of, 130; Chaghan Temür in, 138-39; Bolod Temür and Li Ssu-ch'i conflict in, 145; warlord alliance in, 151-52, 154; Chu Yüan-chang attack on, 155; *see also* Agricultural development; Currency
Shidebala, 18, 20, 26, 37-38, 44, 175, 186*n*35, 188*n*48, 204*n*58
Shih, unit of measure, *see* Picul
Shih P'u, 119, 214*n*2
Shih Wei-liang, 185*n*32, 200*n*4
Shih-cheng fu, palace office, 54
Shih-tsu, *see* Qubilai
Shinggi, 114, 131
Shiu Ta-ta, tribe, 23
Shu-mi yüan, *see* Chief Military Commission
Shun-ning, princely fief, 195*n*30
Shun-ti, *see* Toghon Temür
Sinicization, 3, 33
Ssu-ma Kuang, 2
"Stick" Hu, 66
Sübü'ütei, 53
Sügürchi, 194*n*8, 205*n*60
Su-wei, *see* Imperial Guards
Sung, rebel dynasty, 130, 132, 135-42
Sung Lien, 209*n*28
Sungari region, 23
Szechwan province: Qubilai's invasion of, 85; and 1328 coup, 40, 218*n*53; rebellion in, 52, 66, 184*n*29; Esen Temür exiled to, 122

Ta fu-chün-yüan, military bureau, 153, 155
Ta-hsi tsung-yin-yüan, palace office, 50, 192*n*78
Ta-tu, 7, 10-11, 13, 15, 24, 26-27, 38-42, 51, 53-54, 105, 120, 140, 149, 155-56
Ta-tu-tu-fu, military bureau, 47, 190*n*61
Taghai, 190*n*54
Tai Buqa, Baya'ud, 100, 199*n*79, 205*n*65
Tai Buqa, Qunggirad, 96, 106, 134-37, 218*nn*52, 54, 221*n*84
T'ai-p'ing, Prince of Yang-chai, 185*n*35
T'ai-p'ing, princely fief, 48, 57, 191*n*67
T'ai-p'ing, *see* Ho Wei-i
T'ai-p'ing-nu, 194*n*13
T'ai-ting, *see* Yesün Temür
T'ai-tsu, *see* Chinggis Qan
T'ai-tsung, *see* Ögödei
Talas convention, 10
Tamachi, 107, 110, 132, 212*n*68
*Tangkish, 49, 57, 175
Tangut region, 13, 24
T'ao Tsung-i, 210*n*44
Taraqai, 188*n*48
Tarbagatai region, 20, 28, 178*n*32
*Targi, 13, 37
Tarim area, 23-25, 27, 181*n*53
Tarmashirin, 182*n*62
Tegüder, 199*n*79
Temüder, 37-38, 43, 52, 85, 183*n*6, 190*n*54
Temür, 10, 12, 24-25, 175, 180*n*50
Temür Buqa, *iduq qut* and Prince of Kao-ch'ang, 70, 175, 190*nn*54, 61, 199*n*87
Temür Buqa, Prince of Hsüan-jang, 71

Temür Buqa, Chancellor of the Left, 75-76
Temür Tash, 76, 84, 96, 203*n*39
Teri Temür, 139, 142, 219*n*71
T'ien Feng, 145
T'ien-hsia, Qaishan's concept of, 16
Ting, see Ingot
Ting Wen-yüan, 62
Ting-chu, 76, 96, 147, 175, 195*n*25, 207*n*3
Toghon, 76
Toghon Temür, 49, 98, 101, 105, 118, 175; in exile, 56, 59, 196*n*39; enthronement, 56, 58; as factional symbol, 59; and partial revival of monarchic power, 92-93, 162-63; conflict with Ayushiridara, 147-55; paternity of, 58, 195*n*37; Confucian education of, 201*n*10
Toghto, Prince of Liao, 185*n*35
Toghto, 175; and overthrow of Bayan, 72-74, appointees in first administration, 75-76; policies in first administration, 78-80, 162-63; attack on Berke Buqa, 89-93, 95-96, 100, 166; policies in second administration, 96-99, 101-3, 123, 128-29, 163, 212*n*79; private wealth, 78, 117; princedom awarded to, 214*n*96; and suppression of Red Turban rebellions, 105-9; and centralization of pacification effort, 109-17; campaign against Chang Shih-ch'eng at Kao-yu. 119-20, 127-28, 214*n*5; dismissal of, 121-27, 162-63, 167; and monarchy, 125-26, 215*n*18; popular view of his policies, 210*n*44; *see also under* Censorate; Central Chancellery; Confucianism; Ethnic class system
Toghus Temür, 215*n*16
Töre Temür, *see* Döre Temür
Törebeg, 151, 154
T'ou-hsia, appanaged Mongol nobility, 35, 183*n*6, 187*n*38
Transoxania, 12, 23, 27-28, 181*n*53
Tributary terminology, use of, 181*n*56
Tuan-pen-t'ang, palace school, 97
Tugh Temür, 9, 18, 20, 26-27, 29, 38, 175, 195*n*37; and 1328 coup, 39, 44, 54; role as emperor, 46, 48, 50-52, 55, 158-59; posthumous vilification of, 75
Tughchi, 105-6, 110, 210*n*48, 211*n*55
Tughlugh, 102
Tughtugha, 43, 175, 190*n*54, 191*n*68
Tului, line of, 10, 178*n*20
Tuman Temür, Prince of Wu-p'ing, 181*n*54
Tümender, sworn brother of Berke Buqa, 95
Tümender, Liaoyang Chief Administrator, 186*n*35
T'un-t'ien, military agricultural colonies, 24, 103, 107
Tung T'uan-hsiao, 107
Tung-lu Meng-ku myriarchy, 186*n*36, 190*n*61
Tung-p'ing school, 32-36, 183*n*6

Ubaid-ullah, 51
Üch Qurtuqa, 96, 207*n*5
Uighur, Turkish tribe, 53, 113; *see also Iduq qut;* Qaraqojo
Üldüchi, 205*n*60
Uriangqatai, 221*nn*84, 88

Viceroy *(kuo-wang),* Jalair title, 69, 95, 187*n*38; *see also* Dorji; Naimantai
Volga River, 45

Wang An-shih, 2, 79-80, 93
Wang Chieh, 201*n*10
Wang Hsi, 209*n*28
Wang Hsin, 153-54
Wang I, Confucianist, 201*n*11, 202*n*19
Wang I, Chief Administrator, 204*n*55
Wang K'o-ching, 224*n*3
Wang Pao-pao, *see* Kökö Temür
Wang Shih-ch'eng, 145
Wang Ssu-ch'eng, 123, 138, 214*n*10
Wang Wen-t'ung, 33
Wang Yün, 183*n*6
Water Tatars, *see* Shui Ta-ta
Wei Sain Buqa, 217*n*42
Wen-tsung, *see* Tugh Temür
White Lotus Society, 104; *see also* Red Turbans
Wu Ch'i, 97-98
Wu Chih-fang, 74, 77, 82, 162, 201*nn*12-14, 224*n*2
Wu Lai, 201*n*13
Wu Qudu Buqa, 76
Wu Tang, 214*n*9
Wu T'ien-pao, 203*n*48, 217*n*47
Wu-ku-sun Liang-chen, 207*n*2

Wu-p'ing, princely fief, 49, 181*n*54
Wu-tsung, *see* Qaishan

Yaghan-shah, Prince of Hsi-ning, 113-14, 213*n*81
Yaik River, 45
Yao-chu, 107, 113
Yaqudu, Prince of Ch'u, 178*n*20
Yang Dorji, 184*n*17
Yang Yü, 70, 195*n*32, 200*n*12
Yeh Tzu-ch'i, 67, 209*n*26
Yeh-erh-chi-ni, 16, 175, 178*n*17, 189*n*50
Yellow Army, 108, 110
Yellow River: flood and shift of course, 83-84, 87, 89; rechanneling of, 99, 101, 103, 208*n*16, 209*n*28, 210*n*37
Yesü, 153
Yesüderchi, 199*n*79
Yesün Temür, 26, 38-39, 95, 158, 175-76, 185*n*35, 188*n*48, 201*n*10; conciliation policy toward factions, 20, 38, 44
Yin, 36, 207*n*2
Ying-ch'ang, 23
Ying-tsung, *see* Shidebala
*Yochichar, 11, 176, 188*n*48
Yü Chi, 73, 93; on Shensi famine, 185*n*31; on access to emperor, 191*n*65; on agricultural development in North China, 202*n*24
Yü Ch'üeh, 165, 209*n*28
Yü-shih-t'ai, see Censorate
Yü-wa-shih, 189*n*48
Yüan armies: composition of under Toghto, 105-10, 120; viability of, 213*n*89
Yüan Ming-shan, 197*n*56
Yüan Sain Buqa, 123
Yunnan province, 18-19, 107; Qubilai's invasion of, 85; and 1328 coup, 40; rebellions in, 52, 80, 184*n*29; Toghto exiled to, 122